# Spreadsheet and Database Applications for Accounting Information Systems

Roy D. Johnson/Denise Nitterhouse

Addison-Wesley Publishing Company, Inc.
Reading, Massachusetts • Menlo Park, California • New York
Don Mills, Ontario • Wokingham, England • Amsterdam • Bonn
Sydney • Singapore • Tokyo • Madrid • San Juan

In memory of        Nellie Elizabeth Bent Nitterhouse

Roy Donald Johnson, Sr., Ph.D.

Louise Tate

# Preface

This book integrates Accounting Information Systems (AIS) concepts with the learning and using of popular microcomputer software. The book was developed in the belief that concepts are learned better and retained longer if they are reinforced with examples and practice. The text incorporates AIS concepts and uses AIS examples in the cases and exercises that develop and strengthen students' microcomputer skills. The Lotus® 1-2-3® electronic spreadsheet and the dBASE III PLUS™ database management system software were chosen because they are widely used and powerful.

## Organization

Part I introduces AIS and provides an overview of microcomputer hardware, software and operation. Part II covers the use of Lotus 1-2-3, including its integration with other types of software. Part III covers the use of dBASE III PLUS, and provides a brief introduction to its programming and integration with other types of software.

## Acknowledgments

We would like to thank all those who have helped, directly and indirectly, in the preparation of this book.

We are indebted to the administration, faculty and staff of DePaul University and Roosevelt University for providing environments that support efforts to improve teaching effectiveness.

Special thanks is due to Gary W. Dickson and A. Milton Jenkins for conducting the AACSB Beginning and Advanced Information Systems Faculty Development Institutes, and for their personal support and encouragement of our efforts in the IS field.

Marilyn Freedman of Addison-Wesley provided invaluable editorial support, guidance and feedback. Juliet Silveri of Addison-Wesley supplied excellent technical support. Students at Roosevelt University provided feedback on drafts. Ken Macur of the University of Wisconsin-Whitewater provided valuable insights and suggestions.

Because feedback is an important part of working with information systems, please send your suggestions, corrections, and recommendations for improving this text to:

Roy D. Johnson, Ph.D.
Department of Management
Roosevelt University
430 S. Michigan Avenue
Chicago, IL 60605

# Contents

# PART I: Microcomputers and Accounting

Computers are now an important part of most Accounting Information Systems (AIS). The most commonly used types of software are electronic spreadsheets, database management systems, and accounting packages. Many organizations use a combination of these different types of software to accomplish the various tasks required.

Chapter 1 briefly reviews the relationship between computers and accounting and the relationship between AIS concepts and PC skills. The chapter introduces report design, documentation, and controls (general and applications), which are the AIS concepts most relevant to the remainder of the book. The chapter concludes with an overview of electronic spreadsheets and database management systems and the importance of being able to integrate different types of software.

Chapter 2 provides a brief overview of IBM-compatible microcomputer hardware, software, and operations. The chapter explains the basic components of a microcomputer, how to start one, the nature and purpose of the operating system, filename conventions, running applications software, and saving and backing up your work. This chapter should be used in conjunction with any handouts provided by your school PC lab or with your DOS manual if you are using your own machine.

Part I will provide the necessary framework and background for using Lotus 1-2-3 and dBASE as part of an Accounting Information Systems course.

# Chapter 1: Concepts of Spreadsheet and Database Usage

## Accounting Information Systems (AIS) and Computers

During their brief history, computers have had a tremendous impact on many aspects of our society. Accounting systems were among the earliest areas to be affected and one in which many far-reaching changes have occurred. Although mainframe and mini computers influenced transaction processing systems in many large and medium-size organizations, it was the arrival of the personal computer (PC), or microcomputer, and the electronic spreadsheet that brought the computer to virtually every accountant's desk during the 1980s. The low prices of PCs and user-friendly **electronic spreadsheet, database management system (DBMS)**, word processing, and accounting software make computerization a reality for even the smallest business and CPA firm.

## Computer Use in Accounting

Accounting functions are among the first applications to be computerized in most organizations. In the 1960s and early 1970s, accounting was often the only functional area to be computerized. **Electronic data processing** (EDP) was performed by the accounting department. Other functional areas, e.g., marketing and production, often had difficulty getting computer applications developed to meet their needs, since accounting jobs typically had first priority. In many organizations today, the **information systems** (IS) department is an independent department comparable to the accounting department, and accounting is only one of the several functional areas it supports. Under these circumstances, accounting applications no longer automatically take first priority, but compete with marketing, production, finance, human resources, and other areas on the basis of their relative importance to the organization and their expected costs and benefits. The trend today is away from department-specific applications and toward integrated systems that support the concept of **information resource management (IRM)**. This requires that the various departments, including accounting, cooperate in designing and developing systems to support those business activities that are critical to the organization.

In medium-size and large organizations, the transaction-processing systems that account for basic organizational functions, such as sales, accounts receivable, accounts payable, and payroll, are typically implemented by IS professionals on mini- or mainframe computers. However, these transaction-processing systems seldom completely meet the needs of the accountants (or other users), especially when it comes to analysis and planning. The PC and the electronic spreadsheet have stepped in to fill this gap.

PCs are used in many ways in accounting systems. In some organizations, they replace dumb terminals as the primary input and output devices for large accounting systems. Data can be entered and edited locally (on the PC) and later **uploaded** (sent electronically) to the larger system. Also, several parts of the accounting function do not have the high volume and frequency of items or transactions necessary to warrant a mainframe application, such as fixed assets or miscellaneous receivables or payables. These parts are often candidates for PC-based spreadsheet or database applications, depending on the specific situation. In other cases, the transaction-processing systems may capture part, but not all, of the data that the accountant needs, or they may not produce the specific reports that are needed. It is becoming more common that accountants can get direct access to data using the mainframe database language, or they can **download** data to a PC and import those data into a microcomputer-based DBMS such as dBASE®. This allows data to be manipulated or modified by the accountant without compromising the integrity of the transaction-processing system.

## Computers and Auditing

The preceding discussion addresses accountants as users of computers. Accountants also have another important relationship with computer-based systems, that of auditors. A major responsibility of accounting is to ensure that internal controls over the assets and operations of the organization are adequate. This relates to all systems of the organization, not only those that are strictly accounting applications. In addition, the increasing systems integration means that the integrity of any single system also depends on the integrity of all other systems with which it is integrated. Accountants are involved in auditing the operational systems to ensure that they are functioning effectively and efficiently and that adequate internal controls are functioning properly. Because it is much easier and cheaper to incorporate good internal controls in the initial design than to add them after the system is operational, accountants and auditors are also often consulted about internal controls during project development. It is important that the auditors are not so heavily involved in the systems design that they compromise their ability to function as independent auditors of the system at a later date. PCs, spreadsheets, and generalized audit software (which has many of the features of a DBMS) are valuable in conducting both internal and external audits. A portable PC is now almost as common a sight on an audit as the traditional leather workbag.

## AIS Concepts and PC Skills

Because of the importance of computers in accounting, many AIS courses also cover microcomputers, spreadsheets, and/or DBMS software. Too often, this hands-on part of the course bears no relation to the conceptual materials covered in the AIS textbook. This is unfortunate, since the AIS concepts should and could easily be reinforced by the hands-on work and vice versa.

This text focuses on using spreadsheets and DBMS software in AIS. In addition to covering the technical skills of using spreadsheets and DBMS software, it integrates hands-on computer use into the accounting information systems course by explicitly linking AIS concepts to the hands-on use of hardware and software. A unique feature of this text is the correlation of AIS concepts to the types of problems and issues typically found in an AIS text.

The growing emphasis on systems integration makes it important for students to understand the related concepts and how to apply techniques for integrating data within and among various accounting applications. Although PC software is rapidly becoming more integrated and more easily integratable, substantial effort is still needed to transfer data among different software packages. Two chapters in this book are devoted to how and why spreadsheets and databases can be integrated. Both linking and transferring data within a single type of software and various options for transferring data among different software packages are addressed.

Students with no prior microcomputer experience can use this text to learn the fundamentals of the most popular spreadsheet (Lotus 1-2-3) and database management system (dBASE) software. This text uses accounting applications in its illustrations and practice exercises, thus exposing accounting students to how PCs, spreadsheets, and databases can be used to perform accounting-related tasks. It can be used alone or with a more extensive reference text on PCs and software. If students already know how to use Lotus 1-2-3 and/or dBASE, this text provides them with an opportunity to practice and reinforce their skills using accounting applications and to learn how the accounting concepts relate to hands-on use.

The AIS concepts most relevant to the use of spreadsheets and DBMS relate to report design, documentation, application controls, and general accounting controls. Relevant concepts are applied in the examples, and students are encouraged to apply them in the practice exercises.

# Report Design and Documentation

Although perhaps not typically thought of in terms of communication skills, good report-design skills are important to accountants. The object of most accounting output is to communicate to the user the financial status of the organization (balance sheet), the results of operations (income statement), the proposed financial activities and performance (budgets), or virtually anything else that can be communicated using tables of numbers. This is true whether the outputs are generated manually or using a computer.

A well-designed report helps the user comprehend the relevant information quickly and correctly and facilitates making a good decision based on the reported information. What constitutes a good report depends on the decision to be made. A report that serves one purpose well will serve other purposes poorly or not at all. Therefore, the first consideration is to include only data that are **relevant** to the decision being made. All relevant data should be included for **completeness**, and only relevant data should be included for **conciseness**. The data should also be as **accurate** and as **precise** as is appropriate to the data and the problem at hand. For example, less precise data would be acceptable for a report containing price estimates, but exact price data are required for the report that specifies what checks are to be paid today.

While using only and all relevant data is a necessary condition of good reporting, it is not sufficient to ensure effective and efficient communication. Using relevant data is much easier if the data are appropriately **organized** and **summarized**. If the user has to rearrange the data or do additional calculations to get the needed information, the report should have organized the data in a different order and performed the necessary calculations. Since computers are very fast and accurate at reorganizing and calculating, it is appropriate to have computers do those clerical tasks and let humans spend their time doing the problem solving and decision making that computers are not capable of doing. Usually, a specific organization is more appropriate than others for a given decision. For example, the white pages of a phone book (which is a detailed report of all the listed phone numbers in an area) are useful when the data are organized alphabetically, but they would be useless if the data were organized randomly or by the date each number was first put in service. A second way of organizing certain parts of the data in a phone book was considered so useful that the Yellow Pages were developed, and businesses are willing to pay to have their data presented in this differently organized (alphabetically within type of business) report. Data are summarized with sums, average counts, and other statistics. Generally, the higher the organizational level of the decision maker, the more summarized a report should be. Data are also **transformed** by calculating percentages or differences or by performing other arithmetic manipulations of numeric data. Transformations often improve the ability of the data to show relationships.

The visual display of a report should contribute to easy, accurate perception of the data. In addition to data organization, appropriate use of lines and spacing also greatly facilitates data perception. Data can be grouped (signifying relatedness), separated by lines or spaces (signifying differences), or highlighted by special characters (signifying importance). Although conciseness is desired, a report should not look cramped or cluttered.

Documentation is an important part of report design. At a minimum, documentation should include the report title and the data descriptions in column headings and rows. It should usually also include other data identifying who generated the report, the date (and possibly the time) it was generated, and the name of the file the hard-copy report was generated from, if it is a computer-generated report. It may also include information on data sources, data descriptions, units of measure, calculations, formulas, and the purpose of the report. This information can be contained in a separate documentation section of the report, within the body of the report, or in footnotes.

In general, all parts of a report should be complete, concise, and easy to comprehend. Poorly designed reports waste time and introduce the likelihood of human error. The higher the position of the managers using a report and the larger the number of managers using it, the higher the cost of the time being wasted. Perhaps even more important is the cost of making a bad decision based on a poorly formatted report.

## General and Application Controls

Many systems developed by end users lack even the most basic controls. As responsible end users, accountants should be aware of proper controls and incorporate them in their own information systems. Because they are responsible for the integrity and security of data and other assets, accountants must also be able to evaluate the controls in other parts of the information system.

Input controls are among the most important applications controls and involve making sure that only correct data enter the system. Some input controls are found in most end-user-oriented packages, such as spreadsheets and DBMS. These controls usually cause the system to display an error message on the screen while simultaneously making an annoying beeping sound when the user tries to enter incorrect data. The **redundancy** of having two signals increases the probability that the message will be received. Although often perceived as bad, redundancy is sometimes useful and appropriate. These types of errors generally involve such things as incorrect punctuation, spacing, or spelling of commands.

Content errors, such as entering the number 36 instead of 63, are more difficult to detect. Some content checks can be programmed. For example, a limit check can be set to prevent amounts above a specified number to be entered. If an extra 0 is deliberately or inadvertently added to a check amount, this type of control would catch it. Designing data-entry screens to have the same format as a familiar hard-copy document from which data are being transcribed decreases the likelihood that a user will attempt to enter erroneous data. In integrated information systems, it is possible to have the computer check each entry against a table of allowable values before accepting the data. It should be noted that adding such controls often requires substantial additional work to get a system operational. The time and effort required to incorporate such controls must be compared to the risks and costs of operating the system without the controls.

Debugging and testing refer to the process of making sure a system works properly before putting it into operation. This involves having the system perform tasks for which you know the correct results and making sure the system produces the correct results. Often this is as simple as making a manual calculation or manually selecting records that meet specified conditions. The tricky part is determining the effect of all possible data oddities or errors and making sure you have tested the system under the worst possible conditions as well as the best. Sometimes it is painfully obvious that the results are not what you desire, such as the generation of a blank piece of paper that should have contained a report. However, a sum that accidentally excludes the last row of data is much more difficult to detect. The process of constructing a worksheet, displaying the results, reviewing the output, then making adjustments to correct errors or omissions is a testing and debugging process.

Another common weakness in end-user-developed systems involves security, backup, and recovery procedures. Security is making sure that only authorized persons have access to data, software, and hardware. Leaving a backpack unattended is a common security breach in a student environment and often leads to time and money costs of replacing books, notes, papers, and homework assignments. Some of this property, such as detailed class notes, may be irreplaceable. Backup is the ability to recover from such a situation or from a natural disaster such as a flood in the basement where your materials are stored. If you can borrow books from a friend and have copies of your notes, data disks, and software in a different place, you are unusually well backed-up and positioned to recover from the disaster. When working with a computer, you should save your work frequently and always keep an up-to-date copy of your data file under a different name on the same disk, as well as under the same name on a different disk that is stored in a separate place. The more common disasters in end-user computing involve user error (such as deleting the wrong file or formatting the wrong disk), spilling coffee, leaving disks in a hot car, or having a briefcase stolen. Although they do require some time (to make copies and store them) and expense (extra disks), good backup procedures and other security practices will save much needless grief, aggravation, and expense.

# Electronic Spreadsheets

Accountants have always been among the heaviest users of spreadsheets. In fact, manual spreadsheet paper, organized into rows and columns, was associated almost exclusively with accountants and accounting applications. Any task that requires you to arrange numbers in rows and columns and to perform calculations is a likely task for a spreadsheet. The user enters formulas in the spreadsheet location where they are to be displayed, and the spreadsheet performs the calculations. If any of the numbers referenced in the formula change, the spreadsheet recalculates and changes the displayed value without further effort by the user. In a manual spreadsheet, if a number changes or an error is discovered, all the totals and other items that were calculated using that number must be erased and recalculated. Not only is the process time consuming and error prone, it is likely that one or more items that should be changed will be missed. Any time you find yourself with a paper full of numbers and a calculator, consider using Lotus 1-2-3 instead.

Although features continue to be added, the ability to use formulas to model the relationships among data is the distinguishing characteristic of a spreadsheet. Spreadsheets are commonly used in "what if?" analysis, to examine the effects of different assumptions or changing conditions on some item of interest, such as profits or sales. This "what if?" modeling capability allows managers to use spreadsheets as simple, but effective, **decision support systems**. Many accounting tasks can be performed faster and better with an electronic spreadsheet. Consolidations, budgeting, automated audit work papers, capital budgeting, fixed-asset analysis, and trial balances are but a few of the accounting tasks that have benefited from the application of spreadsheet technology.

In addition to the numeric calculations and modeling, many spreadsheets incorporate the ability to display numbers graphically and to do simple data-management functions. Graphs are generally considered superior to tables of numbers for communicating information about relationships and trends. Users can enter data in a spreadsheet, easily define and display the data graphically, enter a few new numbers into the spreadsheet, and immediately display the same type of graphs based on the new data. This has caused a dramatic increase in the use of graphics in financial analysis and reporting. Although the graphics capabilities of spreadsheets are much less powerful than those of dedicated graphics software, they are adequate for most users' needs and are improving with each new software release. The data-management functions of spreadsheets are also much more limited than those of a DBMS, but sufficient for doing many simple tasks of sorting, extracting, and locating data that meet certain criteria. Some spreadsheets have a command language that provides powerful programing capabilities, and word-processing capabilities (although still generally poor) are also improving.

## Database Management Systems (DBMS)

Just as your calculator should remind you to use Lotus 1-2-3, a file drawer, rolodex, or index file should prompt you to consider using a DBMS. Any task that involves locating data that meet certain conditions, reorganizing data, or linking different types of related data is a good candidate for DBMS software. The ability to enter data only once and use it in many different types of output contributes to data consistency and integrity. Although the financial cost of storing data in several places can be significant, it pales beside the cost of trying to keep several sets of data consistent.

Unlike electronic spreadsheets, DBMSs were initially designed to be used primarily for implementing transaction-processing systems, and they include a powerful programming language with which to do so. Unfortunately, this has meant that DBMSs tend to lack menus and other user-friendly attributes that are taken for granted in spreadsheets. As the user community has demanded easier-to-use, as well as more powerful, software, the DBMS vendors have made substantial improvements in the user friendliness of their systems. PC DBMSs typically include only data-management capabilities. They do not have the formulas and data-modeling capabilities found in spreadsheets, although they can perform arithmetic calculations. They also do not typically include graphical display capabilities.

## Integrating Software

While some packages integrate spreadsheet and DBMS capabilities, they typically are not as good at either task as a stand-alone spreadsheet or DBMS. Since each type of software has advantages for certain purposes, it is valuable to be able to transfer data among different types of software. The ability to share data in this manner can save time, facilitate communication, and lessen the opportunity for users to introduce data-entry errors.

It is also important to be able to get data from and send data to larger systems. The PC is no longer purely personal, as both local area networks (LANs) and wide area networks (WANs) continue to expand. For example, an auditor might use a DBMS to extract selected data items from a mainframe data file, then transfer the selected data into a spreadsheet to analyze the selected items and balances. A corporate accountant responsible for fixed-asset accounting may be able to extract the fixed-asset transactions from the larger system's database for use in the fixed-asset subsidiary records.

## Chapter Review

This chapter has discussed several AIS concepts, and their relation to computers and PC skills. You should keep in mind the AIS concepts related to report design, documentation, and controls (general and applications) as you develop your PC skills throughout the reminder of the book. Notice how these concepts are applied in the hands-on case examples, and remember to apply them as you complete the practice exercises and perform other computing activities. Also notice the similarities, overlaps, and differences between electronic spreadsheets and database management systems and the kinds of tasks to which each applies. If you have to perform tasks that require different types of software but involve the same data, the integration chapters will help you transfer data to the appropriate software environment.

The remainder of this book focuses much more on the technical aspects of using PC spreadsheets and DBMS software. Since PC skills can be learned only by practice, which includes a lot of trial and error, you will spend a substantial amount of time at the computer screen and keyboard. Although it is easy to get lost in the technical details of which button to push, try to keep in mind the concepts and issues discussed in this chapter and recognize them when they recur throughout the text. The person with the best technical skills can aspire to be an expert technician, but the person with good technical skills and an understanding of when, why, and how to use them can aspire to be a manager.

# Chapter 2: Getting Started on a Microcomputer

Computers have had a significant impact on our society, especially on business and accounting practices. The introduction of the microcomputer, or personal computer (PC), during the late 1970s brought the power and speed of electronic processing to the desk top, giving large numbers of individuals direct access to computers for the first time. The penetration of business and society by computers continues to drive the technological revolution in information processing and accounting.

Computers come in many different sizes. This book deals only with microcomputers, which are the smallest, least expensive, and most popular. Many accountants now use a microcomputer on a daily basis in the office, at client work sites, and at home. Both hardware (the computer) and software (an operating system and applications software) are required for the computer to do useful work. This chapter briefly introduces computers and the computing process, emphasizing the skills and knowledge you need to use the programs discussed in the rest of this book.

## Hardware

Think of computer hardware as the physical things you can touch. This simplistic definition distinguishes the physical devices from the software (programs). This book covers only IBM® PCs and compatible computers. There may be occasional slight differences between this book and how your system works. If you run into a problem, consult the manual for your system, your lab manager at school, or your information center at work.

## Central Processing Unit (CPU)

The central processing unit (CPU) is the engine that powers the computer. In general, the faster the processor, the more powerful and expensive the computer. The CPU (often called the "processor") is divided into three parts: the **arithmetic/logical unit**, which processes data with arithmetic operators (+ - * /) and logical operators (= < >); the **control unit**, which directs the flow of data; and the **primary storage** or **main memory**, which holds data and instructions for processing. Primary storage is temporary random access memory (RAM) storage within the computer. The copy of the program and the data in main memory are lost as soon as the power is turned off.

# Input Devices

The user sends data or instructions to the computer with an input device. The most common input device is the *keyboard*, which has three sections: function keys, numeric keypad, and main section (Figure 2.1).

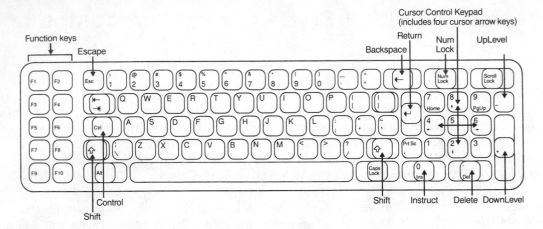

**Figure 2.1  IBM Keyboard Divided into Sections and Labeled**

The **function** keys are located on the left side (or across the top on some keyboards) of the keyboard and labeled F1, F2...F10. They perform special functions, or activities, which vary depending on the software you are using at the time. The F3 key, for example, does not do the same thing in Lotus 1-2-3 that it does in DOS or dBASE. The **numeric key pad** is located on the right side of the keyboard. It serves two purposes, depending on whether Num Lock is on or off. With Num Lock on, it is used to enter numeric data. With Num Lock off, it is used to control the movement of the cursor around the screen. For this reason, these keys are also called **arrow** keys or **cursor-control** keys. Accountants often use the numeric key pad to enter numeric data quickly. For added convenience, many newer keyboards have separate cursor-control keys.

The main section of the keyboard, which looks like a conventional typewriter keyboard, contains letters, numbers, symbols, and special keys. The **Backspace** key (upper right corner of the main section, sometimes labeled with a ⇐. ) deletes the character to the left of the cursor. The **Delete** key (bottom center of the numeric keypad) removes the character under the cursor. The **Return** key (right side, middle row) sends commands to the computer. The Return key is often labeled with a ↵, or it is larger or shaped differently than the other keys. The Return key is sometimes also called the Carriage Return or Enter key, although most keyboards have a separate **Enter** key (lower right corner of the numeric keypad), which can be used interchangeably with the Return key. The **Print Screen** key sends the screen contents to the printer when the Shift key is held down. The **space bar** (long key, center bottom row) sends a "blank" symbol to the computer. It is important to note that a computer uses a separate symbol to represent and store a blank, unlike typewriters, which simply skip a space.

The **Escape** key, located in the upper left corner of the keyboard, is used to cancel or interrupt a command. It is a very important key in Lotus 1-2-3 and other software because it can get the user (you) out of trouble. The **Shift** key is used as it is on a typewriter; holding it down and pressing another key gives an uppercase letter, or the topmost symbol on keys with two characters. The **Alternate** and **Control** keys, located on the left side of the keyboard, also work by being held down while another key is pressed. They are used in combination with other keys to perform special functions, which, like the function keys, vary depending on the particular software you are using.

Some keys in the keyboard turn "on" and "off" and are called "toggle" keys. Pressing a toggle key once turns a feature on, and pressing it again turns the feature off. When **Num Lock** is on, the numeric keypad enters numbers; when it is off, the cursor-control keys are in effect. **Scroll Lock** affects the appearance of screen movement and depends on the program being used. **Caps Lock** makes all letters uppercase. The **Ins** (insert) key affects whether data are entered between existing characters or replace them. Except for Shift, Control, Alternate, and the toggle keys, a key automatically repeats when it is held down.

The keys that contain symbols are found mainly on the upper and lower rows and at the right side of the main section of the keyboard. They include ! @ # $ % ^ & * ( ) _ - + = : " ' ~ \ < , > . ? /. Other keys that contain symbols are the arrow keys found on the numeric keypad (← ↑ → ↓). The Return key is represented on many keyboards as ↵ and the Backspace key as ⇐. For consistency, in this book the symbol ↵ indicates either the Return or the Enter key unless otherwise specified. The word "enter" means "type the indicated characters and press ↵." For example "enter DIR" means type the letters DIR and press ↵. This book uses square brackets ([ ]) to indicate specific named keys to be pressed during an exercise. For example, the Escape key is shown as [Esc]. The named keys are as follows:

**Keyboard**

| Key | Description |
| --- | --- |
| [Alt] | Alternate |
| [Backspace] | Backspace (same as ⇐) |
| [Caps Lock] | Capital Letter Lock |
| [Ctrl] | Control |
| [Esc] | Escape |
| [Num Lock] | Number Lock |
| [PrtSc] | Print Screen |
| [Return] | Return (same as [Enter] or ↵) |
| [Scroll Lock] | Scroll Lock |
| [Shift] | Shift (sometimes seen as ⇧) |

**Numeric Key Pad**

| Key | Description |
| --- | --- |
| [Del] | Delete |
| [End] | End or last |
| [Enter] | Enter (same as [Return] or ↵) |
| [Home] | Home or beginning |
| [Ins] | Insert |
| [PgDn] | Page Down |
| [PgUp] | Page Up |

## Output Devices

Output devices present data in a form that users can read. The most popular output devices are monitors and printers. The **monitor,** which displays output on the computer **screen,** is the primary microcomputer output device. Monitors provide only temporary, or soft-copy, output and can be monochrome or color. **Monochrome** monitors use two contrasting colors to project a clear, crisp image on the screen and are excellent for text output. **Color** monitors are excellent for presenting graphics, graphs, and games, but they are poor for text because they lack clarity. The quality of a color monitor can be enhanced considerably if a graphics adapter board is placed in the computer.

A **printer** provides permanent, or hard-copy, output on paper. The printers you are likely to be using include dot-matrix, ink-jet, and laser printers. **Dot-matrix** printers strike an inked ribbon with pins to form images on the paper. **Ink-jet** printers spray ink from jets onto the paper. **Laser** printers are similar to photocopiers in that a laser beam traces the image onto a photosensitive drum that bonds the toner to the paper with heat.

## Storage Devices: Disks

Long-term storage of data and programs in computer-readable form is provided by **secondary storage**, usually on disks and occasionally on tape. Disks and tapes must be inserted into disk and tape drives, which read data from and write data to the disks and tapes.

You will store data on **magnetic disks**. **Floppy disks** such as the ones packaged with this book are available in 3.5-inch and 5.25-inch sizes and different densities and can store varying quantities of data. Find out from your instructor which type of disk you will need for backup disks. A **hard disk** holds much more data than a floppy disk and is usually built into the computer. If a computer has two floppy disk drives, they usually are labeled A and B.

Following a few simple procedures for dealing with your floppy disks will increase your chances of having the data available when you need it:

- Save and back up files frequently.
- Store disks in their protective paper envelopes in a safe place.

- Do not bend or fold disks.
- Do not expose disks to extreme temperatures (in a car, on a window sill).
- Do not store disks inside books (use plastic diskette carriers).
- Do not touch the exposed disk surface.
- Do not write on a disk. Make the label first and then paste it onto the disk. If you must write on the disk, use only a felt-tip pen. Never use a ballpoint pen or a pencil!

## Starting a Microcomputer

To start a microcomputer with the power **OFF** (cold boot):
1. If you do not have a hard drive and are not connected to a network, insert the DOS disk into disk drive A with the label side up and your thumb on the label.
2. Close the disk-drive door.
3. Turn power on for printer, monitor, and any other peripherals.
4. Turn power on for the computer system

To start a computer with the power **ON** (reset or warm boot):
1. Reinsert the DOS disk if needed.
2. Hold down both the [Ctrl] and [Alt] keys, press [Del] once, then release all three keys.

# Operating Systems

Software is a set of instructions to the computer that makes the hardware perform useful tasks. The **operating system** software controls and manages the computer's hardware operations and the input, output, storage, and manipulation of data. It manages the interaction between the user or application programs and the hardware and contains a number of useful commands for dealing with data files and programs. IBM-compatible PCs use the disk operating system (**DOS**).

## DOS Prompt (A>)

When it is started, or booted, the computer first checks memory to ensure that it is working correctly and then loads the DOS system file (named COMMAND.COM) into main memory so that the computer can respond to the user's commands. If you are prompted for the date and time, enter the date as month/date/year in numbers and the time in European or military time, based on a 24-hour clock (after noon, add 12 hours to the time). For example, 3:45 p.m. on February 6, 1990, would be

```
Enter new date: 02-06-90 ↵
Enter new time: 15:45 ↵
```

A series of messages, including a copyright notice, is then displayed on the screen, followed by the **DOS prompt** (A>), which indicates that DOS is waiting for a command to be entered. The "A" of the DOS prompt indicates that the disk in drive A is the **default,** the one DOS will use for commands unless instructed differently. If you are booting from a hard drive, the DOS prompt is C:\>. Change the default drive by entering the drive letter and a colon. For example, to switch from the hard drive (C) to the A drive, the command would be **A:↵**, which you would type immediately following the DOS prompt, C:\>. DOS would then display A> on the next line, telling you that A is now the default drive.

Notice the blinking underline or rectangle of light immediately to the right of the DOS prompt. This is the **cursor,** which shows you where you are on the screen. This is the point at which the characters will appear when you type anything on the keyboard. If you make a typing mistake that you notice before pressing ↵, you can use the Backspace key (⇐) or the left arrow key (←) to back up and correct the error. If you have already pressed ↵ , DOS will tell you that you made a mistake with the message "Bad command or filename." Reenter the command correctly.

If your computer has a hard drive or is connected to a network, you may be presented with a different set of messages or menus on the screen. The possible variety is infinite, but most of these screens will either give you explicit instructions for using the various programs that are available or provide you with a **menu** of items from which you will select the one you want. With most menus, you use the arrow keys on the numeric keypad (8 moves up, 2 moves down, 4 moves left, and 6 moves right) to highlight, or point to, the item you want and then press ↵ to select it. These arrow keys are used in many programs to control movement around the computer screen.

## DOS Commands

DOS commands tell DOS to perform an operation. A few of the most important DOS commands are listed next with examples and descriptions. Other commands can be found in the DOS manual. The examples assume A is the default drive. The location of blanks (spaces) and punctuation in a command line is important. If a DOS command doesn't work, recheck the command line for blanks. The commands are the same whether you have one or two disk drives; a one-drive machine just takes a little longer.

| Command | Example | Description |
|---|---|---|
| CLS | **CLS** | Clear the screen. |
| COMP | **COMP** ABC XYZ | Compare file ABC to file XYZ. |
| COPY | **COPY** ABC B: | Copy file ABC on drive A to drive B. |
|  | **COPY** ABC DEF | Copy file ABC to file DEF, both on drive A. |
|  | **COPY** ABC B:DEF | Copy file ABC to file DEF on drive B:. |
| DEL | **DEL** ABC | Delete file ABC from the default-drive disk. |
| DIR | **DIR** | List all files on the disk in the default drive. |
|  | **DIR** B: | List all files on the disk in drive B. |
| DISKCOMP | **DISKCOMP** A: B: | Compare disk in drive A to disk in drive B. |
| DISKCOPY | **DISKCOPY** A: B: | Copy disk in drive A to disk in drive B. |
| ERASE | **ERASE** XYZ | Erase file XYZ; same as DEL. |
| FORMAT | **FORMAT** A: | Erase disk in drive A and prepare for use. |
| RENAME | **RENAME** ABC XYZ | Change the name of file ABC to XYZ. |
| TYPE | **TYPE** ABC | Print file ABC on the screen. |

The **FORMAT** command must be used to prepare a new disk for use. A disk cannot be used until it is formatted. Most disks will be formatted only once, since formatting a used disk *erases all data* on the disk. **DIR** tells you what files are on a disk. **COPY** is used in making backups, and **DEL** is used to get rid of files you no longer need. These are the DOS commands you will use most. Figure 2.2 shows the screen as it appears after you boot the computer and enter the date and time. Note that only a single DOS command should be typed immediately following the DOS prompt, and sent to the computer by pressing ↵. When the DOS prompt appears again (after DOS has carried out your last command, or told you that it can't do it), you can enter the next command.

```
Current date is Wed 12-20-1989
Enter new date (mm-dd-yy): 1-1-90
Current time is 16:45:14.67
Enter new time: 10:15

MS-DOS Version 3.30
A:\>_
```

Figure 2.2 DOS screen

## Filenames and Extensions

A **file** is a collection of related instructions or data with a unique name. The unique **filename** is from one to eight characters long and can be followed by a one- to three-character **file extension** with a *period* to separate the two parts e.g., (STUDENT.TXT).

Spaces (blanks) and the symbols % , < > \."/ [ ] are not allowed in filenames. Some programs (e.g., Lotus 1-2-3 and dBASE) create file extensions for you; other programs require you to enter them.

## Wild Cards (? *)

**Wild cards** let DOS commands work on more than one file at a time. The two wild cards used by DOS are ? and *. The ? in a filename or extension in a command indicates that any *one character* can occupy the ? position. For a directory listing of all versions of a file named RESUME1.TXT, RESUME2.TXT, and so on, the DOS command is: DIR RESUME?.TXT. The result is a list of all files with names that start with RESUME, followed by any single character (represented by the wild card ?), a period, and the extension TXT.

A * in a filename or extension in a DOS command indicates that *one or more characters* can occupy that position. For the directory listing of all files starting with the letters RES, the DOS command is DIR RES*.*. The result is a list of all files with RES as the first three letters of the filename.

## Application Programs

**Application programs** or **application packages** do specific work, such as word processing, spreadsheets, database management, accounting, graphics, and telecommunications.

There are many accounting application programs, ranging from simple, inexpensive systems to complex, expensive ones. The modules most commonly available in accounting systems are accounts receivable, accounts payable, payroll, general ledger, and inventory or cost accounting. Although extremely valuable, these accounting systems seldom meet all the needs of accountants and managers. This book covers two of the most popular types of software used by accountants, electronic spreadsheets and database management systems.

The two application programs used in this book are the Lotus 1-2-3 electronic spreadsheet program and the dBASE III PLUS database management system. The hands-on use of the software is integrated with explanations of the relevant accounting information systems concepts, so you can apply AIS concepts as you learn to use the software. Lotus is used for numerical modeling and analysis and for displaying output graphically. dBASE is used for answering ad hoc questions, generating reports, and processing transactions.

## Loading Application Software

Perhaps the most important operation that DOS performs is loading application software into the computer so it can be used. This is done by entering a command at the DOS prompt, usually the software name or an abbreviation of it.

## Versions and Release Numbers

Most commercial software has a version number, which indicates major changes in the program, and a release number, which indicates minor modifications. For example, Lotus 2.2 went through one major change since starting as version 1.0 and two minor changes since version 2.0. Both Lotus and dBASE also have student editions, which have their own differences. Work done using one version can usually run on newer versions but will seldom run on older versions. If you use version 3.0 to work on a project, then try to use version 2.1 to do more work or even just to print output, you will be unable to do so. If you plan to do work in more than one location and will not be using your own version of the software, make sure the version and release numbers are the same or compatible. Appendices B and D discuss different versions of Lotus and dBASE.

## Saving and Backing Up Data and Software

Work in an application program like Lotus is done in the main memory of the computer. If you want to **save** that work for later use, it must be copied onto a disk, where it is saved in a file. Each application has its own series of commands to save work on a disk. If you make *any* changes to your work, you must save it again to keep those changes.

Backing up means making a second copy of a file or files that have already been saved on a disk. Although the examples of the COPY and DISKCOPY commands above show *how* to copy files using DOS, it may not be clear *why* you need to make copies. Many end users learn the answer to this question the hard way, by losing valuable software, data, and time because they did not make a copy when they should have. Backup deals with when, where, why, and under what name to make copies of files.

## Save Frequently!!!

Saving is a vital function in any computing environment, but it is especially important in PC work. It is a good habit to save your work every 15 minutes in case of a disaster caused by nature or you. Good saving and backup practices, consistently performed, are an important aspect of good internal control in an AIS. Your own experience will probably provide you with concrete evidence of the importance of well-thought-out backup procedures (for naming files, labeling and storing disks, and making the necessary copies). The importance of following backup procedures consistently and (for some of you) the unpleasant consequences of inadequate backup and recovery planning and implementation cannot be overemphasized.

## Backup Files

Many backup copies are made on the same disk with different names. One major reason for making a backup file on the same disk under a different name is that some software (e.g., dBASE) can occasionally lose or damage the file it is working with. While some software is more prone to such accidents than others, no software is completely fail-safe. Although software and power failures are rare, when one occurs it is crucial to have a **backup**, or a second copy of the file. It is common to use the same filename with the extension .BAK. Much of the software available today will provide automatic saving and backup at a time interval specified by the user. This is an excellent system design feature to enhance backup and recovery procedures, which are important in having a high-quality, reliable AIS.

At other times, you may want to save different versions of a file for other reasons, such as to document your progress or to examine the effects of different design features. In this situation, it is common to use a sequence of numbers in the filename or extension to indicate the different versions. For example, to keep different versions of a file called RESUME.TXT, you might name the different old versions RESUME1.TXT, RESUME2.TXT, and so on, leaving the basic RESUME.TXT as the current version of your resume.

## Backup Disks

Although floppy disks are fairly durable, they do occasionally fail for no obvious reason. They have coffee spilled on them, are chewed by pets, are lost or stolen, or meet a fate that has nothing to do with the disk quality. Although hard disks are less susceptible to most of these disasters, they still occur. If any of these disasters occurs, and you do not have your work backed up, you will lose hours of work and the additional time to reenter your data. A **backup disk** is a separate disk that contains copies of all of your important software and data files. We will not deal with backing up entire hard disks here; if that is necessary, see your computer and DOS manuals. It is good practice and safer to store the backup disk in a separate location from the main disk, although you will need to have both disks to make and update the backup disk. Generally, a backup disk should be updated at the end of each computer session or day.

You can always use DOS to make backup copies of files and disks, no matter what software was used to generate the data files. However, some software packages (e.g., Lotus) make it just as easy to place a copy of a file on your backup data disk when you save it on the data disk. For the exercises contained in this book, the Student Data Disk and one backup data disk should be sufficient. If you own your own software, such as the Student Edition of Lotus or dBASE, follow the instructions in the manual(s) on making backup copies.

## Ending a Computer Session

When you want to stop working on the computer, be sure to save your work before leaving the application program. **EXIT** or **QUIT** are the commands most often used to close the files and return to DOS, where you will again see the DOS prompt (A>). Use the COPY command to back up any files that you worked on during the session. Remember to periodically make a copy of important files on a separate disk. Remove your disks from the drives, place them in their protective paper envelopes, and turn off the power to the computer. Then turn off the monitor, printer, and any other peripherals.

## Chapter Review

This chapter introduced the basic hardware components of an IBM-compatible PC, and the DOS operating system used to run it. A few crucial DOS operations (such as formatting disks, copying files, and running applications programs) and conventions (such as file names) were discussed, and different ways of backing up your data were introduced. This level of coverage should be sufficient to allow you to complete the Lotus and dBASE topics covered in Parts II and III. You can explore the many additional DOS capabilities by using your DOS manual.

# PART II: Lotus 1-2-3

Electronic spreadsheets are the type of software most widely used by accountants, and Lotus 1-2-3 is the best-selling electronic spreadsheet software available today. Electronic spreadsheets are commonly used by accountants in even the smallest accounting firms, businesses, and nonprofit organizations. The next four chapters will show you how you can use Lotus 1-2-3 to be a more efficient and effective accountant in whatever career setting you choose.

Performance reports that compare actual costs to budgeted costs and calculate variances are among the most common and most important accounting tools. Some form of performance reporting can be found in almost every accounting information system. Since Lotus is extremely useful for generating and modifying performance reports, we use a performance reporting system as the sample accounting application throughout the next four chapters. The work you will do here is typical of the kind of work that recent accounting graduates might find themselves required to perform on the job.

Chapter 3 introduces you to the basics of getting into and out of Lotus 1-2-3, manipulating data, using Lotus commands, formulas, and functions, and printing, saving, and retrieving your work. By the time you have completed this chapter, you will have created, saved, and printed a simple performance report for the laundry department of the Argon County Hospital. The material in Chapter 3 assumes only that you have read the preceding two chapters in this book.

In Chapter 4, you will learn to use additional Lotus features to modify your performance report to make it more powerful and flexible. Although initial planning and design are important, changes and enhancements are likely as the report is used. Fortunately, Lotus makes it easy to implement improvements or corrections. Chapter 5 covers advanced Lotus topics of displaying output with graphs, writing macros to save time, and using Lotus' database management capabilities. Chapter 6 covers integrating separate Lotus worksheets using the File commands, as well as integrating Lotus with other application software by importing and exporting data in a variety of formats.

The objective of Part II is to provide you with a solid foundation of Lotus skills and knowledge to implement accounting information systems. While it is impossible for this book to cover all aspects of all the features of Lotus, you will be introduced to most of the capabilities of Lotus. That foundation will allow you to continue to learn more about Lotus on your own, in other courses, and during your accounting career. You will continue your learning by using more extensive Lotus reference manuals and, most important, by experimenting with using Lotus yourself.

# Chapter 3: Getting Started with Lotus 1-2-3

Lotus 1-2-3 consists of a set of programs designed to harness the power of computers to help accountants and managers perform tasks they would otherwise do manually using a pencil and eraser, a calculator, and paper organized in rows and columns. The user must first decide whether Lotus is most appropriate for the task at hand. Chapter 1 discussed the kinds of tasks for which spreadsheets are most useful. The case and practice exercises have been selected to provide examples of relevant Lotus applications. You will gain a better understanding of how to spot such tasks by completing the case and the practice exercises.

The first step is to understand the task or problem at hand. The relevant information is provided for you in the next section of this chapter. The following sections will teach you to load the necessary Lotus software, understand what is displayed on your computer screen, move around the worksheet, enter and modify data, use Lotus commands to modify the worksheet appearance, and print, save, and retrieve a worksheet.

## Case Setting

Argon County Hospital is a small hospital in the county seat of a popular summer resort area. The hospital had been experiencing rapidly increasing costs and operating deficits. A new controller, who has five years' experience as an auditor in the health-care practice of a large CPA firm, was recently hired to improve the financial performance of the hospital. The new controller has decided to provide quarterly performance reports to each department as the first step in helping department heads manage their operations better. You have just been hired as the special assistant to the controller, and your first assignment is to use Lotus 1-2-3 to develop a performance report for the laundry department of the hospital. Once a good report form has been developed, it will be implemented for other departments. Although the controller knows what types of data the performance report should contain, the department heads are expected to provide input and suggestions for improving the content of the report or the underlying assumptions. Lotus is ideal for performing the necessary calculations and will allow the report to be modified easily once the basic data is entered.

Performance reports are used in many different situations to help managers evaluate the performance of a department or other organizational unit. They contain actual performance measures, standard performance measures (usually a budget), and differences between the actual and the standard (variances). Variances as a percentage of budget are also frequently calculated and shown, to give a better understanding of the significance of the variance in relation to the standard amount. In this case, the relevant output performance measures are considered to be pounds of laundry processed and patient days, and the relevant input performance measures are expenses of the laundry department.[1]

This chapter will take you step by step through the construction of a simple performance report for the laundry department of Argon County Hospital. As you read through this chapter, follow the instructions by actually performing them, using Lotus 1-2-3 on an IBM-compatible microcomputer or personal computer (PC). If you are a new Lotus user, it may be a good idea to read through the chapter once before starting, then go through the chapter again performing each step on the computer as instructed. By the time you complete this chapter, you will have constructed, saved, and printed the performance report shown in Figure 3.1, which is what the controller wants the report to look like.

```
        Student Name: Sandy Student
              Course: AIS 200


Documentation:
    The quarterly report calculates the VARIANCE
(BUDGET minus ACTUAL), then divides VARIANCE by the
BUDGET to give % over or under budget.

Argon County Hospital
Performance Report - Laundry Department
July - September 1990

                                      VARIANCE
                                       (OVER)  VARIANCE
                                        UNDER    % OF
                      BUDGET   ACTUAL   BUDGET   BUDGET


Patient Days          9,500    11,900  (2,400)   -25%
Pounds Processed    125,000   156,000 (31,000)   -25%


        COSTS
Laundry Labor        $9,000   $12,500 ($3,500)   -39%
Supplies              1,100     1,875   (775)    -70%
Water                 1,700     2,500   (800)    -47%
Maintenance           1,400     2,200   (800)    -57%
Supervisor's Salary   3,150     3,750   (600)    -19%
Allocated Admin. Costs 4,000    5,000 (1,000)    -25%
Equipment Depreciation 1,200    1,250    (50)     -4%


TOTAL               $21,550   $29,075 ($7,525)   -35%
```

**Figure 3.1 Laundry department performance report (Final)**

---

[1]   From CMA Examination. Taken from Barry E. Cushing and Marshall B. Romney, *Accounting Information Systems*, Fifth Edition. Reading, MA: Addison-Wesley Publishing Company, 1990, 55–56.

## Loading Lotus

Now that the problem is understood, the relevant accounting report has been designed, and the decision to use Lotus has been made, you must instruct the computer to let you use Lotus. To start the Lotus 1-2-3 application program you must have already loaded the operating system and be at the operating-system level, as discussed in Chapter 2. If you are using a PC that is on a network or a PC with a hard drive, enter LOTUS or 123 at the DOS prompt or select "Lotus" or "1-2-3" from the menu, if your computer has one. Remember: "enter" means *type* and press ↵. If you are working with a computer system that requires you to load Lotus 1-2-3 from a floppy disk, insert the 1-2-3 system disk (backup copy) into the A drive. At the A> prompt, enter LOTUS. The next screen you will see is the "1-2-3 Access System" with a series of menu options at the top of the screen (Figure 3.2).

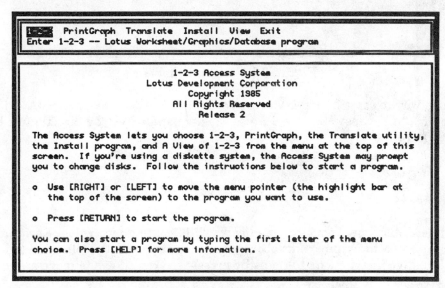

Figure 3.2  Lotus 1-2-3 access system

The default selection is 1-2-3, which is highlighted in inverse video and located first on the menu. Press ↵ to select the highlighted option, 1-2-3. A copyright screen will display a large 123 while Lotus is being loaded into main memory. You then will see a blank worksheet (Figure 3.3). If you entered 123, you will not see an Access System, but will immediately see a blank worksheet. You must enter 123 instead of LOTUS if you are using the Student Edition.

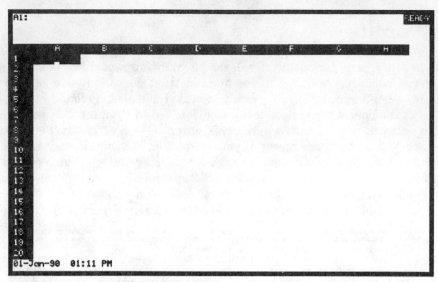

**Figure 3.3  Blank worksheet**

An alternative way to start Lotus, if you are working from the DOS prompt (A>), is to enter 123. This command bypasses the 1-2-3 Access System and takes you directly to a blank worksheet (Figure 3.3).

# Screen Tour

This section describes how Lotus communicates with you and vice versa. Each area of the screen tells you something important about what Lotus is currently doing and the status of your work. You give instructions to Lotus by pressing various keys to move around the screen and enter commands or data.

## When in Trouble Press [Esc] !

To begin the screen tour of the blank worksheet, you should know that there is one key that will get you out of almost any trouble you can create — the Escape key. This key is the single most important key on the keyboard for all new Lotus users and many experienced users. The Escape key will get you out of almost anything and back to the worksheet where you can try again. Remember, when in trouble press [Esc]!!!

## Columns, Rows, Cells, and Cell Addresses

A Lotus worksheet consists of a series of columns and rows that form a grid. The columns are represented by the letters A through Z, followed by AA, AB...AZ, then by BA...BZ, CA...CZ, and so on. The rows are represented by numbers, beginning with 1. The column letter and row number are indicated on the upper and left borders of the worksheet. This border of letters and numbers is always visible on the screen.

This combination of columns and rows provides a method of locating any intersection on the worksheet. This layout is similar to a street map that has the borders labeled with letters and numbers. The intersection of a column and a row is called a **cell**. Each cell has a unique **cell address**, which represents its location in the worksheet. The cell address consists of a column letter(s) followed by a row number. Legitimate cell addresses include A1, Z58, and BQ395. An individual cell within the worksheet is used to store information.

## Cell Pointer and Cursor

The block of light that highlights a cell on the worksheet is called the **cell pointer**. The **cursor** is the blinking underline (_) in the center of the cell pointer. The cell pointer indicates (points to) the active cell in which data can be entered and stored. When you first enter a blank worksheet, the cell pointer is always positioned at cell address A1. When you enter a worksheet that already contains data, the cell pointer will be wherever it was positioned when that worksheet was saved. The control panel at the top of the screen provides additional information about the active cell and its contents.

## Control Panel and Mode Indicator

The top three lines on the screen form the Lotus **control panel**, which indicates the address, contents, and settings of the active cell. The first line of the control panel is the **status line**. At the left margin of the status line is the current cell address (A1). Special codes and the cell contents appear immediately to the right of the cell address as you enter them. Since you have entered nothing in this cell, nothing appears immediately to the right of the current cell address; this tells you the cell is empty. To the extreme right on the status line is the **mode indicator** (READY). The mode indicator tells you what Lotus is doing currently. The READY mode means that Lotus is ready for you to enter data or ask for the command menu. We will discuss other modes as you encounter them. The possible Lotus modes are as follows

| Mode | Meaning |
|------|---------|
| EDIT | Changing the contents of a cell |
| ERROR | Waiting after a mistake (press ↵ or [Esc]) |
| FILES | Listing files |
| FIND | Searching a database |
| HELP | Using a Help screen |
| LABEL | Entering text |
| MENU | Using the Command Menu |
| POINT | Pointing to a cell (or range of cells) |
| READY | Waiting for instructions |
| VALUE | Entering a number or formula |
| WAIT | Calculating or moving data (no input allowed) |

In EDIT mode, the second line of the control panel contains a copy of the data being entered (or edited) in the active cell. In MENU mode, the second line of the control panel will show the Lotus Command Menu and the third line will show the submenus or briefly explain the highlighted command. The Lotus Command menu is discussed in detail later in this chapter.

If an **error** occurs during the processing of your worksheet, Lotus will sound a beep, the mode indicator will change to ERROR, and a description of the error or instructions for recovering from it will appear in the lower left corner of the screen. To remove the error message, press ↵ or [Esc].

# Date and Time

The bottom line at the left side of the screen contains the **date** and **time** currently in your computer's clock calender.

# Status Indicator

A **status indicator** is displayed on the right side of the last line of the screen. This status line indicates special worksheet conditions and when certain keys have been pressed. These conditions and keys are listed below.

| Condition | Meaning |
| --- | --- |
| CALC | Need to calculate (press [F9]) |
| CAPS | Using [Caps Lock] (all characters in uppercase) |
| CIRC | Circular reference in a formula |
| CMD | Waiting during execution of macro |
| END | Using [End] |
| NUM | Using [Num] (numeric keypad entry) |
| OVR | Using [Ins] (overwrites the characters) |
| SCROLL | Using [Scroll] |
| SST | Processing macros one step at a time |
| STEP | Single-step mode for processing macros is turned on |

To examine how these keys work, let's take a look at a key often used by accountants. The [Num Lock] key allows you to enter numbers using the numeric key pad.

## NUM

Press the [Num Lock] key in the upper right corner of the keyboard. NUM should appear in the lower right corner of the screen. This means that the numeric keypad will type numbers instead of controlling cursor or cell-pointer movement. Press → and notice that the cell pointer does not move, but that a 6 appears on the second line in the control panel. Press other arrow keys or [PgUp] or [PgDn] and notice that more numbers appear and the cell pointer does not move. The mode indicator has now changed from READY to VALUE. Press [Esc] to make the numbers disappear. Press [Num Lock] again to make NUM disappear from the screen and allow the numeric keypad to control movement instead of typing numbers. Try using the directional arrow keys again just to be sure. If you ever try to use the arrow keys but end up typing numbers into your worksheet instead, check for the NUM indicator and press [Num Lock] to turn it off. More modern keyboards have separate keys to control cursor movement, so the numeric keypad can be left in numeric mode for data entry. With a bit of practice, you will find the numeric keypad a much faster way to enter numbers than using the numeric keys at the top of the keyboard.

# Moving around the Screen

When accountants need to enter or change data in a manual system, they move to the desired location by turning pages and moving down the columns or across the rows until they find the data entry area. In Lotus 1-2-3, keystrokes are used to move around the electronic worksheet and to indicate where the data are to be entered or changed. A **screen** is everything you see on the computer monitor. One screen in an electronic spreadsheet is similar to one page in an accounting ledger or report; it may require several screens of data to represent a complete ledger or report. A variety of key combinations allow quick and precise location of individual cells in the worksheet.

## Directional Arrow Keys

You move around the worksheet by using the directional arrows, or **arrow keys** ($\uparrow \rightarrow \downarrow \leftarrow$). If you are at cell address A1, pressing the right arrow ($\rightarrow$) once moves the cell pointer one cell to the right to column B. You stay in row 1 and make the active cell address B1. Notice that the cell pointer appears to move over the worksheet.

Continue to press $\rightarrow$ until you reach cell I1. Notice that column A is no longer visible; it has shifted off the screen and out of view. This movement is called **scrolling** off the screen. As you use the down arrow key ($\downarrow$) to reach row 21, row 1 scrolls off the screen (Figure 3.4).

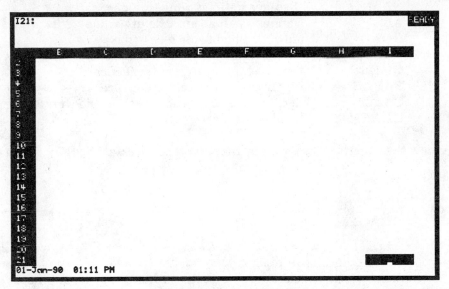

**Figure 3.4 Scrolling**

## Page Up [PgUp], Page Down [PgDn]

Moving around a large worksheet one cell at a time is tedious. You can use the page down [PgDn] and page up [PgUp] keys to move down or up 20 lines at a time. Lotus will beep at you when you hold down an arrow key and try to move the cursor left of column A or above row 1.

## Screen Right [Tab], Screen Left [Shift] [Tab]

The [Tab] key moves the window one screen to the right; [Shift] [Tab] moves the window one screen to the left.

## Scrolling [Scroll Lock]

Another way to move around the screen is to use the scroll feature. Press the [Scroll Lock] key once to turn on the scroll feature; the lower right corner of the screen will indicate that

[Scroll] is locked on. Press [PgDn] once and notice that instead of the cell pointer appearing to move over the worksheet, the worksheet now appears to move under the cell pointer, and the cell pointer appears to remain stationary. Press [Scroll Lock] once again to turn off the scroll feature.

# F Keys

One of the most common shortcuts in computing is the use of the function keys (or F keys). This becomes a time saver for accountants because a series of special functions have been assigned to the function keys. The function keys in Lotus perform the following tasks:

| F Key | Task | Meaning |
|-------|------|---------|
| F1 | HELP | Displays a help screen |
| F2 | EDIT | Edits the contents of a cell |
| F3 | NAME | Displays defined range names |
| F4 | ABS | Defines a cell as an absolute value |
| F5 | GOTO | Moves the pointer to a cell |
| F6 | WINDOW | Jumps from one window to another |
| F7 | QUERY | Performs the last query sequence |
| F8 | TABLE | Performs the last table sequence |
| F9 | CALC | Recalculates all the formulas in the worksheet |
| F10 | GRAPH | Displays the last graph |

Let's explore how the function keys work by taking a closer look at the [F5], or the GOTO, key.

## GOTO [F5]

If you know the exact cell address you want to move to, you can use [F5] to go directly to that cell. When you press [F5], Lotus will prompt you with "Enter address to go to:" and display the current cell address. Enter the address of the cell you want to go to, and Lotus will move the cell pointer there. Press [F5], type AX190, and press ↵. When you have entered a legitimate cell address, Lotus shows the new cell address in the upper left corner of your screen. Do not leave any spaces when you type an address. If you do, the mode indicator will flash ERROR, and a message at the bottom of the screen will indicate "Invalid cell or range address." If ERROR appears in the mode indicator, press [Esc] to back out of the mistake.

Experiment with using the various keys to move around the worksheet until you feel comfortable with how they work. Press [Home] to return you to cell A1 from anywhere in the worksheet.

## On-line Help [F1]

Accountants are very busy individuals and seldom have time to go searching through books to look up answers. Lotus provides users with on-line help as long as the Lotus System Disk (or other disk with Help files on it) is in the disk drive. The [F1] key calls up the Help screen relevant to the area Lotus thinks you need help in: this is called context-sensitive help. Since you are in READY mode, pressing [F1] will bring up the READY mode Help screen, seen in Figure 3.5. Notice the mode indicator has changed to HELP.

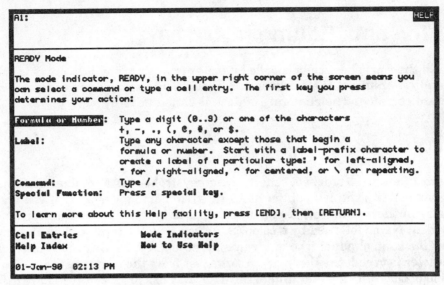

**Figure 3.5 READY help screen**

Use the arrow keys to highlight the desired area, then press ↵. Related topics are displayed on the bottom of the screen for further help. Move down to the Help index at the bottom of the page and press ↵ (Figure 3.6).

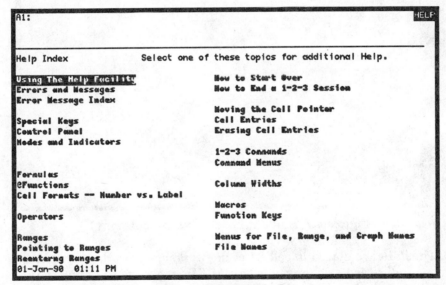

**Figure 3.6 Help index**

You access the Help index topics by using the directional arrows or by pressing ↵. Leave the help screens by pressing [Esc] as many times as necessary to return you to the worksheet in READY mode.

# Data Entry and Editing

Putting data in the worksheet cells is called **data entry**. Accurate data entry is critical to the success and reliability of the worksheet. Although data entry seems easy enough, data entry errors are common. The changing of data is called **editing**.

## Data Entry

You enter data in an electronic worksheet using keystrokes; in a manual system, you use a pencil and paper. With the cell pointer at A1 (use [Home] to move to A1 if you are somewhere else in the worksheet), begin entering data in the performance report worksheet by typing Student Name followed by a colon (:). As you type the letters, they appear on the second line of the control panel (the entry line), preceded by the flashing cursor. As soon as the first character is typed, the flashing cursor moves from the center of the cell pointer to the second line of the control panel, where the data that has just been typed are displayed; the mode indicator switches to LABEL (Figure 3.7).

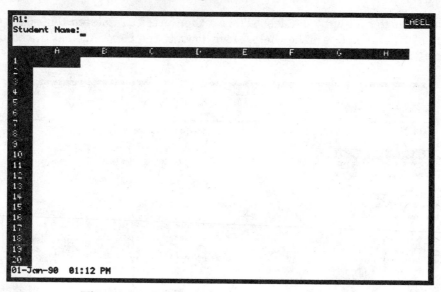

**Figure 3.7 Student Name: (before entering)**

Now press ↵. The data are placed in cell A1 of the worksheet. On the far right side of the screen, the mode indicator has changed from LABEL (as you were typing in the entry) to READY (after you pressed ↵). The status line of the control panel now shows that the cell pointer is highlighting cell A1 and the cell contents are 'Student Name:. The single quote (') indicates that the data in the cell is a label, which will be displayed left-justified. Lotus automatically enters a single quote before any entry that begins with a letter (alpha character). Your entry now appears in cell A1 and is automatically left-justified (aligned with the left margin of the cell), as seen in Figure 3.8.

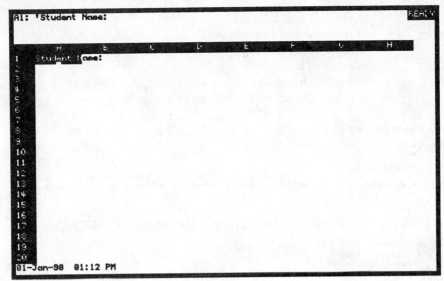

**Figure 3.8  Student Name: (after entering)**

Press the [Caps Lock] key once. Notice that CAPS appears in the lower right corner of the screen. If you find you are accidentally typing only capital letters into the worksheet, press [Caps Lock] to turn off CAPS.

If you make a typing error and notice it before you press ⏎, use [Backspace] and retype the letters to correct your mistake. Once the word is typed correctly, press ⏎.

Move to the following cell addresses with [↓] and enter the material in the cells as listed. The list includes only the cells in which you are required to make an entry.

| Cell | Contents |
|------|----------|
| A2 | Course: |
| A4 | Documentation: |
| A9 | Argon County Hospital |
| A10 | Performance Report - Laundry Department |
| A11 | Yuly - September 1990 |
| | (Leave this misspelling in cell A11) |

## Editing [F2]

You can edit, or change, the contents of a cell after entering data by using the F2 key. This is especially useful for editing long entries. Move the cell pointer to the cell you want to edit and press [F2]. The mode indicator changes to EDIT, and the contents of the active cell appear on the entry line, followed by the cursor. You can move the cursor one character at a time with the left or right arrow, to the beginning with [Home], or to the last character with [End]. Once you position the cursor below a character, you can delete that character with [Del]. You can remove the character to the left of the cursor with [Backspace]. New characters you type are inserted before the character the cursor is currently under. When you have completed your editing, ⏎ places the revised material in the cell just as it does in any other data-entry operation.

When you entered the list of labels, you entered "Yuly" instead of "July" in cell A11. To correct this error move to cell A11 and press the following keys:

| Key | Reason |
|---|---|
| [F2] | to change to EDIT mode |
| [Home] | to move to the beginning of the cell contents |
| → | to skip over the single quote (') |
| [Del] | to remove the Y |
| J | to insert the correct character |
| ↵ | to place the revised contents into Cell A11. |

This sequence of steps applies the editing concepts just described and works for cell contents of any length. Check to see that your worksheet looks like Figure 3.9.

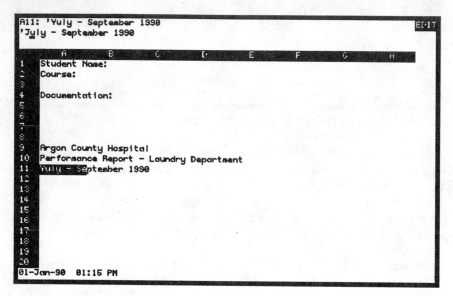

**Figure 3.9  Editing cell A11: July - September 1990**

You have just used the delete key and the insert function to edit the contents of cell A11. But you can also use the overstrike (or type over) to make corrections in the EDIT mode. Overstrike allows you to type directly over existing characters and is controlled by the [Ins] key. With the NUM LOCK off, press [INS]. Notice that OVR appears in the lower right corner of the screen. This feature is convenient in certain editing situations, such as replacing one or two mistyped letters in a word. Remember to toggle OVR off when you have finished using it. If you leave OVR on, you may type over characters that you do not want to change. You cannot change to OVR while NUM LOCK is on. The [Ins] key, which controls OVR, is on the numeric keypad and thus is not available when NUM LOCK is on.

When an entry is short, it is often simpler to retype the whole cell entry than to bother using [F2] to edit. You can replace the contents of a cell by entering the new data just as you would if the cell were empty. However, the longer the cell entry, the more valuable [F2] becomes.

## Empty Cells to the Right of Text

Notice that some of the cell contents in column A have flowed over into column B. If the cell to the right is empty, a LABEL entry that is longer than the cell's width overflows into the space of the cell(s) to the right.

Use the [F5] to move to cell A17 and enter the following data in the specified cells. Note how the labels extend into the cells in the B column.

| Cell | Contents |
|------|----------|
| A17 | Patient Days |
| A18 | Pounds Processed |

## Label and Cell Justification ( ' ^ " )

Labels can be left-justified, centered, or right-justified in a cell. Cell justification means that the data are placed at the left edge, the center, or the right edge of the cell. In cell A20, type ^, using the [Shift] and the 6 key on the top row of the keyboard, then type COSTS ↵. The word COSTS should appear centered within the cell (Figure 3.10).

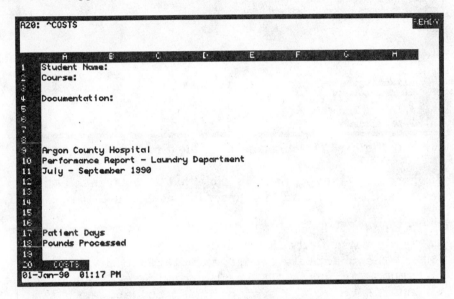

**Figure 3.10 Centering COSTS**

The ^ symbol centers the label in the middle of the cell, just as the single quote (') left-justified a label. A double quote (") right-justifies a label. Labels always begins with ', ^, or ". These symbols tell Lotus that the entry is a label. When a cell entry begins with one of these label justification characters or a letter, the mode indicator changes to LABEL as the entry is typed. Enter the following data in the specified cells.

| Cell | Contents |
|------|----------|
| A21 | Laundry Labor |
| A22 | Supplies |
| A23 | Water |
| A24 | Maintenance |
| A25 | Supervisor's Salary |
| A26 | Allocated Admin. Costs |
| A27 | Equipment Depreciation |
| A29 | TOTAL |

Let's review the material we have discussed so far, moving the cell pointer around the screen, editing, and justifying. Move to A1 using [Home] and edit the cell to make it right-justified ([F2] [Home] [Del] " ↵). Repeat this process on cell A2. Move to B1 using [F5] and enter your name. Notice that your name covers up the material that previously overflowed from cell A1. Move back to cell A1. The contents line shows that the entry in cell A1 is still intact. Since cell A1 is too narrow to display the entire contents on the screen, only the part that fits within that cell width appears if there is anything in the cell to the right of A1 (Figure 3.11).

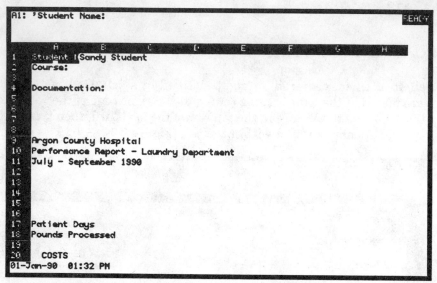

**Figure 3.11  Long label example (Student Name:)**

Enter the following data in the specified cells. Note that the entry in cell A5 begins with three blank spaces, and the entry in B15 begins with a double quote to right-justify.

| Cell | Contents |
|------|----------|
| B2 | '(your course #) (the single quote indicates a label) |
| A5 | '     The quarterly report calculates the VARIANCE |
| A6 | '(BUDGET minus ACTUAL), then divides VARIANCE by the |
| A7 | 'BUDGET to give % over or under budget. |
| B15 | "BUDGET |

# Numeric Cell Entries (Numbers)

Entering numeric data is similar to entering labels. If you are a new computer user, remember to use the upper row on the keyboard for numeric entry rather than the numeric key pad. Move to cell B17 and type 9500. As soon as you type the first numeric character, 9, Lotus changes the mode to VALUE, which means you are entering a number, a function, or a formula. Press ↵ to complete your first numeric entry. The number 9500 should appear in cell B17. Its appearance may be somewhat different on your screen, such as having zeros after a decimal point or even a $ in front of it. However, it should essentially be the number 9500 (Figure 3.12).

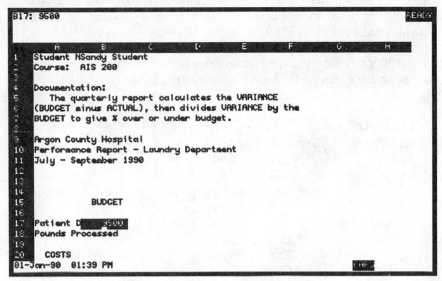

**Figure 3.12 Numeric entry**

If you entered 9,500, Lotus would beep, display an error message, and automatically switch from VALUE to EDIT mode. Try entering 9,500, then correct this data entry error with ← to position the cursor under the comma, [Del] to delete the comma, and ↵ to enter the corrected data. Attempting to enter commas in numbers is a common mistake. Lotus understands only numbers and a single period for a decimal. Most formatting is for the convenience of the human user, not the computer. So enter only numbers and the decimal point (if needed) *without* commas. You will soon learn how to make Lotus display numbers in other formats, such as with dollar signs and commas, but for now you need to enter just the number. The result of attempting to enter the number 125,000 (with the comma) in B18 is that nothing is entered in B18, and that Lotus 1-2-3 switches to edit mode, as shown in Figure 3.13.

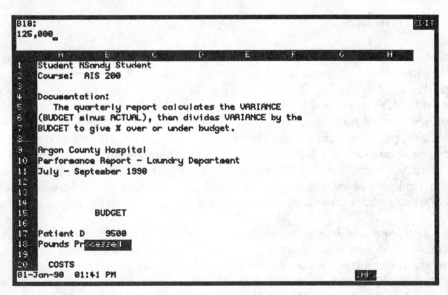

**Figure 3.13 Attempted numeric entry (with comma)**

This detection and prevention of data-entry errors is a good system design feature of Lotus. It is generally easier and cheaper to correct errors at the data-entry stage than at later processing stages. Although this is only one of many possible types of data-entry error, every error that is prevented avoids correction costs and enhances data quality. This is a programmed input-validation control.

All numbers used in calculations are automatically right-justified by Lotus. Unlike labels, you cannot change the justification of numbers. Enter the following data in the specified cells.

| Cell | Contents | Cell | Contents | Cell | Contents |
|------|----------|------|----------|------|----------|
| B18 | 125000 | C15 | "ACTUAL | D12 | "VARIANCE |
| B21 | 9000 | C17 | 11900 | D13 | " (OVER) |
| B22 | 1100 | C18 | 156000 | D14 | "UNDER |
| B23 | 1700 | C21 | 12500 | D15 | "BUDGET |
| B24 | 1400 | C22 | 1875 | | |
| B25 | 3150 | C23 | 2500 | | |
| B26 | 4000 | C24 | 2200 | | |
| B27 | 1200 | C25 | 3750 | | |
| | | C26 | 5000 | | |
| | | C27 | 1250 | | |

# Formulas and Cell References

You have now entered the basic data in your worksheet. All the remaining numbers on the report (variances and totals) are calculated from the data that have already been entered. The next section focuses on using formulas to make Lotus do calculations for you. Once a correct formula is entered, Lotus automatically recalculates the value accurately whenever data are changed anywhere in the worksheet. The computer ensures the correct calculation, but you must ensure the correct formula and data.

## Writing Formulas

Take a minute to look at your task and visualize how you would complete it using a pencil, paper, and a calculator. You want to calculate the variance between the budgeted amount and the actual amount. The VARIANCE (column D) is calculated by subtracting the ACTUAL (column C) from the BUDGET (column B). The formula is variance = budget – actual. If you were working manually with a paper spreadsheet, you would subtract the numbers yourself, perhaps using a calculator, and enter the result in the appropriate location. You could use Lotus 1-2-3 as a calculator by entering 9500–11900 in cell D17, and Lotus would calculate and display the answer for you just as your calculator does. Some users discover this simple calculating feature and think it is so great that they never get beyond it. However, an electronic spreadsheet can be used in much more powerful ways.

When you enter a **formula** in a cell, Lotus carries out the operation for you. Instead of retyping numbers, the formula references the cells that already hold the numbers. If a number in one cell changes, all other cells that refer to that one cell change automatically. This ability to reference the contents of other cells is what allows you to build a "model" using an electronic spreadsheet. Each cell address in a formula is a **cell reference**, because the cell address tells Lotus which cell to refer to for the needed data.

The formula for finding *variance* is *budget* minus *actual*. The first formula would be B17–C17. Move the cell pointer to D17 to make it the active cell and enter +B17–C17. Your screen

should display the correct result of –2400 in cell D17, while the control panel status line
shows that D17 contains the formula +B17–C17 (Figure 3.14).

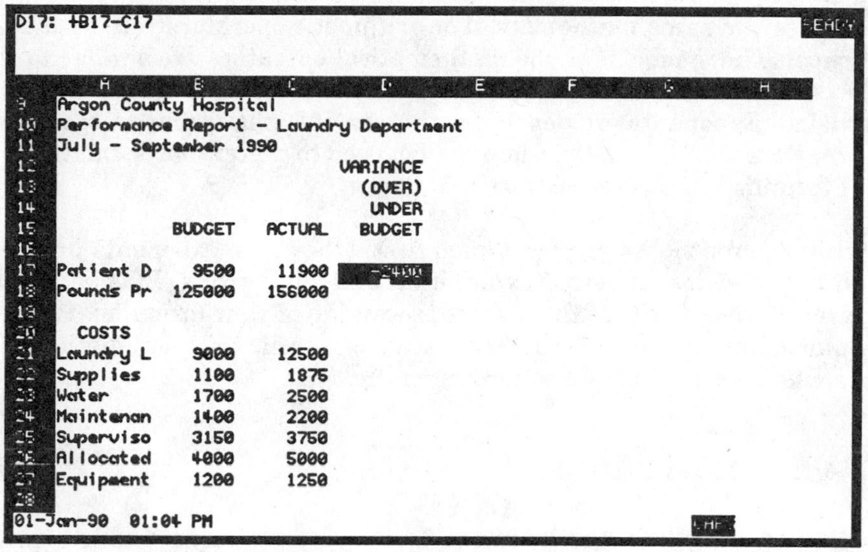

```
D17: +B17-C17                                                              READY

         A        B        C        D        E        F        G        H
  9  Argon County Hospital
 10  Performance Report - Laundry Department
 11  July - September 1990
 12                                   VARIANCE
 13                                    (OVER)
 14                                    UNDER
 15              BUDGET   ACTUAL       BUDGET
 16
 17  Patient D    9500    11900        -2400
 18  Pounds Pr  125000   156000
 19
 20    COSTS
 21  Laundry L    9000    12500
 22  Supplies     1100     1875
 23  Water        1700     2500
 24  Maintenan    1400     2200
 25  Superviso    3150     3750
 26  Allocated    4000     5000
 27  Equipment    1200     1250
 28
01-Jan-90  01:04 PM                                                       LMF
```

Figure 3.14  Formula entry

A common mistake is to try to enter the formula as B17–C17. If you entered this, the
worksheet would display B17–C17 in the cell and 'B17–C17 in the control panel. You would
expect to see a number in the worksheet, not the letters of the cell addresses. On the control
panel, the ' at the beginning of the cell contents would tell you that Lotus made this entry a
label because the letter B defines a label entry. If you had noticed, the mode indicator would
have shown that you were entering a label as soon as you typed the B. Always remember to
begin a formula with one of the special mathematical characters, usually +, which will
make the mode indicator display VALUE. Any of the other special characters, such as a
period, left parenthesis, minus sign, pound sign, dollar sign, or at sign ( . ( – # $ @ ) also
indicate to Lotus that a value is being entered. When you expect to see a number displayed
in a cell and instead see a label that looks a lot like a formula, check for this type of data-
entry error (Figure 3.15).

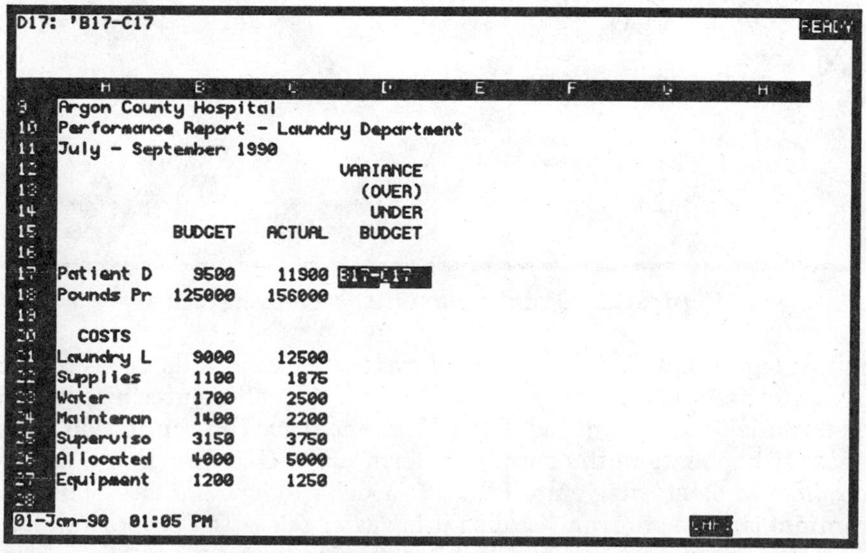

```
D17: 'B17-C17                                                              READY

         A        B        C        D        E        F        G        H
  9  Argon County Hospital
 10  Performance Report - Laundry Department
 11  July - September 1990
 12                                   VARIANCE
 13                                    (OVER)
 14                                    UNDER
 15              BUDGET   ACTUAL       BUDGET
 16
 17  Patient D    9500    11900      B17-C17
 18  Pounds Pr  125000   156000
 19
 20    COSTS
 21  Laundry L    9000    12500
 22  Supplies     1100     1875
 23  Water        1700     2500
 24  Maintenan    1400     2200
 25  Superviso    3150     3750
 26  Allocated    4000     5000
 27  Equipment    1200     1250
 28
01-Jan-90  01:05 PM                                                       LMF
```

Figure 3.15  Attempted formula entry

## Mathematical Operators and Precedence

Lotus formulas use the same mathematical or arithmetic operators you have used since elementary school. The symbols for the mathematical operators are similar to the ones you are used to: + is used for addition and – for subtraction. * is used for multiplication, and / is used for division. Exponents are denoted with ^, so 4^3 means four raised to the third power, or 4*4*4. Note that this is the same symbol used to center labels, but in a mathematical formula it raises a number to a power.

Operations within parentheses are performed first; otherwise, exponents precede multiplication and division, followed by addition and subtraction. It is generally a good idea to use parentheses to ensure the correct processing of your formulas. Parentheses can be nested by placing one set inside another. Lotus uses basic business math, which works just as it does when formulas are written manually.

## Pointing versus Typing

Instead of typing an entry into a cell, you can "point" to the reference cells with the cell pointer and have the computer enter the cell addresses for you. This lowers the probability of errors from mistyping or misidentifying the cell address. Highlight cell D18 and type a plus sign (+) to tell Lotus a formula is coming; note that the mode indicator changes to VALUE as soon as the + is typed. Move the cell pointer to cell B18 by using ← twice to put the cell address B18 into the formula in cell D18 immediately after the + sign (Figure 3.16).

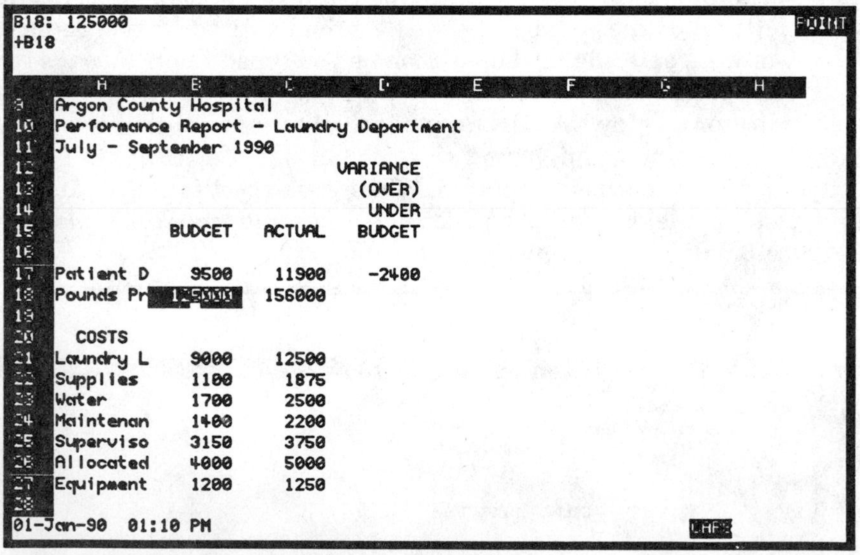

Figure 3.16 Pointing to enter a cell reference

Now type a minus sign (–), which enters the address of B18 and tells Lotus the next character in your formula is a minus sign. Notice that the cell pointer jumps back to the cell where the formula is being entered (D18). Use ← to move the pointer left one cell to C18. The cell address C18 appears in the formula to form +B18–C18. Pressing ↵ tells Lotus the formula is complete and returns you to READY mode. The formula has been entered in the cell with a minimal chance of error, because it is easier to see the proper cell locations when they are highlighted, and having Lotus type the address for you eliminates the chance of typing errors. This technique is important to use no matter how experienced you are. Enter the following headings in the specified cells.

| Cell | Contents |
|------|----------|
| E13  | "VARIANCE |
| E14  | "% OF |
| E15  | "BUDGET |

The last column contains the variance as a percent of budget, calculated with the formula % variance = (budget − actual) / budget. That is, to calculate the VARIANCE % (column E), subtract the ACTUAL (column C) from the BUDGET (column B) and divide the result by the BUDGET (column B). When you write out this formula, if you do not use parentheses, the precedence rules will cause the computer to perform the division first instead of the subtraction. Using parentheses to indicate that the subtraction is to be done first, then the division, means the formula entered in cell E17 must be (B17−C17)/B17.

To practice the material you have just learned, use the pointing technique to enter the formula for the percent of variance in cell E17.

| Action | Reason |
|--------|--------|
| ( | to start formula by changing to VALUE mode |
| ← ← ← | to move B17 into the formula |
| — | to enter B17 and return to E17 |
| ← ← | to move C17 into the formula |
| ) | to enter C17 and return to E17 |
| / | to divide |
| ← ← ← | to move B17 into the formula, as seen in Figure 3.17 |
| ↵ | to enter B17 and return to E17 |

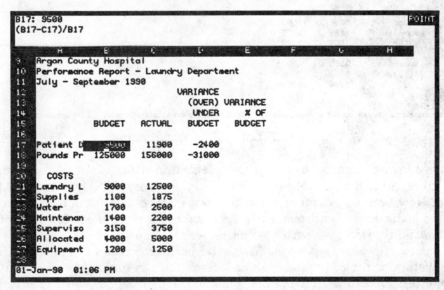

**Figure 3.17  Pointing to enter a formula**

This concludes the section dealing with data entry and formulas. You are now armed with the basic tools necessary to set up, use, and understand an electronic spreadsheet. The next section deals with using commands to save your work and to perform other activities.

# Command Menu

Lotus uses commands to affect the appearance of the worksheet, to save and retrieve data, to copy data, to get out of Lotus, and to do a variety of other useful things. By now, you should be anxious to save your work; perhaps you are even anxious to quit Lotus for a while.

## Accessing the Lotus Command Menu (/)

You access the Lotus Command menu by typing a slash (/), when in the READY mode. The / on most keyboards is in the lower right area below the ?. Press /. Notice that the second line of the control panel now has a series of words, each of which is a Lotus command, with subcommands on the third line (Figure 3.18).

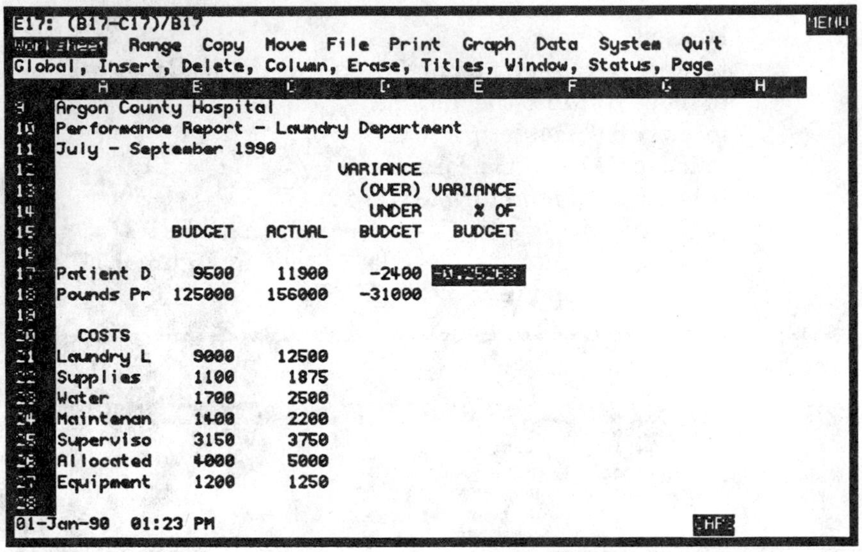

**Figure 3.18 Lotus Command menu**

The commands on the Command menu can be **selected** in either of two ways: (1) use the arrow keys to highlight, or point to, a command and then press ↵; (2) type the first letter of the command. New Lotus users often prefer the first method, because a brief description of the highlighted command or subcommands appears on the next line below the commands. This feature is useful (even to experienced users) when you are not quite sure which command to select. However, typing the first letter of the command is a much faster method and worth learning for the commands you use often. You can highlight the option and then still type the letter (instead of ↵) to use the command. This is a good way to start; you will soon find yourself automatically entering the command letter without highlighting the command first or even looking at the menu.

The availability of two ways to select commands is an example of how Lotus is user friendly. Its designers recognized that different users may have different needs and preferences for how they interact with the computer. Such design considerations are becoming increasingly important in accounting information systems as the growing body of nontechnical users and higher-level managers demand software that meets their needs.

After you select a command, Lotus prompts you to select additional commands or to provide information. *Be sure to read the screen* if you are unsure of what is happening, or what to do, or you need help. If you need help, remember to access the Help Screen with [F1]. Anytime you want to get out or undo a command use [Esc]. Each time you type [Esc], you move one step or level out of the command menu until you are back at the worksheet level in READY mode. Press [Esc] now.

## Saving Files (/FS)

The most important command in Lotus is Save. All the work you do is stored in the main memory of the computer, but it is not automatically stored permanently on a disk. Saving a file means placing a copy of it on a disk for permanent storage. If you have not saved your file, and the power goes out, the system crashes, or you do something to destroy or damage the file in main memory, you would have to start over from the beginning. Save your work on your disk as soon as you have done any work that you do not want to lose.

Place your Student Data Disk in drive B (if you are working with a hard drive, use drive A and enter that as your drive designation) and close the door of the disk drive. You will use this disk to save all your worksheets. Use the following commands to tell Lotus to use the disk in drive B in response to all Save commands.

| Action | Reason |
|--------|--------|
| / | to get the Lotus Command menu |
| File | to select the File command |
| Directory | to select the File subcommand |
| B: | to enter the drive designation |
| ↵ | to execute the subcommand |

Now save your worksheet in a file with the filename PRACTICE by using the following commands, as shown in Figure 3.19.

| Action | Reason |
|--------|--------|
| / | to get the Lotus Command menu |
| File | to select the File command |
| Save | to select the File subcommand |
| **PRACTICE** | to Enter saved filename: |

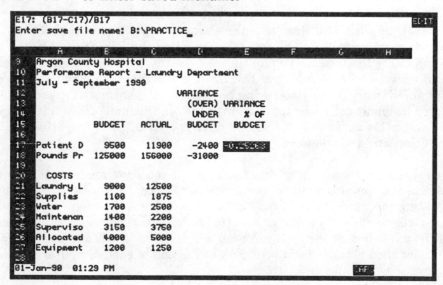

**Figure 3.19  Saving a worksheet file**

Press ↵ to execute the subcommand. Lotus adds one of the file extensions .WKS, .WK1, or .WKE to the filename, so that the actual complete name of the file is PRACTICE.WK?. (Remember that the ? is a wild card, which indicates that any of several different characters may actually be found in that position in the filename or extension.) Lotus uses file extensions to indicate which version of Lotus created the file. The exact file extension depends on the version of Lotus you are working with; see Appendix B for more information on the various Lotus versions.

Normally, saving the file should be the last thing you do before stopping work on a spreadsheet. When you return to the worksheet later, the copy of the file on disk will look just as the file in main memory did the last time you saved the worksheet. Any changes made *after* your last save were lost when you exited Lotus.

## Same Filename

After you have saved your worksheet once, Lotus makes it easy for you to save the worksheet again (under the same name). This is an important feature because you want to save every 15 minutes, as discussed in Chapter 2. Part of good AIS design is making it easy for the user to follow good backup and other "safe computing" and internal control practices. Enter the following sequence.

| Action | Reason |
|--------|--------|
| / | to get the Lotus Command menu |
| File | to select the File command |
| Save | to select the File subcommand |
| ↵ | to enter saved filename: PRACTICE.WKS |
| Replace | to copy new version in main memory over the old file |

If you decide you do not want to save the file, select Cancel instead of Replace. From now on, we will begin to write familiar commands without listing the reasons. For example, the list of commands above would be written with as /File Save ↵ Replace.

## New Filename

There might be a time when you want to make a second copy of the worksheet so you can use it later. Remember, when you use the same filename and the Replace command, the previous version of the file is destroyed. In the hospital case, you may want to keep a copy of your first draft and therefore would give this draft a new filename. Saving the worksheet under a new name is very much like saving a new worksheet. Enter the sequence /File Save, and Lotus automatically prompts you with the old filename, PRACTICE. Type in a new filename and press ↵. To save a file on a different drive, enter the drive letter followed by a colon and the filename.

You can save a file as early and as often as you like. If you have made some changes that you want to keep, but you also want to keep an earlier version, save the worksheet under a new name. Adding the numbers 1, 2, etc., to the filename is a common way of keeping track of the various versions by relative age. However, be careful not to get so many versions of a file on your disk that you can't tell which is the "good" one. It is a good idea to delete all the unneeded old files from your disk at the end of each computer session while you still remember which file is which.

## Backup Copies

Although floppy disks are fairly durable, they do occasionally fail. If you lose or damage a disk and do not have a backup disk, you will lose hours of work. See Chapter 2 for the commands used to make copies of files and disks using DOS. In Lotus, it is easy to place a copy of a file on your backup disk when you save it on the Student Data Disk (SDD). Just save the file on the SDD, remove the SDD from the drive and insert the backup SDD, and save the file again exactly as you just saved it on the SDD. When the file has been saved, replace the SDD in the disk drive. This procedure will not necessarily work in all other software packages.

Remember that good backup practices, consistently performed, are an important aspect of good internal control in an AIS. Use your own experience with backups to help you understand this important aspect of internal control.

## Quitting Lotus (/QYE)

Make sure you have saved the latest version of your file before you exit! If you do not save it, any changes you made since the last save will be lost when you leave Lotus, even if you do not turn off the computer. If you turn off the computer without leaving Lotus, the unsaved work will also be lost. When you have finished working with Lotus, it is a good idea (although not mandatory) to exit from Lotus to the operating system before turning off the computer (this is crucial for some software, such as dBASE). End a Lotus session by using the command sequence /Quit Yes. This will either take you back to the Lotus Access menu, where you select Exit, or return you directly to the operating system level.

Lotus does not keep track of whether you have made any changes to your file since the last save, but it does ask you whether you want to save again before exiting. A common user-friendly feature on other software helps remind you that you have made changes to a file that have not yet been saved to disk and that will therefore be lost if you leave the program without saving the file. Omission of such a feature is a weakness in the design of Lotus. Lotus does ask you if you are sure you want to exit, which allows recovery from an accidentally typed /Exit command sequence.

This is an excellent point to take a break. Even if you intend to continue working, practice exiting from Lotus, making a backup disk, and reentering Lotus the same way you first entered it at the beginning of this chapter.

## Retrieving Files (/FR)

When you reenter Lotus, you see another blank worksheet. While you could begin a new worksheet from scratch, this is not what you want to do. The ability to save work would be useless if it were impossible to get it back to view, print, and work with. Transferring a copy of a file from the disk on which it was saved to main memory is called **retrieving** a file. A copy of the work saved earlier is loaded into main memory by Lotus with /File Retrieve. Put your data disk back in drive B, and enter /File Retrieve. Lotus provides a horizontal, alphabetized listing of all Lotus files available on the disk in the default drive. If the default drive is B, where your data disk is, Lotus will list all the files on your data disk (Figure 3.20).

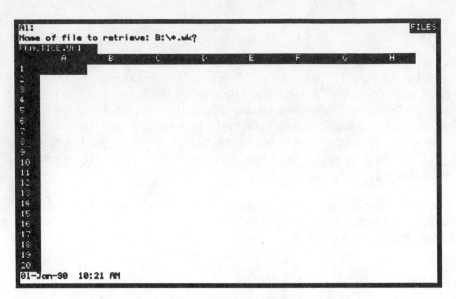

**Figure 3.20 Retrieving a worksheet file**

If your Lotus program is set up with any other drive as the default, press [Esc] twice and enter B:.

If you saved your PRACTICE file on the Student Data Disk, you should see several files listed. You can highlight and retrieve any of the files using the arrow keys to point to and ⏎ to select the file. Unlike commands, files cannot be retrieved using the first letter of the filename. You do always have the option of typing in the name of the file to be retrieved instead of using the highlight and ⏎ sequence. If all the files do not fit on the screen at once, use the → arrow or [Tab] to see the rest of them. Select the file PRACTICE to retrieve it so that you can finish your performance report for the laundry department. /File Save and /File Retrieve are two important commands that you will use every time you deal with Lotus. Remember to practice saving every 15 minutes, so you will not have to reenter your work later.

## Copy (/C Relative Cell Addresses)

Looking at the PRACTICE worksheet, you remember that you have already entered all the basic label and numeric data and some formulas in the VARIANCE and VARIANCE % columns. You need to enter similar formulas in the other rows of the report in these same columns. It is possible to enter every formula individually, as you did earlier, either by typing cell addresses or by pointing to them. However, you know that the formulas in the first row are correct and that entering the formulas one at a time will take several minutes to do and provide many opportunities to enter an incorrect formula. Entering each formula individually would require repeating a very similar set of keystrokes, especially if you entered them by pointing. One of the principles of AIS is to let the computer do the structured, repetitive work. A major advantages of electronic spreadsheets is that they implement this design principle by providing the capability to copy the existing formulas, suitably modified, into the appropriate cells with just a few keystrokes.

## Copying a Formula from a Single Cell to a Single Cell

The Copy command from the Lotus Command menu allows you to copy a formula to one cell or many other cells. The formula in cell E17 is (B17–C17)/B17. The same formula is needed for E18, except that the row number needs to be changed from 17 to 18. For row 18, the row number should be 18 throughout the formula, etc. Go to cell E17, type / to get the Command menu, and select Copy (either type **C** or highlight Copy and press ↵). Lotus will prompt you with "Enter range to copy FROM: E17..E17" (Figure 3.21).

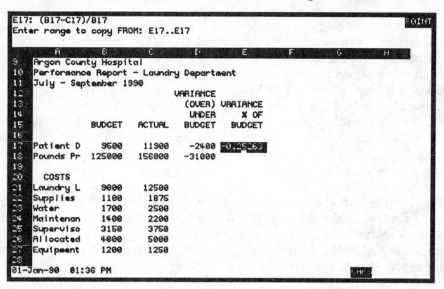

**Figure 3.21 Copy command (FROM)**

Telling the worksheet the source of the formula (the cell you want to copy from) is easy because you positioned the cell pointer on the formula before selecting the Copy command. While this is not necessary, it is usually most convenient. Press ↵ to verify that E17..E17 is the cell you want to copy from.

The prompt "Enter range to copy TO: E17" asks for the location of the new formula. Although you could enter E18 by typing, instead point (using ↓) to E18 and press ↵. Notice that Lotus enters the cell address as E18. After entering the final cell address, Lotus automatically returns to the cell you started in, E17.

Copying this formula works because Lotus handles cell references in terms of their position relative to the cell the formula is entered in. Thus, Lotus treats the formula +B17–C17 in D17 as "add the number two columns to the left in this row (B17), subtract from it the number one column to the left in this row (C17), and display the result in this cell (D17)." The copied formula will always contain the addresses of the cells that have the same relative position to the copied formula as the original cell addresses have to the original formula. When you copy a formula from one row to another row in the same column, Lotus changes only the row number. The same is true of copying formulas from one column to another in the same row; the column letters are adjusted in the same way to preserve the relative values.

## Anchoring a Range (..)

So far, we have dealt only with individual cells. Lotus also allows you to deal with several cells at once. To copy either to or from several cells at once, you must specify the range of cells to be used. A range of cells must be a rectangle. The range begins with the top left cell in the rectangle and ends with the bottom right cell. The range beginning with cell A1 and ending with B3 is typed A1..B3. A range can be specified by typing in these two cell addresses or by pointing to the corners of the rectangle to highlight it.

Specifying a range by pointing is very powerful. Move the cell pointer to the cell that will be the upper left corner of the range. When you press any of the arrow or other cursor-control keys, the cell pointer should respond normally and continue to highlight only one cell. If the highlighted block begins to cover more cells at this point, press [Esc] or [Backspace] to make the cell pointer move properly. When the cell in the upper left corner of the range is highlighted, press the period to **anchor** the upper left corner of the range. Use the arrow keys to move the cell pointer to the lower right corner of the range. The block of light should expand to cover the entire group of cells that make up the range you want to specify. When the lower right corner of the highlighted block is at the cell that ends the range, press ↵ to tell Lotus that the currently highlighted range is the one you want to use.

Either the [Esc] or the [Backspace] key will remove an anchor from a cell, allowing you to move around the screen. You will need to use this feature if the cell pointer accidently becomes anchored. When the anchor is released, the second cell address in the range on the "Enter range to copy FROM:" line disappears. When you find the cell that you want to use, pressing a period will again anchor the range.

You will now use these features to copy the two different formulas from cells D18 and E18 into the multiple cells of the range D21..E27. Move to cell D18 and use /Copy. At the prompt "Enter range to move FROM: D18..D18," use → to expand the range to D18..E18 and press ↵. Notice that the movement of the cursor highlights both cells D18 and E18 to give you additional visual feedback to check your work. At the prompt "Enter range to copy TO: D18," move down three rows to D21, using ↓, and anchor the beginning of the range at D21 with a period (.). Notice the display now says "Enter range to copy TO: D21..D21." Since you need to put the two formulas you copied into both columns D and E, use → to highlight both columns and make the TO range prompt display D21..E21. Do not press ↵ yet; if you have, simply start over again at the beginning of this paragraph. Notice how you have now highlighted the two cells D21 and E21. You also want to copy these two formulas (from D18..E18) into the other rows in these columns, so use ↓ until you reach row 27, as seen in Figure 3.22. Now the area from D21 to E27 is highlighted, and the status line says "Enter range to copy TO: D21..E27."

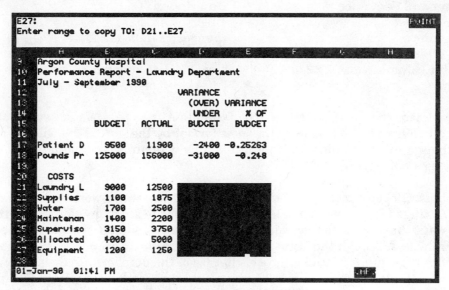

**Figure 3.22  Copy command (TO)**

The final step in this process is to press ↵. Watch how fast the formulas are both copied and calculated as the highlighted area is filled in. Copying formulas rather than typing them saves time and improves accuracy. This is a powerful feature of Lotus, and you should practice it at every opportunity. If you ever find yourself entering formulas that are similar to others you just entered, with only a row or column change, stop! You should probably be making Lotus copy them for you. Any cell can be copied. When cells containing labels or numbers are copied, the contents of the cell(s) copied to will be identical to the contents of the cell(s) copied from.

# Worksheet Appearance

Because the appearance of a report can have a significant impact on how easy it is to use and how likely it is to be used, it is important to have your work look good. If you compare your performance report on the screen to the one in Figure 3.1, you notice that the one in the Figure 3.1 is much neater and easier to see. Some of the numbers have dollar signs and percentages, and columns appear to be different sizes, etc. Once the data and formulas are entered, Lotus provides a great deal of flexibility in allowing you to display your data in different ways.

## Worksheet Global (/WG)

Commands that affect the entire worksheet are found under Worksheet. They are Global Insert Delete Column Erase Titles Window Status Page. We will cover only a few of them here; you will examine several others in later chapters.

Most worksheets look better and are more readable if some of the individual columns are widened or narrowed. The command for this procedure is found under Worksheet, because it affects all rows of the column indicated. To widen column A so you can read the labels, move the cursor to any cell in column A and enter the following:

| Command Sequence | Description |
|---|---|
| / Worksheet | affects worksheet |
| Column | changes column attribute |
| Set-Width | changes individual column width |
| "Enter column width:" 22 | new width in number of characters |
| ↵ | enters command sequence |

This command sequence changed the width of column A from the default setting of 9 to 22. Notice that all cells in column A show this new format by the "[W22]" on the command line. This change in the column width affected only column A. Individual column widths must be changed one at a time.

The /Worksheet Global command affects the format of the entire worksheet and changes the default settings for that worksheet. Since it is tedious to set many column widths one at a time, you want the default column width to be the one you will use for most of the columns in your worksheet. Although the Lotus default of 9 is a popular column size, you may prefer to have a different column width because of the size of the numbers or labels in your data. To change the default column width to 12, you would use /Worksheet Global Column -Width "Enter global column width:" 12 ↵. This command sequence changes the widths of all the columns except A to 12. It changes the widths of only the columns that were not individually set with a /Worksheet Column Set-Width command.

All global commands are overridden by specific settings, so think carefully about how you want your finished worksheet to look. Make the global changes that will affect most of the worksheet before you start changing individual column widths or other formatting features.

Selecting /Worksheet Global Format shows the available formats: Fixed Scientific Currency , General +/− Percent Date Text Hidden Reset. To change the default format to display numbers with commas, rounded to the nearest whole number, you would select /Worksheet Global Format , "Enter number of decimal places:" 0 ↵. The entire worksheet would be converted to this format.

## Range (/R)

Many settings can also be changed for individual cells or ranges of cells. Ranges of cells are dealt with using the Range command. The commands under Range are Format Label Erase Name Justify Protect Unprotect Input Value Transpose. Ranges can be specified or changed anywhere they are used by entering the cell addresses or by pointing and anchoring, as discussed earlier.

To format the amounts in column E as percentages, use / Range Format Percent 0 ↵ and specify the range E17..E29. Remember, the global settings of formats, cell widths, and anything else are overridden by changes to a specific cell or range of cells. Format rows 21 and 29 of columns B, C, and D for dollar signs (Currency) with no decimal places.

When a number is longer than the cell width, Lotus displays ******** in the cell to indicate there is insufficient room in the cell to print out the number. However, if you highlight this cell, the control panel will show the number or formula that the cell actually contains. You can make the number display properly by changing the column width. When designing a worksheet, be sure to include enough room for Lotus to display the largest expected number in each column, including a space for the decimal point, negative sign, dollar sign, commas, and any other formatting characters.

Just as erasers and correction fluid are vital to manual systems, the ability to remove entries is vital to an electronic spreadsheet. The following exercise will illustrate why.

Move to B10 and press the space bar and ⌐. Notice that the last part of the contents of A10 are no longer visible even though cell B10 appears to be empty. In spite of appearing to be empty, cell B10 now contains a space, which is a character that the computer must store. The computer must keep track of numbers, letters, and all special characters, including spaces. To confirm that there is really something in the cell, the status line shows that the contents of cell B10 is a label (') or a left-justified space. Lotus automatically entered the ' for you when you began your cell entry with a space character, which it recognizes as a label.

This is the one situation where you cannot change what is in the cell by reentering what you want to be there. There is no key that means nothing; every key on the keyboard means something. The only way to remove the space in B10 is by using a series of commands that tells Lotus to erase what is currently in the cell, leaving it empty. Position the cell pointer on the cell to be erased and select the command sequence **/Range, Erase,** ⌐. Notice now that the contents of A10 again overflow into cell B10.

# @Functions

To speed the process of performing standard, sometimes complex calculations, Lotus provides functions that contain built-in formulas. A function performs a calculation or logical operation, just as a formula does. The result of a function is displayed in the cell in which the function is entered. If a function is used in a formula, the result of the function is used in the formula. A function always starts with an @, followed by the function name and the arguments, which are enclosed in parentheses. The **arguments** specify the information the function needs to accomplish its task. Different functions require different arguments. Arguments are usually numbers or cell references. Other arguments are labels, formulas, or even other functions. The @functions are different from the F (function) keys; unfortunately, they are both referred to by the word "function." The functions fall into several groups: mathematical, statistical, financial, logical, date, database, string, and special. @SUM is the only function used in this chapter; other similar functions are discussed briefly. We will use only a few functions in this book; you may use Lotus Help, the Lotus manual, or another Lotus reference book to learn how to use other functions. Appendix A contains a list of @functions and their arguments.

## @SUM

The numbers in the last row of the performance report (Figure 3.1) are totals, or sums, of the expenses in the columns above them. Although you could type in the formula +B21+B22+B23+B24+B25+B26+B27, it is obvious that this would become tedious if there were more numbers to be added, as there often are in AIS. An @SUM function adds all the numbers in a specified range of cells and displays the answer in the cell that contains the @SUM function. The argument of @SUM must be a range of cells. For example, the cell entry @SUM(B21..B27) tells Lotus to add all cells in the range beginning with B21 and ending with B27. Apply this to the worksheet, by going to B29 and typing **@SUM(.** Point to cell B21, anchor the cell range by pressing period (.) and move down to B27. As usual, the range is highlighted to allow you to check visually that the correct cells will be summed (Figure 3.23). Finish the formula by typing ) and pressing ⌐. The sum of the numbers displayed in the range of cells B21..B27 is displayed in cell B29. A common error is to forget to type the end parenthesis; Lotus will remind you to do so with a beep.

```
B27: 1200                                                        POINT
@SUM(B21..B27

             A              B          C          D          E
10  Performance Report - Laundry Department
11  July - September 1990
12                                                  VARIANCE
13                                                  (OVER)     VARIANCE
14                                                  UNDER      % OF
15                            BUDGET     ACTUAL      BUDGET     BUDGET
16
17  Patient Days             9,500      11,900      (2,400)    -25%
18  Pounds Processed         125,000    156,000     (31,000)   -25%
19
20           COSTS
21  Laundry Labor            $9,000     $12,500     ($3,500)   -39%
22  Supplies                 1,100      1,875       (775)      -70%
23  Water                    1,700      2,500       (800)      -47%
24  Maintenance              1,400      2,200       (800)      -57%
25  Supervisor's Salary      3,150      3,750       (600)      -19%
26  Allocated Admin. Costs   4,000      5,000       (1,000)    -25%
27  Equipment Depreciation   1,200      1,250       (50)       -4%
28
29  TOTAL
01-Jan-90  02:02 PM                                          CHP
```

**Figure 3.23  @SUM function (selecting range)**

This function was applied to only seven cells but could have been applied to many more just as easily. Although @SUM is most commonly used on a range in a single row or column, it can add up the values in all the cells of a multirow and multicolumn range. Other functions that work in a similar manner include @MIN (the minimum or smallest number in a cell range), @MAX (the maximum or largest number in a cell range), and @AVG (the average of all the numbers in a cell range).

Comparing your worksheet to Figure 3.1 shows you that you have only three more cells to complete. To finish the calculations for the worksheet, use the Copy command to fill in the last three cells. While still in cell B29, copy the @SUM function into C29 by performing the command sequence /Copy FROM: B29 TO: C29. Then copy the two formulas from D27.. E27 to D29..E29.

Why not also copy the @SUM function from B29 to cells D29 and E29? Would it give the same result as what you did? Think through the meaning of the calculation, then try it and see. The amount in D29 should be the same, but the amount in E29 is very different! In general, you cannot sum columns of percentages; instead, you must calculate the percentage based on the totals. In situations like that in D29, where you expect either of two approaches to give you the same answer if your worksheet is correctly designed and implemented, a common accounting internal control procedure is to calculate both and compare them to make sure they do provide the same result. When done manually, this is referred to as footing and cross-footing. Here, we could have Lotus do it for us, although it is beyond the scope of this chapter. Your worksheet should now look like the one in Figure 3.1.

# Printing  (/PP)

In spite of long-standing predictions to the contrary, computers have caused more paper used instead of less. Most reports are still printed, rather than only viewed on the screen. You can get a paper printout (**hard copy**) of the worksheet by using the Print command. If you can send your output directly to a printer, use the command sequence /Print Printer. If you are not connected to a printer, but want to make a file that can be printed later without using Lotus, use /Print File instead and provide the filename you want Lotus to use for the file to be printed. After this point, the options under /Print Printer and /Print File are the same: Range Line Page Options Clear Align Go Quit.

Select Range and tell Lotus the range of cells to be printed by highlighting the range A1..E29 and pressing ↲. The entire area highlighted on the screen will be printed on paper (Figure 3.24).

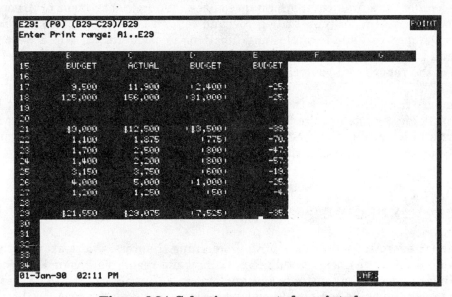

Figure 3.24 Selecting range to be printed

If you are working with a dot-matrix or daisy-wheel printer, make sure the print head is at the top of the paper just under the page perforation. No matter what kind of printer you are working with, enter Align to let the computer know the print head is positioned at the top of the page. To send the data to the printer, select Go. The printer should begin printing your worksheet. The Mode indicator displays WAIT while the printer is printing. When the printer is almost done printing, the Mode indicator returns to MENU. To get out of the printing menu, use Quit.

If you sent your output to a printable file that was stored on a disk for printing in the future, to print your report you must find a computer which has a printer attached. At the DOS prompt, enter "PRINT *filename*.PRN," where *filename* is the name you told Lotus to use for your output file and PRN is the extension Lotus automatically assigns to such files. The file is printed exactly as it would have been if you had printed it directly.

Once you have a printout of your work that looks like the report in Figure 3.1, you are done with this chapter. Remember to save your work on the disk with the File Save command before ending a Lotus session. If you made any changes since the last time you saved, you must save again to keep them. It is a good habit to always save as the last thing you do before you leave Lotus or any other application. Save with the following command sequence: /File, Save, ↲, Replace. End this Lotus session with /Quit Yes Exit to return to the operating system. This concludes the first case designed to walk you through Lotus step by step.

# Chapter Review

This chapter introduced you to many of the important features of Lotus and discussed related AIS concepts. It addressed starting and leaving Lotus and the physical layout and meaning of the different areas of the screen. You can now move around the worksheet; get help; enter and edit data, formulas, and @functions; and use several powerful Lotus commands and function keys. While learning how Lotus works, you actually built a worksheet to reflect the financial performance of the laundry department of Argon County Hospital. You entered proper report titles, row and column labels, budget and actual amounts for the quarter, and formulas and functions to calculate variances, percentage variances, and totals. You also used the principles of report design to improve the appearance of the report, and you printed a hard copy.

Although you are far from being a "power user," you have learned quite a bit about Lotus 1-2-3. Completing one or more of the following practice exercises will reinforce what you have learned and let you know what material, if any, you need to review before going on to Chapter 4. Chapters 4 and 5 assume that you have mastered Chapter 3 completely.

# Practice Exercises

A set of practice exercises follow each of the remaining chapters. These exercises are designed to improve your Lotus and dBASE skills while reenforcing your knowledge and understanding of accounting systems and applications. Completing the exercises will require you to use the skills you developed by working along with the cases in the chapters. For most of the Lotus exercises, we provide a partially completed worksheet to minimize your data entry time, allowing you to focus on developing formulas and manipulating the data and report form. You will start most exercises by retrieving the worksheet named in the practice exercise from the Student Data Disk that came with this book. Much of the data have already been entered; your job is to complete what was left undone and fix any mistakes that might have been made.

To help you get started, a set of reminders is provided for each of the first two exercises. The items in parentheses at the end of each reminder indicate the cells to which the reminder applies. Try to complete the necessary work without using the reminders, then check them to make sure you have done everything necessary to complete the exercise. Compare your outputs to the finished reports. Remember that examination of output by the user is an important output control; in fact, it is the only one that can catch certain types of errors. Do as much as you can by yourself and then check your answers against the reminders. Be sure to save your work at least every 15 minutes.

To begin work on a practice exercise, use /File Retrieve to move a copy of the file from the disk into main memory. This is the same operation you used to retrieve your PRACTICE worksheet after you had saved it and exited from Lotus. With a blank worksheet on the Lotus screen, select /File, Retrieve, and the filename given to the practice exercise. A copy of the partially completed worksheet will be placed in main memory and displayed on your screen. Continue by performing the necessary steps to generate the required output. Each worksheet will include documentation in the upper left corner indicating the source of the material.

Exercise 3-1

**Filename: 3EX1.WKS**

A common and important task in AIS is the evaluation of proposed systems changes.
Although other factors are also important, an accountant frequently analyzes the
quantitative factors, by estimating and calculating cost and revenue changes expected to
occur if the proposed system is implemented.

As the administrative services specialist for the CPA firm of Xeron, York, and Zapata, you
have been assigned to analyze the feasibility of a computer acquisition. The necessary
configuration and related operating costs and cost savings have already been determined,
and entered into the feasibility study report. The monthly costs consist of the indicated
amounts for hardware rental, software rental, personnel, and overhead. Cost savings
consist of reductions in clerical costs and inventory carrying costs. Accounts Receivable
will need three fewer clerks, a cost savings of $1,200 per clerk; Accounts Payroll will need
one less clerk, saving $1,200; and Inventory will need two fewer clerks, a savings of $1,000
each. Clerical cost savings will be the number of clerical personnel that can be eliminated
times their monthly salaries. Inventory carrying cost savings will, due to reducing the
current $1,600,000 Inventory balance by 20%, generate savings at the firm's 15% cost of
capital rate. Calculate the total monthly operating costs and the total monthly cost savings
for the proposed system during the month immediately following its implementation. Your
completed report should look like the following.[2]

```
CPA Firm: Xeron, York, and Zapata
Client: Avalon Electronics Company
Feasibility Study: Computer Acquisition

Monthly Operating Costs


ITEM                                          AMOUNT


Hardware Rental                               $3,000
PERSONNEL
Analyst-Programmer            $2,400
Operator                       1,600
CRT Operator - FTime           1,000
CRT Operator - PTime             500
TOTAL PERSONNEL                                5,500
Software Rental                                  500
Other Overhead                                 2,000


TOTAL                                         $11,000


Monthly Cost Savings:
```

---

[2]  After Barry E. Cushing and Marshall B. Romney, *Accounting Information Systems*,
     Fourth Edition, Reading, MA: Addison-Wesley Publishing Company, 1987, 524–526.

```
CLERICAL COSTS          NUM    SAVINGS   TOT SAV
Receivables Clerks       3     $1,200    $3,600
Payroll Clerk            1      1,200     1,200
Inventory Clerks         2      1,000     2,000


TOTAL                                             $6,800


Inventory Carrying Costs:


                 INVENTORY    COST of      PER      MONTHLY
                 BALANCE RED  CAPITAL     MONTH     SAVINGS

                 $1,600,00020%    15%     0.083     $4,000


TOTAL                                             $10,800
```

## Reminders

1.  Check entries for accuracy, make any necessary changes, and fill in missing data.
2.  Edit cells with the [F2] key.
3.  Change justification of column headings.
4.  Construct functions and formulas by "pointing" to ensure accuracy; use parentheses to ensure values are processed in the proper order.
5.  Dollar Variance calculated as the Budget minus Actual.
6.  Percentage Variance is the Budget minus Actual divided by the Budget.
7.  Keep all of the columns the same width (except for A).


Exercise 3-2

**Filename: 3EX2.WKS**

Performance reports are common in manufacturing environments. At the Carlton Manufacturing Company, the supervisors of three production departments (Machining, Assembly, and Finishing) and one service department (Maintenance) report to the plant manager. The plant manager makes recommendations concerning salary increments for these subordinates as well as his own staff and makes recommendations concerning equipment purchases for the departments under his control. An assistant supervisor began work on the performance report for the Assembly Department for May 1990. Retrieve the file and complete this report by entering any missing data, correcting any errors, and entering the appropriate formulas and functions to calculate the totals and variances. The completed report should look like the following.[3]

---

[3]  Adapted from Barry E. Cushing and Marshall B. Romney, *Accounting Information Systems*, Fifth Edition, Reading, MA: Addison-Wesley Publishing Company, 1990, 57–59. Reprinted with permission.

```
Carlton Manufacturing Company
May 1990

Assembly Department
Performance Report - All Costs, Fixed Budget
```

|  | | | VARIANCE (OVER) UNDER | VARIANCE % OF |
|---|---|---|---|---|
| COST | BUDGET | ACTUAL | BUDGET | BUDGET |
| Direct Labor | $10,500 | $12,000 | ($1,500) | -14% |
| Materials Spoilage | 600 | 630 | (30) | -5% |
| Overtime Premium | 1,500 | 1,740 | (240) | -16% |
| Reassembly | 1,200 | 1,170 | 30 | 3% |
| Supplies | 900 | 930 | (30) | -3% |
| Supervisor's Salary | 1,950 | 1,950 | 0 | 0% |
| Allocation of: | | | | |
| Depreciation-Bldg. | 300 | 300 | 0 | 0% |
| Depreciation-Equip. | 300 | 360 | (60) | -20% |
| Salary-Plant Mgt. | 600 | 600 | 0 | 0% |
| Salary-Plant Staff | 750 | 780 | (30) | -4% |
| Maintenance Costs | 3,200 | 3,290 | (90) | -3% |
| TOTAL | $21,800 | $23,750 | ($1,950) | 9% |

## Reminders

1. Enter data where necessary (complete description of the worksheet; documentation).
2. Justify.
3. Edit.
4. Enter formulas.
5. Copy formula.
6. Enter function.
7. Copy function.
8. Change column width.
9. Change formats.
10. Check output and edit data.

## Exercise 3-3

### Filename: 3EX3.WKS

The Perry Corporation has four new computer applications under development or scheduled to begin development shortly. The monthly requirements for computer and system analyst-programmer time (A-P) over the next two years are indicated in the worksheet for each of the next four six-month time periods.

Operational requirements for the company's existing applications total 400 computer system hours and 200 A-P hours. These requirements increase by 10% at the end of each six-month period. The firm currently employs six A-Ps who work eight hours a day for an average of 22 days per month. There is a total of 720 hours of available computer time per month (30 days x 24 hours per day). However, for each hour of computer time used, an average of only 80% is available for productive work, with the other 20% used for equipment maintenance, reruns, etc.[4]

Open the template provided and complete the formulas and formatting to match the report below. Print a copy of the report and answer the following questions.

1. When will a significant increase in the capacity of Perry's computer system become necessary? Why? *19-24 current capacity is 720*
2. The new computer system is projected to be complete as of the first day of month 13. One A-P will devote full-time effort to implementing the project for the six months prior to the first day of month 13. How many full-time A-Ps must Perry employ during each six-month period?

```
Perry Corporation
Long-Range Systems Plan
January 1, 1990

Monthly Computer System Hr Use:


                              ----------------MONTHS----------------
                               1-6       7-12      13-18     19-24
         -------------------------------------------------------------
Existing Systems               400       440       484       532
Project A                       20        75        80        88
Project B                       30        30       100       150
Project C                       25        30        30       100
Project D                                            20        30
         -------------------------------------------------------------
TOTAL SYSTEM HR USE - CURRENT  475       575       714       900
                               =============================================
TOTAL SYSTEM HR USE - NEW      475       575       238       300
                               =============================================
ADJUSTED FOR UNPRODUCTIVE TIME 594       719       298       375
                               =============================================

************************************************************************
Analyst-Programmer Hours used per Month:


                              ----------------MONTHS----------------
                               1-6       7-12      13-18     19-24
         -------------------------------------------------------------
Existing Systems               200       220       242       266
Project A                      240       380       100       110
Project B                      352       400       550       120
Project C                      264       280       300       500
Project D                                120       380       410
```

---

[4] Adapted from Barry E. Cushing and Marshall B. Romney, *Accounting Information Systems and Business Organizations*, Fourth Edition, Reading, MA: Addison-Wesley Publishing Company, 1987, 425–426.

Conversion                                          176

```
---------------------------------------------------------------------
TOTAL A-P  HOURS  REQUIRED        1056      1576      1572      1406
                                 =========================================

A-P  REQUIRED  (rounded)            6         9         9         8
                                 =========================================
```

**********************************************************************************

Exercise 3-4

**Filename: 3EX4.WKS**

The R&D Consulting firm specializes in AIS and has just moved its data from a database program into Lotus 1-2-3 for analyzing. The data in the file pertain to the employees, their rate of pay, the projects they have worked on, the number of hours worked, the pay week, and whether the project has been completed that week. Calculate the gross pay for each employee and determine the minimum, maximum, and average of the pay rate, hours worked, and gross pay for all employees. Format your report to look like the following example.

```
***************************************************
 PAY WEEK     EMP     RATE    PROJ    HRS     GROSS
01-Jun-90     345     8.75    133     40     350.00
01-Jun-90     432    20.55    140     40     822.00
01-Jun-90     654    15.65    140     40     626.00
01-Jun-90     678    10.75    133     40     430.00
08-Jun-90     234   100.00    133     14    1400.00
08-Jun-90     345     8.75    133     40     350.00
08-Jun-90     432    20.55    133     20     411.00
08-Jun-90     432    20.55    147     20     411.00
08-Jun-90     567    80.00    145      8     640.00
08-Jun-90     654    15.65    133     28     438.20
08-Jun-90     654    15.65    140     12     187.80
08-Jun-90     678    10.75    133     24     258.00
08-Jun-90     678    10.75    140     16     172.00
15-Jun-90     345     8.75    133     40     350.00
15-Jun-90     432    20.55    147     40     822.00
15-Jun-90     654    15.65    147     40     626.00
15-Jun-90     657    75.00    147     12     900.00
15-Jun-90     678    10.75    133     40     430.00
22-Jun-90     234   100.00    133     16    1600.00
22-Jun-90     345     8.75    133     40     350.00
22-Jun-90     432    20.55    133     40     822.00
22-Jun-90     455    85.00    133     12    1020.00
22-Jun-90     654    15.65    151     40     626.00
```

```
22-Jun-90    678    10.75    133    40    430.00
29-Jun-90    234   100.00    150     6    600.00
29-Jun-90    345     8.75    150    40    350.00
29-Jun-90    432    20.55    151    40    822.00
29-Jun-90    625    70.00    151     6    420.00
29-Jun-90    654    15.65    151    40    626.00
29-Jun-90    678    10.75    151    40    430.00
-----------------------------------------------------
   Minimum:           8.75           6.0    172.00
   Maximum:         100.00          40.0   1600.00
   Average:          31.18          29.1    590.67
***********************************************************
```

Check all formulas to ensure that you understand the logic and the processing in Lotus to arrive at the answers in the above cells.

# Chapter 4: Additional Lotus 1-2-3 Features

As you work through the case in this chapter, notice how easily the spreadsheet can evolve to become increasingly more complex as your understanding of the problem improves. You will modify the performance report for the laundry department of Argon County Hospital to better reflect the operations of the department. In doing so, you will be introduced to several more commands and functions, as well as absolute cell references. Also discussed in this chapter are data reference areas, documentation, and worksheet/report design. The importance of structuring a worksheet to facilitate "what if?" analysis is illustrated by examination of the impact of different levels of price changes and volumes on the laundry department performance report.

## Case Setting

The controller knew that the performance report you prepared in Chapter 3 would probably need to be modified, since relatively simple (expenses equally spread throughout the year) and optimistic (a 3% budget reduction below the prior year's expenses) assumptions were used to estimate the budgeted expenses and activity levels. Analysis of the prior three years' costs had shown that all costs increased each year, with more rapid increases between the second and third year. The controller had considered setting the budget at an average of the prior three years' costs, but realized that that was so extreme that it would probably be discouraging and would not be taken seriously by the department heads. Therefore, the 1990 budget was set at the latest year's costs, less three; the three % decrease was what the controller believed could be attained by efficiency improvements and careful cost-containment measures. Since activity levels had been stable over the past three years, they were budgeted to remain unchanged for 1990. Quarterly budgets for both expenses and activity levels were computed as one-fourth of the annual budget.

The purpose of the initial performance report was to get the department heads to think about how their departments actually operated, which could then be reflected in the final performance reporting system. Once the system accurately reflects the departments' operations, department heads can realistically be expected to use the reports to help them improve the efficiency of operations, and upper management can legitimately use them for evaluation and control. The controller realizes the power of the accounting system to shape how managers view their operations. A crucial aspect of systems analysis and design is to get input from the people who are expected to use the reports. To accomplish this, the performance report from Chapter 3 was sent out with a note stating that it was a first draft and requesting feedback and input from the departmental supervisors. The process of designing a working system, letting the users use it and provide feedback, and then modifying the systems in response to the user input is called prototyping. Software, such as Lotus 1-2-3, that allows you to develop a working system quickly and to modify it easily has made the prototyping approach to systems development increasingly common.

The laundry department supervisor was understandably upset to receive the initial performance report, since it showed that the laundry department was over budget in every line item by a substantial amount! The laundry supervisor requested a meeting with the controller and you, the special assistant, to discuss the assumptions that had been used to determine the quarterly budget. This was just what the controller wanted. During the meeting, the laundry department supervisor pointed out that since Argon County is a summer resort area, the county population doubles during the vacation months (May-August), and hospital activity more than doubles during these months. Also, labor rates and other prices have been rising steadily and give no sign of leveling off. Together, you discussed how these factors could be incorporated into the performance reporting system to make it more accurate, meaningful, and useful for managing costs of operations. Because Lotus is so easy to use, you were able to implement the proposed changes in the performance report as they were discussed. By the end of the meeting, all three of you were much happier with the performance reporting system and better understood the operations of the laundry department and the objectives of the controller's cost-containment program.

# Worksheet Design

You are often admonished to plan ahead, and developing a worksheet is no exception. The payoff for planning is a clearer, better organized worksheet, completed in a minimum of time. However, since even the best designs are seldom perfect, Lotus makes it easy to change the worksheet contents and appearance. So, do the best you can to plan a well-designed worksheet and make improvements as they occur to you or are suggested by others.

The general principals in designing worksheets are as follows:

1. **Document thoroughly.**

   - Answer any questions a user might have.
   - Identify where data are to be entered in the worksheet.

2. **Organize for consistency and logic.**

   - Progress from the general to the specific.
   - Keep reference data together in one area.
   - Place items to be compared next to each other.
   - Order items in a meaningful sequence.

3. **Design for visual impact.**

   - Separate areas with blank spaces, lines, or special characters.
   - Allow sufficient space between columns to distinguish numbers.

4. **Let Lotus calculate.**

   - Never perform a calculation yourself; make Lotus do it.
   - Use cell references instead of retyping or copying numbers.

# Documentation

Always document your worksheets thoroughly. Good documentation is important to accountants because it facilitates using, evaluating, and auditing information systems. Unfortunately, documentation is often done poorly or neglected altogether in end-user computing. Poor or nonexistent documentation can lead to costly mistakes if it is not clear what a worksheet does, and to time-consuming, frustrating efforts to figure out how a worksheet functions if the person who initially developed the worksheet has left the department. You may even forget how your own worksheets function if you have not used them recently.

The case in Chapter 3 provided the worksheet documentation without discussing its purpose. In the real world, the person who designs or modifies a worksheet is responsible for designing the documentation as well as entering it. Treat documentation as though the next user will begin with no idea what a worksheet does; try to anticipate and answer any questions he or she might have. Be as clear and concise as possible. The objective of documentation is to describe everything necessary to understand and use the worksheet and includes the following:

- **Worksheet identification data**: the name of the file, the date it was created or modified, and by whom
- **Explanatory documentation**: the general purpose of the worksheet, what the worksheet does, assumptions and the logic behind them, source(s) of the data, and where data are to be entered or changed
- **Report identification data**: the organization and the unit, the name of the report, and the time period it covers

In addition, some users consider all labels in a worksheet or report to be documentation. Whether viewed as documentation or data, labels such as column headings and row descriptions should meet the criteria of accuracy, clarity, conciseness, and readability.

You entered report identification data in the case in Chapter 3, stating the type of report, the department, and the time period covered. The other types of documentation listed above are discussed throughout this chapter.

# Worksheet Organization and Components

Organization refers to the location of the various items in the worksheet. The worksheet should be organized consistently and logically. Keep in mind that the purpose of organization is to enable users of both the electronic worksheet and the related hard-copy reports to use them more effectively and efficiently. With this in mind, the worksheet designer must consider the ease of viewing the worksheet on screen, of printing it, and of modeling the necessary relationships.

A good rule of thumb is to start with the more general information and progress to the more specific information. The worksheet identification data is usually placed in the upper left corner of the worksheet, followed by explanatory documentation, the reference data area, and the report or worksheet body. The size, complexity, and nature of the items in a worksheet, as well as individual preferences and company standards for formats, all affect the organization of a worksheet. Although there is usually no single best way to organize a worksheet, some ways are definitely better than others.

It is a good idea to keep all reference cells together in one area, which typically follows the explanatory documentation. Within reports, group related items together, place items to be compared next to each other whenever possible, and order items in a meaningful sequence (such as alphabetical order, numerical order, or size) if one exists. It is seldom possible to follow all these suggestions simultaneously, because they often conflict. Choose an organization that serves your purpose well; reorganize the worksheet if you find a different organization that works better.

Many companies and CPA firms have developed worksheet documentation and organization standards that all worksheets must meet. If users can expect to find certain types of information at certain places in reports, they can understand a new report more quickly. Standards make it easier for users to interpret reports, which is especially important when users get new reports frequently.

## Reference Data Area

If a piece of data will be used several places in the worksheet, enter it in a single cell and reference that cell any time that data is needed. Such data values are grouped in the **reference data area** of the worksheet, which is typically part of the documentation in the upper left corner of the worksheet. Each data item is labeled to explain how it is used and its relevance to the rest of the worksheet. Inflation or interest rates are examples of data commonly entered here.

Referencing is much more efficient than typing or copying the data in several worksheet locations. Referencing does not necessarily help you prepare the initial worksheet faster, but it makes it much faster and easier to modify the worksheet to reflect changes in data. If the data value itself is entered in the formulas, all the formulas must be retyped or edited and copied if the data value changes. However, if a cell reference is entered in the formulas, the data value needs to be changed only once to have its effects reflected everywhere in the worksheet that cell is referenced. Any data value that is likely to change or that you want to use to test the effects of different values should be referenced. If a cell reference is not used, you must remember to change the number everywhere it occurs in the worksheet, which is a time-consuming and error-prone task.

## Worksheet Body

The calculating area that contains the analysis is referred to as the **worksheet body**. It is the area that contains much of the data and the models, in terms of formulas and cell references, of how the data are related. Although this area sometimes consists entirely of formulas that are dependent on the reference data area, it is more commonly a combination of constant data, formulas, and cell references. The performance report worksheet you are working on is such a combination.

New data values are entered in the reference data area, and the impact of those changes are reflected in the worksheet body. The worksheet becomes a dynamic instrument for aiding decision making, called a decision support system (DSS), to help you answer "what if?" questions, such as "What if some of my assumptions change or are different from what I expect?"

## Visual Clarity (Lines and Spacing)

Lines and spacing can be used in a worksheet to delineate or draw attention to material. Blank rows are used to separate distinct sections of the worksheet, such as sections of a report. A blank column can be inserted or the column width can be increased to give the appearance of a wider spacing between columns. Rows can be filled with repeating characters to make lines between areas. Vertical lines can be made using a narrow column in which each cell contains a label entry that consists of the straight vertical line character ('I).

## Worksheet Insert (/WI) or Delete (/WD)

Additional columns or rows are often inserted in a worksheet to provide additional blank space or room to expand existing material or to add new material. To add columns or rows, select /Worksheet Insert Column (or Row), highlight the location at which you want to insert the rows or columns, and press ⏎. Rows are inserted above and columns are inserted to the left of the highlighted area. To delete columns or rows, select /Worksheet Delete Column (or Row), highlight the rows or columns you want to delete, and press ⏎. It is convenient, but not necessary, to move the cell pointer to the desired location before beginning the insertion or deletion command sequence.

To start the case for this chapter, retrieve the file 4CASEA.WKS using /File Retrieve. This file contains the properly completed worksheet from Chapter 3, plus worksheet identification data (the file name, preparer's name, course, date, etc.). You have already seen this type of documentation if you completed any of the practice exercises in Chapter 3. Enter your name, the course, and the date.

Additional room is needed for the documentation and reference data area in the revised performance report. To insert five additional rows, move to A15 and enter /Worksheet Insert Rows "Enter row insert range:" A15..A19, as shown in Figure 4.1.

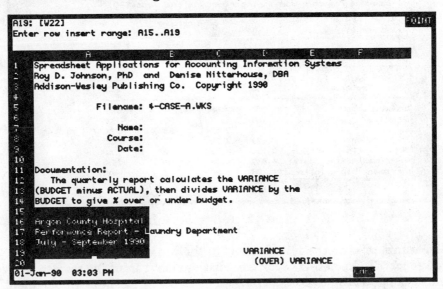

Figure 4.1 Inserting rows

Press ⏎ to insert the rows. Return to A1 by pressing [Home], then press [PgDn]. The title of the report now begins in the upper left corner of the screen. This positioning will let you move around the screen using [PgDn] much more conveniently than moving only a row at a time using the arrow keys. Use /Worksheet Delete Row to delete row 32.

## Repeating Labels (\)

To visually separate data, rows, or columns even more clearly, you can make horizontal lines of various symbols using **repeating labels**. A repeating label begins with a backslash (\). Note that the backslash (\) is *not* the same as the slash (/), which brings up the command line or signals division in a formula. When \ is the first character entered in a cell, whatever characters follow it will be displayed in a repeating pattern across the entire width of the cell. If the column width is changed, the display also changes so that the repeating characters appear to fill the entire cell. The characters most frequently used in repeating labels are the hyphen(-), the underline (_), the equals sign (=), and the asterisk, or star (*). Hyphens or underlines are used to make horizontal lines within reports, usually to separate column headings from numeric data and to separate numeric data from the related totals and other summary statistics. The equals sign is used to make a double underscore, commonly used to designate final totals in balance sheets, income statements, and other accounting statements. Rows of asterisks are used to separate areas of the worksheet or reports. Asterisks are used in this worksheet to separate the reference data area from the performance reports.

Move to A20 and enter \* ↵. Copy this cell across to F20 (/Copy FROM: A20..A20 TO: B20..E20). A line of asterisks now separates the documentation and the reference area from the performance report. Using repeating labels, place hyphens in row 28 below the headings, in row 31 between activity levels and expenses (below Pounds Processed), and in row 39 above the TOTAL (\- ↵) (Figure 4.2).

```
A39: [W22] \-                                              READY

         A              B          C          D          E          F
20  *********************************************************************
21  Argon County Hospital
22  Performance Report - Laundry Department:Initial Report
23  July - September 1990
24                                      VARIANCE
25                                       (OVER)   VARIANCE
26                                       UNDER     % OF
27                     BUDGET   ACTUAL   BUDGET    BUDGET
28  ------------------------------------------------------------
29  Patient Days        9,500   11,900   (2,400)   -25%
30  Pounds Processed  125,000  156,000  (31,000)   -25%
31  ------------------------------------------------------------
32  Laundry Labor      $9,000  $12,500  ($3,500)   -39%
33  Supplies            1,100    1,875     (775)   -70%
34  Water               1,700    2,500     (800)   -47%
35  Maintenance         1,400    2,200     (800)   -57%
36  Supervisor's Salary 3,150    3,750     (600)   -19%
37  Allocated Admin. Costs 4,000 5,000  (1,000)   -25%
38  Equipment Depreciation 1,200 1,250     (50)    -4%
39  ------------------------------------------------------------
01-Jan-90   01:15 PM
```

**Figure 4.2 Repeating labels**

The controller wants to keep the initial report in the worksheet, so it can be easily compared to the revised report. To keep this report and distinguish it from the revised one you are planning, add a colon at the end of "Performance Report - Laundry Department" in cell A22 and enter "Initial Version" in cell D22. (Alternatively, the initial report could be eliminated entirely, or it could be kept in a separate file with a different name.) The revised report will be placed below the initial report and will have similar rows and columns. The labels in the left margin of the report will be displayed using cell references, since you want the line-item names in the revised report to appear and remain *exactly* the same as those in the initial report. The revised budget amounts will be calculated by using formulas that refer to the original budget and to the reference data area.

## Range Label (/RL)

The column headings in the revised performance report will be similar to, but not exactly the same as, the headings in the first report. Therefore, you will copy the headings and edit them. Move to A21 and copy the report title and column headings with /Copy FROM: A21..E27 ⏎ [PgDn] TO: A41 ⏎. You can indicate just the starting cell of the copy TO range without specifying the whole target range exactly. Although this saves time, there is a danger that the copy will overwrite needed data. Be cautious when using this double-edged sword of maximum convenience and minimal control.

The revised report title was deliberately placed immediately below the totals of the initial report so the [PgDn] can be used during data entry. Additional rows for better spacing can be added later. Enter the following data in the indicated cells to make the column headings appropriate for the revised report:

| Cell | Contents | Cell | Contents | Cell | Contents |
|------|----------|------|----------|------|----------|
| B44 | LAST | | | D42 | REVISED VERSION |
| B45 | YEAR'S | C45 | REVISED | | |
| B46 | ACTUAL | C46 | QUARTER | | |
| B47 | ANNUAL | C47 | BUDGET | | |

The data you have just entered is left-justified (the default) because you did not enter " as the first character in each cell. You could edit each cell by deleting ' and inserting ", but this would be tedious. Fortunately, a faster way to change the justification of a group of labels is to use the sequence /Range Label Right B44..C47 ⏎ (Figure 4.3).

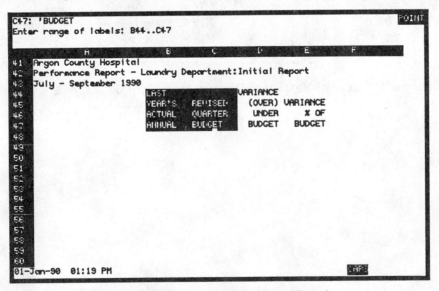

**Figure 4.3 Changing label justification**

This command changes the first (justification) character of all labels in the specified range; it affects only cells that already contain label entries. This ability to change the format of a range of labels parallels the ability to change the format in which a range of numeric data is displayed, which was discussed in Chapter 3.

# Developing and Using the Worksheet Model

The data in the worksheet are related by formulas that model the relationships among the actual entities the data represent. The worksheet formulas represent how the worksheet designer believes the world works. If the underlying assumptions are incorrect or are correct but incorrectly implemented by the formulas, the worksheet will provide misleading results. A crucial part of worksheet design is understanding what the data represent, and how that is reflected in the data and the formulas. The formulas determine what data can be changed conveniently and what the effect of changing any piece of data will be on the other entries in the worksheet.

## Reference Area

The data values that seem to be both most important and most in question are "How much and in what direction should costs be expected to change from the prior year and how much of the annual expenses will be incurred in the current quarter?" Since these numbers are uncertain, and you want to see the effects of different values on the performance report, they should be placed in cells that can be referenced by formulas. This will allow us to change a data value (variable) and see the effects immediately, without having to search for every place that value appears in the worksheet, and to edit and recopy the formulas with the modified variable.

Enter the following reference data and documentation in the indicated cells, making sure a space follows the label indicators in C16..C18 so that the labels are separated from the % by a space.

| Cell | Contents | Cell | Contents |
|------|----------|------|----------|
| A16 | "Reference Data Area: | C16 | ' Budget Change |
| B16 | -.03 | C17 | ' Quarterly Volume Percent |
| B17 | .25 | C18 | ' Exception Level |
| B18 | .1 | | |

Format the range B16..B18 as percentage with zero decimal places, as shown in Figure 4.4.

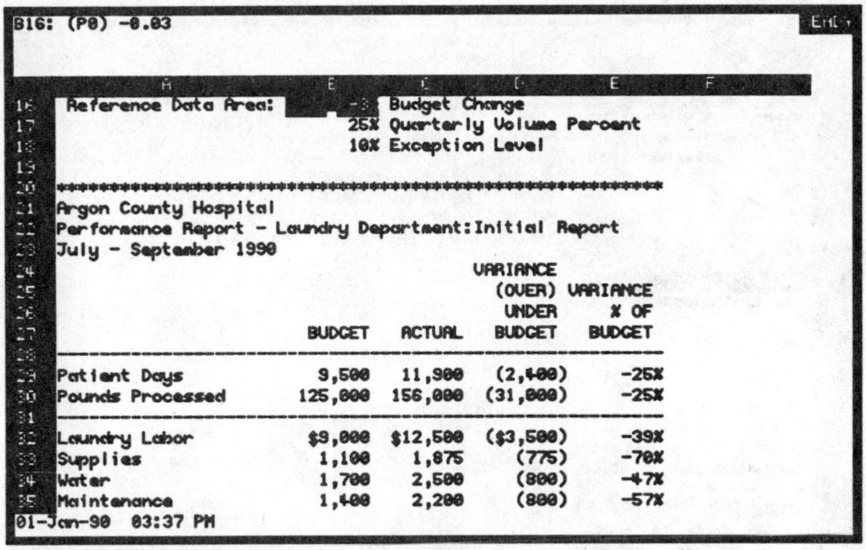

```
B16: (P0) -0.03                                                          END

          A          B          C          D          E          F
16  Reference Data Area:        -3  Budget Change
17                              25% Quarterly Volume Percent
18                              10% Exception Level
19
20  **********************************************************************
21  Argon County Hospital
22  Performance Report - Laundry Department:Initial Report
23  July - September 1990
24                                           VARIANCE
25                                            (OVER)    VARIANCE
26                                             UNDER      % OF
27                         BUDGET    ACTUAL    BUDGET    BUDGET
28  _____
29  Patient Days            9,500    11,900    (2,400)    -25%
30  Pounds Processed      125,000   156,000   (31,000)    -25%
31  _____
32  Laundry Labor          $9,000   $12,500   ($3,500)    -39%
33  Supplies                1,100     1,875     (775)     -70%
34  Water                   1,700     2,500     (800)     -47%
35  Maintenance             1,400     2,200     (800)     -57%
01-Jan-90  03:37 PM
```

**Figure 4.4  Reference area**

## Relative Single Cell References

A **single cell reference** is essentially a formula that contains only one item, the address of the cell to which it refers. A single cell reference can refer to cells that contain *either* labels or values. Formulas that contain multiple cell addresses linked by a mathematical operator, such as +, can contain only addresses of cells that contain values (other formulas, numbers, or functions that result in values). If a cell address in a formula contains a label, the cell containing the formula will display an error message (ERR). Although you could use the Copy command to copy the line-item names, here you will use a cell reference instead. The advantage is that if you change a line-item name in the initial report, the change will be displayed in any cell that references the cell where the change was made. If you used the Copy command to copy the line-item names, changes to the initial report line item names would *not* affect the line-item names in the revised report.

To reference the cell contents of cell A29 in cell A49, position the cell pointer on A49, press plus (+), point to cell A29 with [PgUp], and press ⌐. Use the Copy command to replicate your cell reference for the other line-item names by using /Copy FROM: A49 TO: A50..A60 (Figure 4.5).

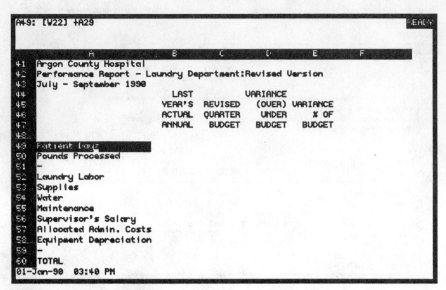

**Figure 4.5 Relative cell reference**

This action results in references in A51 and A59 to cells that contain repeating labels (A31 and A39). When cells containing labels are referenced, the label-justification character is not carried along to the cell that contains the reference. Therefore, cells A51 and A59 contain and display a single dash instead of repeating dashes to make a line. Correct the entries in A51 and A59 to be repeating hyphens. (By now you should realize that there are three ways you could do this: type in the correct entry (\–), edit the cell to delete the ' and enter \, or copy the entry from another cell.) When an empty cell is referenced, Lotus displays a zero instead of an empty cell. To correct this problem if it occurs, use /Range Erase to erase the cells that incorrectly display zeros. Cell references do not reflect formatting of either labels or values, only the cell contents.

These examples should show you that the computer does not always act as you might expect it to. Be aware of the screen contents. Do not assume that because a computer did it, it must be right! Do not assume that the computer has done what you think it would make sense to do. Only careful scrutiny by a human user will detect items like this.

## Absolute Cell Addresses ($ or [F4])

The term "absolute" means that a cell address is fixed and does not change when the cell address is copied. Thus, an **absolute cell address** always refers to the same cell no matter where it is copied to, while a relative cell address changes in relation to the location it is copied to. Absolute cell addresses can be used in single cell references and in formulas. An absolute cell address is indicated by a $ in front of the column and another $ in front of the row designator in the cell address. Mixed cell addresses are those in which either the row or the column is absolute, and the other is relative. If only the column letter is preceded by a $, then the column address letter remains fixed, but the row changes as in a relative cell address. If the row number is preceded by a $, the reverse is true.

The formulas that use the Budget Change and the Quarterly Volume Percent do so by referring to the contents of cells B13 and B14, respectively, and to Last Year's Actual Annual. Enter the following data for Last Year's Actual Annual (which came from the controller's manual files).

| Cell | Contents | Cell | Contents |
|------|----------|------|----------|
| B49 | 38000 | B55 | 5773 |
| B50 | 500000 | B56 | 12990 |
| B52 | 37113 | B57 | 16495 |
| B53 | 4536 | B58 | 4948 |
| B54 | 7010 | | |

Enter an @SUM Function in B60 to add up all the costs. (Remember *not* to include the activity level lines in the range!) The amount displayed in B60, if you have correctly entered the cost data and function, should be 88,865. Checking the results against known correct figures is a valuable type of control on the integrity of an AIS.

The Revised Quarter Budget for activity levels is calculated by multiplying Last Year's Actual for each item by the Quarterly Volume Percent in cell B17 in the reference data area, so move to cell C49 and enter the formula +B49*B17. As usual, you can enter the formula by either pointing or typing.

Normally, the Copy command modifies the column letters or row numbers in the copied formulas automatically. So far, you have found this useful for copying formulas. However, if the formula in cell C49 is copied to C50, the formula in cell C50 is +B50*B18, but you need the reference to cell B17 to remain the same. This can be accomplished by placing a $ in front of both the column letter and the row number of the cell address to make it absolute. The dollar sign in front of the column letter keeps the column letter in a formula unchanged when a column is copied; the $ in front of the row number has the same effect for row numbers. Use edit [F2] to change the contents of cell C49 to +B49*$B$17. Copy the formula from C49 into cell C50. Since B49 is still a relative cell address, it changes as it should for the various line items; since $B$17 is absolute, it does not change.

Although the Patient Days and Pounds Processed activity levels are not affected by the budget change, the cost of the line items are expected to be affected by the budget change and will need a slightly different formula to reflect this. The Revised Quarter Budget for cost line items is calculated by multiplying Last Year's Actual Annual by (1 plus the Budget Change) by the Quarterly Volume Percent. This time, enter the formula by pointing to the cells to be entered in the formula and using the [F4] function key to make the cell reference absolute while pointing to the cell. Move to cell C52, press +, point to B52, type *(1+, then point to cell B16, and press [F4] to enter $B$16, as shown in Figure 4.6.

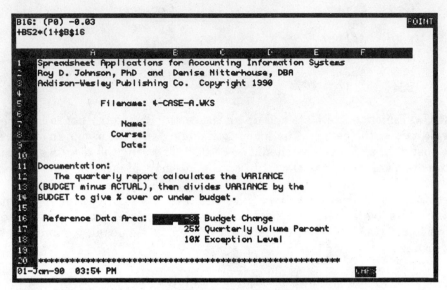

Figure 4.6  Absolute cell reference ($)

Complete the formula by typing )*, pointing to cell B17, pressing [F4] to enter $B$17, and pressing ↵. The formula in cell C52 should be shown on the first line of the control panel as +B52*(1+$B$16)*$B$17. If it is not, erase it and follow the steps again, so that you are sure you understand using pointing and [F4] to enter absolute cell references. Once it is correct, copy the formula to C53..C58.

# Naming Ranges (/RN)

A cell range can be referenced by name instead of address if it has been assigned a name with the /Range Name command. The idea is to use a meaningful, easily remembered name instead of having to point to the cells. Named ranges also make formulas easier to understand, because the range names (instead of the cell addresses) are displayed when the cell is highlighted. Move to cell B16. Name the cell that contains the Budget Change (B16) BUDGET CHANGE with the sequence /Range Name Create "Enter name:" BUDGET CHANGE "Enter range:" B16..B16 ↵. Unlike filenames, range names can contain spaces and can be up to 15 characters long. Repeat the sequence /Range Name Create to see the existing range name displayed on the third line of the control panel, as shown in Figure 4.7.

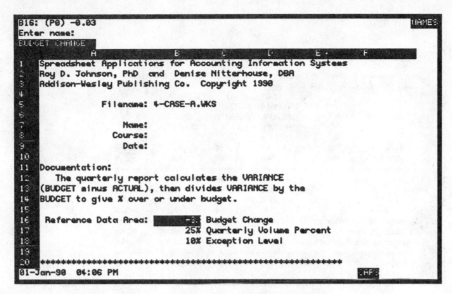

**Figure 4.7 Creating additional range names**

To modify a range, select its name from this list, then change the range by pointing to or typing in the new range. Having the range names listed also helps prevent duplication. If you accidentally try to use an existing range name a second time, Lotus will highlight the cells that are currently assigned that name. If you want to keep the original range, just back out with [Esc] and choose a different name for the new range. When you use certain commands, such as Copy, the [F3] function key lists the stored range names, for easier data entry.

Complete the /Range Name Create sequence with "Enter name:" VOLUME "Enter range:" B17..B17 ↵ to assign the range name VOLUME to the cell B17. The formula in C52 now displays the named ranges as absolute references ($BUDGET CHANGE and $VOLUME) instead of the cell addresses.

Having entered the revised quarterly budget, calculate the variances, percentage variances, and totals, which should be fairly familiar by now. Copy the @SUM function from B60 to C60. Move to cell D49 and enter +C49−C29 to calculate the variance of actual from the revised budget. Enter +D49/C49 in cell E49 to calculate the variance as a percent of budget. To copy both formulas at the same time, use a single Copy command to copy D49 and E49 down to row 60. Improve the appearance of the worksheet by copying the repeating cells where necessary to make lines, formatting the cells in the Laundry Labor and TOTAL rows as currency with no decimal places, and formatting column E as percentages with no decimal places, as shown in Figure 4.8.

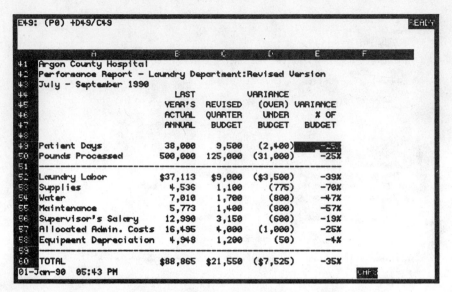

**Figure 4.8 Revised performance report**

Although the revised performance report is now structured to incorporate the alternative budget assumptions, it still contains the same assumptions used for the initial report. Again, this allows you to check the accuracy of your data entry and formulas by comparing the budget numbers in the revised report to those in the initial report. If they are different, you have done something wrong and need to fix (debug) your worksheet by finding the error and correcting it. Do this before continuing. (Notice that the budget is in different columns in the revised and initial reports; be sure you are comparing the correct columns before you panic!)

Once the worksheet is correct, save it. You should have saved the worksheet several times since starting this chapter; if you have not been saving regularly, you are destined to find out the hard way how important it is.

## Move (/M)

At this point, you the controller, and the supervisor stopped to reexamine the organization of the spreadsheet. You have decided to have the revised report to the right of the initial report, instead of below it, and the Actual column before the Budget column in the initial report. It is relatively easy to change the report structure this way, and even to change it back if the new organization doesn't work out as well as expected.

The Move command removes, or cuts out, material from selected cell(s) and puts it in other cell(s). It moves material from one place to another in the worksheet. Go to cell B42 and move the revised report from below the initial report to beside it with /Move "Enter range to move FROM:" B42..E60 "Enter range to move TO:" F22. The beauty of the Move command is that all the cell references are automatically changed to reflect the new locations.

Erase the area you moved your reports from with /Range Erase A41..E60. This removes the contents from cells no longer needed, including any blank spaces entered in the cells by mistake.

Insert a new column B (at B27, select /Worksheet Insert Column ↵) and move the actual data FROM D27..D40 TO B27. Move the documentation and reference data from columns C and D (C1..D20) left TO B1, check to make sure column D is now empty with [End] ↓ and [End] ↑, and delete column D with /Worksheet Delete Column. The worksheet should now look the same as it did earlier, except that the Budget and Actual columns are reversed in the initial version of the report.

## Hiding a Column

You can hide worksheet data by using /Worksheet Column Hide and selecting the column to be hidden. Try this now with column F, Last Year's Actual Annual data. Note that when column F is hidden, the column letters at the top of the screen jump from E to G, which is how you know a column is hidden. Make the column reappear with /Worksheet Column Display. This option is not available in version 1 of Lotus 1-2-3.

## Worksheet Titles (/WT)

Although the movement of the report was successful, it is harder to understand what the numbers mean because the column headings and row titles do not appear on the screen. Fortunately, Lotus has a Titles command to keep titles for columns or rows on the screen. Use [F5] or another method to position A24 in the upper left corner of the screen. The column headings (in rows 24..27) should be the top four rows of the screen, and the line-item names (in column A) should be at the left edge of the screen. Use the arrow keys to move to B29, where you will freeze all of the titles *above* and to the *left* of the cursor with /Worksheet Titles Both.

Now when you move around the worksheet, these title columns and rows will stay on the screen. Move to cell I29 to see how this works. The columns and rows frozen as titles are now treated as the borders of the worksheet, and you can no longer move into them using arrow keys. (Try it.) Pressing [Home] now returns you to cell B29 instead of A1. You can move to a cell in a frozen title or anywhere else in the worksheet by using [F5]. You can also use the arrow keys to move into or beyond titles when you are pointing to a range within a command, such as Print or Copy. Remove the titles now with /Worksheet Titles Clear.

## Worksheet Windows (/WW and [F6])

When a worksheet becomes too large to view on a single screen, it is often convenient to be able to view two distant areas of the worksheet at the same time. To view both the cell reference area and the calculations being performed in the report just completed, you will now create an upper window three rows high and a lower window that uses the rest of the screen. Move to A1 with [Home], move to A4, and enter /Worksheet Windows Horizontal. Two **windows** are now displayed, with the cell pointer located at cell A3 in the upper window. Move the cell pointer down to cell A18 to display the reference area, as shown in Figure 4.9. (You also could have arrived here by positioning the worksheet so that cell A16 is in the upper left corner of the screen, moving the cell pointer down to cell A19, and entering /Worksheet Windows Horizontal.)

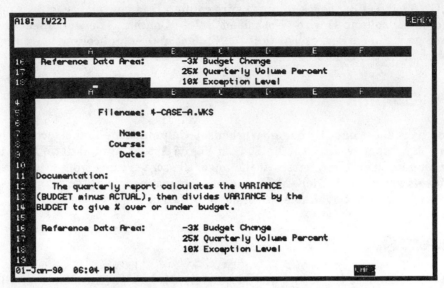

**Figure 4.9  Worksheet windows**

To change windows, press [F6]; the cursor jumps to the lower window at cell A4.

If you press [Tab] to move right to see the revised report, you lose both the reference area and the line-item names. This is because the windows are synchronized; when one moves right or left, so does the other. Use [Shift] [Tab] to return the reference area to the upper screen, then use /Worksheet Windows Unsync to make the windows move left and right independently of each other. In the lower window, position the line-item names and column headings at the left and top edges of the lower window. Cell A24 should be in the upper left corner of the lower window. Move the cursor to C28, and use /Worksheet Titles Both to freeze them as titles. You can now move anywhere in the worksheet in the lower window and still view the cell reference area in the upper window. Position the worksheet so the revised report is visible. Return to the upper window with [F6] and move to cell B17.

The use of the Windows command makes it possible to view multiple portions of the worksheet at the same time. The increased clarity and understanding gained from views of different portions of the worksheet are important for communicating your ideas and desk-checking your results. The window feature can be turned off with /Worksheet Windows Clear, but leave it on for now. Since the revised report is easier to view, let's try a "what if?" analysis.

## "What If?" Analysis

The budget should reflect the fact that almost half of the volume is processed during the four months from May through August. Since the laundry department supervisor estimated that the July to September quarter represents about one third of the annual volume, enter 0.33 in cell B17 and watch the worksheet recalculate, as shown in Figure 4.10.

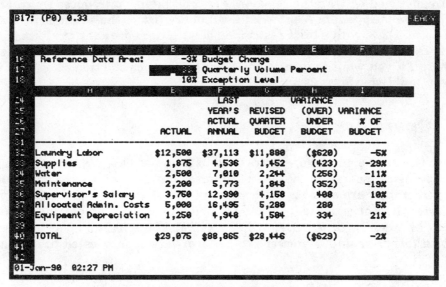

**Figure 4.10 "What If?" analysis**

How does this change the performance picture of the laundry department for this quarter? Do you think the estimate of 33% is reasonable? How might that be tested? Enter 0 in B16, to reflect a budget for the current year that is the same as last year's. As you can see, it is possible to change any variable in the reference area and see the results immediately. Practice changing the values of the Budget Change and Quarterly Volume Percentage to see their effects. What do you think are reasonable values to use for these data?

Flexible budgets can be calculated based on actual activity levels, once those data are available. Although so far you have only entered constants in your reference cells, they can also contain formulas. Instead of guessing at the Quarterly Volume, you can calculate the percentage that this quarter's actual (B30) is of this year's budgeted activity level of pounds processed (F30). In cell B17, enter +B30/F30. (Actual quarter activity divided by Last Year's Actual Annual). You can use Last Year's Actual Annual, since this year's annual activity is budgeted at the same amount. This is a good example of the type of shortcut that can get you into trouble in the real world. While it is perfectly legitimate for the current situation and set of assumptions, if those change, someone must remember or notice that the cell used in this formula is *really* Last Year's Actual instead of this year's annual budget. When you have completed your analysis, turn off windows with /Worksheet Windows Clear.

# @Functions

Lotus has many powerful built-in functions to provide complex calculations or other processing of values and labels. Function names always begins with @ followed by the function name; they are referred to in this book as "at functions." Each @function has arguments that tell it what data to act on and what actions to take. The arguments must be entered in a specific order within parentheses, and the nature and type of arguments differs among @functions. The general form of an @function is @FUNCTION(*argument1,argument2,...*)

You have already used @SUM; the remainder of this chapter introduces several more complex @functions. Appendix A provides a summary list of the @functions available in version 2 of Lotus 1-2-3, with a brief description of what each does and the form of the arguments it requires. Those typically of most interest to accountants are discussed briefly next. In general, if you want to do a complex but common calculation, check the @function list before you build your own formula.

## Logical Operators

In addition to the mathematical operators used in formulas (+ − * /), Lotus has a fairly standard set of logical operators that are used in combination with some of the @functions. These logical operators are equal to (=), less than (<), less than or equal to(<=), greater than (>), greater than or equal to (>=), and not equal to (<>). Combinations of these logical operators can be made with #AND#, #OR#, #NOT#. These logical operators can be combined with formulas and @functions to perform very sophisticated processing.

## Types of @Functions

Several standard **statistical** operations that should be familiar from your business math are found in Lotus @functions. As you know, @SUM adds all the numbers in the specified range. Two simple and common statistics are generated by @AVG, which calculates the arithmetic average of the cells in the range, and @COUNT, which counts the number of entries in the range. @MAX and @MIN find the largest and smallest numbers in the range. Two more complicated statistics are generated by @STD and @VAR, which calculate the standard deviation and the variance of the cells in the range. (See your business math book if you have forgotten these formulas or their meanings.) The statistical functions are commonly used when dealing with a column or a row of like items, for example, to calculate an average price or quantity of items. The **database statistical functions** parallel the statistical functions described above, operate on subsets of databases, and start with the letter D, as in @DAVG and @DCOUNT.

**Financial** @functions are also frequently used by accountants to make calculations relating to loans, annuities, cash flows (investment evaluation), and depreciation. @SLD, @DDB, and @SYD calculate depreciation based on the straight-line, double declining balance, and sum of the years digits methods. @IRR and @NPV calculate the internal rate of return and the net present value; @FV and @PV calculate the future and present values of a stream of cash flows.

The **mathematical** @functions of most use to accountants are @ABS (to return the absolute or positive value), @ RAND (to generate random numbers), @ROUND (to round numbers), and @SQRT (to calculate square roots). **Date** and **time** @functions allow dates and times to be used in calculations; they extract the time and date from the computer's internal clock or work with times and dates in cells of the worksheet. Cells that contain @Date functions should usually be formatted using Date format (/Range Format Date), to display the date in a way that makes sense to human users. Subtracting the due date of an account receivable from the current date to prepare an aged accounts receivable report is an example of a common use of date functions. **String** @functions are used for working with letters, numbers, and special characters as long as they are label data types.

**Special** @functions are used to perform several advanced tasks related to looking up values in cells. @HLOOKUP and @VLOOKUP find a specified value in a row or a column and return the contents of a cell a designated number of rows below it or columns to the right of it. @ERR and @NA force the cell and any cell formulas depending on it to have the value of error or not applicable. @ERR can be used to test for errors and is often used to check for correct values. @NA is used to notify you that a number needed for a calculation is not available.

**Logical** @functions evaluate conditions (whether something is true or false) and return or result in a value of 1 if the statement is true or 0 if it is false.

# @IF

One of the most important and powerful logical functions is @IF. It allow us to implement an important programming concept of selection, or conditional performance, where what you do depends on the veracity of a statement (whether it is true or false). The form of this function is @IF(*logical condition to be tested*, if true *do this*, if false *do this*).

The first argument must be in the form of a logical statement, such as A12=3, or B50<= C16. The items in the condition can be constants, cell references, formulas, functions, or labels.

## Using @IF in a Flexible Budget

During the meeting, the controller and the laundry supervisor discussed whether the various cost line items are fixed or variable and controllable or uncontrollable. They agreed that some of the costs are variable and others are fixed and also that some are within the laundry supervisor's control, while others are not. In this situation, all the Variable costs are also controllable, and the fixed costs are uncontrollable (this is common, but not always true).

To designate costs as variable (V) or fixed (F), insert a new column B and set it to a width of 3. (Move to column B, /Worksheet Insert Column ↵, /Worksheet Column Set-Width 3 ↵). Enter V in B32..B35 to indicate variable costs and F in cells B36..B38 to reflect fixed costs, as agreed to by the controller and supervisor. Since the left-justified labels in column B are not clearly distinct from the material in column A, right-justify the label data in column B using /Range Label Right B32..B38 ↵.

Lotus 1-2-3 version 1 will not allow labels in @IF functions. This activity can be completed by entering 1 instead of V and 0 instead of F in column B, and by substituting in the @IF function.

Variable costs change with activity volume, but fixed costs do not. To properly reflect this, it was agreed that the budget for variable costs should be calculated based on activity levels, whereas the budget for fixed costs should be based on a constant 25% per quarter. You will use @IF to make Lotus test whether a cost is fixed (F) or variable (V) and treat fixed and variable costs differently.

To do this, the formula in cell H32 should multiply Last Year's Actual Annual by (1 plus BUDGET CHANGE) by the Quarterly Volume Percentage if the cost is variable, but by .25 if the cost is fixed and therefore distributed evenly throughout the year. Use edit to change the formula to: +G32*(1+$BUDGET CHANGE)*@IF(B32="V",$VOLUME,0.25).

Why was the .25 not placed in the reference area? Although it is never incorrect to place a variable in the reference area, it is not necessary in this case because you anticipate that a quarter will always be 25% of a year. This was deliberately included as an example of a situation where it is relatively safe to use a constant value rather than a reference in a formula.

This formula provides a good review of many concepts. The arithmetic operator + is used to start a formula. G32 is entered as a relative address so that it will change when the formula is copied. @IF is a function, a left parenthesis indicates the beginning of the arguments, B32= is a logical comparison, "V" is a character string that must be enclosed in double quotes, and a comma (,) separates arguments. The $BUDGET CHANGE and the true condition $VOLUME are absolute addresses that will not move when copied using a named range, so you do not have to remember what the cell addresses are. The false condition, .25, will be the multiplier if B32 is anything other than the letter V. Copy the formula and repeating labels where necessary and use /Range Format Reset to reformat H33..H38 to the global format setting. (See Figure 4.11.)

```
H33: +G33*(1+$BUDGET CHANGE)*@IF(B33="V",$VOLUME\,0.25)                    READY

        B        C         D         E        F        G        H        I
21
22  aundry Department:      Initial Report                         Revised Version
23
24                                   VARIANCE                     LAST             VARIANCE
25                                   (OVER)   VARIANCE          YEAR'S   REVISED    (OVER)
26                                   UNDER    % OF             ACTUAL   QUARTER    UNDER
27               ACTUAL   BUDGET     BUDGET   BUDGET           ANNUAL   BUDGET     BUDGET
28
29              11,900    9,500     (2,400)    -25%           38,000   11,856      (44)
30             156,000  125,000    (31,000)    -25%          500,000  156,000        0
31
32    V        $12,500   $9,000    ($3,500)    -39%          $37,113  $11,232   ($1,268)
33    V          1,875    1,100       (775)    -70%            4,536    1,373      (502)
34    V          2,500    1,700       (800)    -47%            7,010    2,122      (378)
35    V          2,200    1,400       (800)    -57%            5,773    1,747      (453)
36    F          3,750    3,150       (600)    -19%           12,990    3,150      (600)
37    F          5,000    4,000     (1,000)    -25%           16,495    4,000    (1,000)
38    F          1,250    1,200        (50)     -4%            4,948    1,200       (50)
39
40            $29,075  $21,550    ($7,525)    -35%          $88,865  $24,823   ($4,252)
01-Jan-90   02:29 PM
```

Figure 4.11  Flexible budget formula

## Using @IF for Directing Attention

It is important that the reports provided by AIS highlight unusual information and call these exceptions to the attention of managers. Here, you will use @IF to highlight line items that have a variance of more than 10% with <--- (created with the less than sign and hyphens). Line items with a variance less than or equal to 10% will be marked with OK. Insert two new columns to the left of the current G column (Last Year's Actual Annual). Set the width of the "new" column G to 5 and the "new" column H to 2. Enter a vertical line in column H using 'I. In G29 enter @IF(F29>$C$18," <---","" OK"). This formula says, "If the value in F29 is larger than the exception level value in C18, display <--- in cell G29; otherwise, display OK." When this formula is entered, cell G29 displays OK.

This is an example of an entry that is technically successful (it results in a number or label instead of an ERR message or beep) but substantively incorrect. Since the variance in F29 is –25%, you want it to be highlighted with <--- instead of marked OK. Most spreadsheet errors in Lotus involve this type of error, a conceptually incorrect formula or function, rather than technical errors. That is in part because Lotus helps us avoid technical errors by giving us error messages or simply by refusing to allow us to enter technically incorrect entries. Unfortunately, there is no way for Lotus to detect conceptual errors or misapplication of formulas. Only human examination of the output can detect these types of errors.

What makes more sense is to highlight all variance percentages that are more extreme than either +10% or –10%, either greater than a positive 10% or less than a negative 10%. This is easily reflected mathematically by saying you want to highlight any variance with an absolute value greater than 10%. The absolute function for cell F29 is @ABS(F29). The @functions can be combined, or nested, by entering @IF(@ABS(F29)>$C$18," <---"," OK") in cell G29, as shown in Figure 4.12.

```
G29: [W5] @IF(@ABS(F29)>$C$18," <---"," OK")                    READY

         B      C       D        E       F    G H     I         J
  22  aundry Department:     Initial Report
  23
  24                       VARIANCE                        |   LAST
  25                       (OVER)  VARIANCE                | YEAR'S   REVISED
  26                        UNDER   % OF                   | ACTUAL   QUARTER
  27         ACTUAL  BUDGET  BUDGET  BUDGET                | ANNUAL   BUDGET
  28
  29        11,900   9,500  (2,400)  -25% <---|  38,000    11,856
  30       156,000 125,000 (31,000)  -25%     | 500,000   156,000
  31                                          |
  32    U  $12,500  $9,000 ($3,500)  -39%     | $37,113   $11,232
  33    U    1,875   1,100    (775)  -70%     |   4,536     1,373
  34    U    2,500   1,700    (800)  -47%     |   7,010     2,122
  35    U    2,200   1,400    (800)  -57%     |   5,773     1,747
  36    F    3,750   3,150    (600)  -19%     |  12,990     3,150
  37    F    5,000   4,000  (1,000)  -25%     |  16,495     4,000
  38    F    1,250   1,200     (50)   -4%     |   4,948     1,200
  39                                          |
  40       $29,075 $21,550 ($7,525)  -35%     | $88,865   $24,823
  41
01-Jan-90  07:31 PM                                          LHF
```

**Figure 4.12 Killer formula (containing nested functions)**

This formula says, "If the absolute value of the data in F29 is larger than the exception level value in C18, display <--- in cell G29; otherwise, display OK." This is a subtle but important difference from the first entry you used. When the formula is entered correctly, cell G29 now displays <---. Usually, both positive and negative large variances should be highlighted to call them to the attention of management for investigation.

Set the width of column M to 5. Copy the formula from G29 into the other line-item rows of column G and into the rows of the revised report (column M) as well. You will be faced with the dilemma of whether to copy the entry into all rows and then go back and reenter the repeating labels for lines and erase any cells that should be blank or to use multiple Copy commands and only copy the formula into the precise cells you want it in. Either way works, but both are somewhat tedious. To minimize these types of efforts, many experienced users wait until the substantive contents of the worksheet (data and formulas) are finalized before doing the entries that are purely appearance oriented, such as lines and spaces.

## Net Present Values with @NPV

The laundry department supervisor told the controller that new washing machines would decrease labor, maintenance, and water costs, and provided price quotes for the new equipment and estimates of the savings expected in the first three years after installation. However, the board of directors has refused the proposal for new washing machines in the past because of the size of the investment required. Because of the nature of hospital accounting, it is common to view equipment purchases more as operating costs than investments, which is a big mistake. The laundry supervisor agreed that budgets could be lower in the future if the new washing machines could be purchased.

The controller decided to use two alternative ways of evaluating the proposed investment, using a straight payback period and using discounted cash flows. The payback period is how long it will take before the investment "pays for itself" in cost savings or increased revenue. @NPV(*discount rate, cash flows*) calculates the net present value of a series of cash flows at a specified discount rate. Lotus assumes that the first cash flow in the list of cash flows is at the end of period 1. This means that any cash flows at time 0 must be subtracted from the result of the NPV calculation. @IRR calculates the discount rate necessary to make the present value of the cash inflows less the present value of the cash outflows equal to zero. Whereas the initial cash flow can be on a separate line for the NPV calculation, all flows in the IRR must be in contiguous cells.

A new worksheet must now be retrieved. If you retrieve before saving, the last file will be lost along with any changes made since the last time you saved. *Save* your current worksheet and *then retrieve* worksheet file 4CASEB.WKS, which contains the acquisition cost and savings (cash flow) estimates. Enter your name, the course, and the date. Name the following ranges: DISCOUNT (A19), COST (B29), SAVINGS (C30..E30), and NETFLOW (B32..E32). Enter appropriate formulas and functions in B32..E32, B34..E34, C38, and C40. Net annual cash flow is simply Estimated Savings minus Acquisition Cost for each year. Cumulative Cash Flow is the prior year's Cumulative Cash Flow plus the current year's Net Annual Cash Flow. The entry in C38 is @NPV(DISCOUNT,SAVINGS)–COST, as shown in Figure 4.13. The entry in C40 is @IRR(DISCOUNT, NETFLOW). Manually determine that the payback period is less than three years by looking up the year in which Cumulative Cash Flow becomes positive. Enter 3 in C42. In the next section, you will learn how to make Lotus look up the payback period.

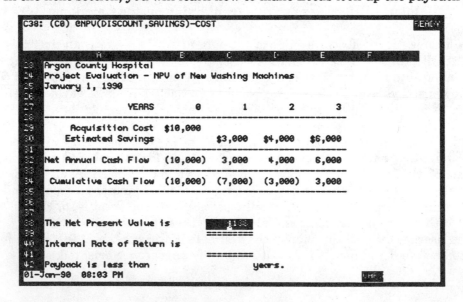

**Figure 4.13 Net present value function**

## LOOKUP Function (@VLOOKUP and HLOOKUP)

Lotus has the ability to look up specified data in a worksheet. A common example of a VLOOKUP table is a tax table, which is searched for the tax basis in the left column (vertical lookup). When the tax basis amount is found, Lotus moves to the right the specified number of columns (offset) to find the tax amount. The form of these functions is @?LOOKUP(*item,range,offset*). *Item* is whatever is to be looked up. *Range* is the area that contains the list in which the item is to be looked up and the related item to be returned as the result of the function. The list of items to be searched must be the leftmost column (VLOOKUP) or top row (HLOOKUP) of the specified range. *Offset* represents the number of columns (rows) @VLOOKUP (@HLOOKUP) needs to move in (down) from the left (top) margin of the lookup range to find the needed data. The leftmost column (top row) is counted as column (row) 0, so that the first column (row) to the right of (below) it has an offset of 1. The list in which an item is to be looked up must be in alphabetical or numerical order.

To look up the payback period, you manually went across the Cumulative Cash Flow row until you found the first cell that had a Cumulative Cash Flow greater than or equal to 0. You then looked up to the row that contained the year and saw that it was year 3. The Lotus @HLOOKUP would do almost the same thing. The differences are that the year must be below the Cumulative Cash Flow row instead of above it and that when an exact match of the searched for item is not found, the @LOOKUP functions stay in the last column (row) *before* where the item would be found in the list. To deal with the first difference, copy or reference the years in row 36. To deal with the second, add 1 to the results of the LOOKUP function. In C42, enter 1+@HLOOKUP(0,B34..E36,2). This tells Lotus to look up the number 0 in the Cumulative Cash Flows, the top row of the range B34..E36. When Lotus reaches the cell that contains the item or the cell immediately before the one that would contain the item if it was there, Lotus moves down two (offset) rows and displays 1 plus the value in that cell. When this is done correctly, 3 should be displayed in cell C42.

To complete a VLOOKUP, retrieve 4CASEC.WKS. This worksheet contains a schedule of doctors' fees and hospital charges for various treatments. The purpose of the worksheet is to let the user enter only the treatment code and the doctor's ID number in the indicated cells (B20 and C20), have Lotus look up and display the doctor's fee (E20) and hospital charges (F20) for that treatment and that doctor. Lotus also calculates the total charges (G20).

Two cells in TABLE are empty because the doctor does not perform surgery. If someone wanted to know how much it would cost to have an appendix removed by doctor number 4, Lotus should respond with NA (not applicable). Cells E30 and E38 contain @NA; this @function requires no arguments and makes Lotus return the label NA. The treatments are in alphabetical order because a LOOKUP function requires it. If the treatment name is not found, the computer will give you an error message (ERR).

Enter APP, for appendectomy, in cell B20 as the code for the first treatment. LOOKUPs are case sensitive; all treatments were entered in capital letters, so use [Caps Lock]. Enter 1, the doctor's identification number, in cell C20. Enter the formula to add doctors' fees and hospital charges in G20. Use the Windows command to make the worksheet on the screen appear as shown in Figure 4.14.

@VLOOKUP's general format is @VLOOKUP(*item to be looked up, range, offset*). The range for the search to occur in is the one named TABLE (A30..G38). Finally the number of columns to move right (offset) for the hospital charges is six, because it is always six rows in from the edge of the table. Try to write and debug the formula yourself and enter it in cell F20. The formula is @VLOOKUP(B20,TABLE,6).

Try to write, debug, and enter the @function to look up the doctor's fees in E20. Recognize that instead of being fixed, the offset number will vary depending on the doctor's ID in cell C20. The formula is @VLOOKUP(B20,TABLE,C20), as shown in Figure 4.14.

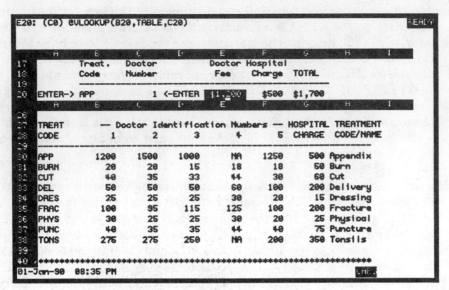

**Figure 4.14 Vertical lookup table**

# Other Worksheet-Management Tips

In addition to the Titles and Windows commands, a variety of other useful features are available to help manage Lotus worksheets. This section introduces a few of the most useful or common: protecting cells, changing recalculation to manual, and circular references.

## Protected Cells

A worksheet is often set up by a professional accountant or manager with the intention that it will be used primarily by clerical personnel. The worksheet 4CASEC.WKS is an example of a situation in which you would like a clerical staff person to be able to enter data only in the cells marked for entry, B20 and C20. To do this, select /Worksheet Global Protection Enable, which protects all the cells in the worksheet that have not been explicitly unprotected. Now try to enter DEL (short for "Delivery of a baby") in cell B20. Lotus should beep, display a flashing ERROR in the mode indicator, and display "Protected Cell" in the lower left corner of the worksheet. Press [Esc] to return to READY mode. To allow data entry in the two cells marked for data entry, use /Range Unprotect and enter B20..C20 when prompted to enter the range. These two cells will now appear to be brighter than the rest of the worksheet, will display a U (for Unprotected) next to the cell address in the control panel, and will allow data to be entered. Now enter DEL (in caps) in B20, Doctor Number 3 in C20, and watch the related numerical data change (Figure 4.15).

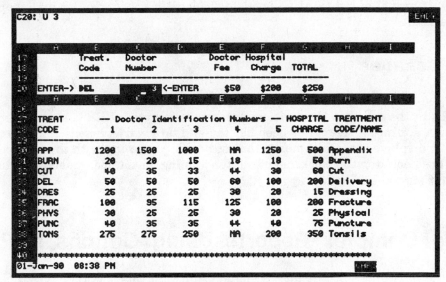

Figure 4.15 Protected cells

## Worksheet Global Recalculation (/WGR)

Notice that the worksheet is recalculated each time you enter data in a cell. While this has not slowed you down so far, it will when you have large worksheets with many complicated formulas. If the worksheet is large and complex, recalculating it can take several minutes, during which time you can not do any other work. If you switch to manual recalculation, Lotus will not recalculate until you tell it to by pressing the [F9] function key. Enter the commands /Worksheet Global Recalculation Manual. Enter FRAC in B20 and note that the Fee and Charge numbers do not change. As soon as the new data value is entered, CALC appears in the lower right corner of the screen, where it will remain as long as data are being entered since the last recalculation. This tells you that the worksheet is not complete and you need to press [F9] to recalculate the worksheet. /Worksheet Global Recalculation Automatic will return the worksheet to automatic recalculation after each cell entry.

## Circular References

As a worksheet becomes more complex, eventually you are likely to reference a cell in one formula that is dependent on the cell in which you are entering the formula. To give a simple example, if cell C5 contains the cell reference +D5, and cell D5 contains the cell reference +C5, there is a circular reference. Circular references are typically much more complex than this example and can occur through a long series of formulas; thus, they can be difficult to locate. Lotus warns you that a circular reference exists by displaying CIRC in the lower right corner of the screen. Unfortunately, it is up to you to find and fix the problem.

The worksheet will still calculate and function with a circular cell reference. In some cases, you may deliberately design a worksheet to include a circular reference, because the items being modeled actually seem to depend on each other (a recursive model). If the circular reference was entered deliberately, you may want to use one of the other Worksheet Recalculation options to control the order in which calculations are done. (For more information, see the reference manual.) If the circular reference was not entered deliberately, it probably indicates a serious deficiency in your formulas and should be found and fixed.

## Error Messages

Sometimes you will attempt to divide by zero, which is impossible. When you do so, Lotus displays ERR in the cell that the division by zero is attempted. ERR is also displayed when a cell to which a formula refers has been deleted and for a variety of other reasons. In general, ERR displayed in a cell means that something is wrong with the cell entry. Again, this does not stop the worksheet from functioning, but it does mean there are mistakes that should be fixed.

# Printing Complex Reports Using Options (/PP)

Since both the controller and the laundry supervisor want copies of the revised performance reports and the new washing machine proposal evaluation, you need to print the reports. At least part of most Lotus worksheets end up being printed, both for hard-copy output and for documentation. As a worksheet becomes larger, it becomes somewhat more complex to print as well as to view. Save the report again *now*, before you make changes to it that you may not want to keep. Clear any Titles or Window settings to make it easier to specify ranges and to work with the entire worksheet for printing.

You want to print both the initial and the revised versions of the performance reports. Since they will not all fit on one page, you have to decide what to print together. There are usually several possible approaches to printing a worksheet, just as there are to designing one; the following procedure is only one option. It has been decided that two pages should be adequate for printing the performance report worksheet and to print the documentation at the top of each report. The leftmost three columns of each report should be the line-item name, the fixed or variable indicator, and the actual data. To accomplish this, several different ranges will need to be specified for printing. Several features needed to print both reports are found in the Options submenu of the Print menu.

## Borders (/PPOB)

The second report to be printed will include the same first three columns (A, B, C) as the first report, followed by data from columns in the middle of the worksheet. This can most easily be accomplished by creating column borders. Column borders are set for printing with /Print Printer Options Boarders Columns Range. Row borders are set the same way, using rows instead of columns. The result of using borders for printing is similar to using the Titles command to view the worksheet on the screen, although they are set in different ways. When you have set borders for printing, the range you specify for printing must *not* include the border columns or rows; if it does, they will print twice. As with many Lotus settings, borders are remembered and reused until you change or clear them. Borders are changed by reusing the initial command sequence and entering a different border range. Borders are cleared with /Print Printer Clear Borders.

For convenience, first name the different ranges to be used in printing. Create the following range names and ranges: DOC for the documentation area in range D1..G20; BORDCOL for the border columns in A1..C1; INITREP for the initial report data in D21..G40; and REVREP for the revised report data in J21..M40. Note that any one row of the columns to be used for borders is sufficient to specify the entire column. Select /Print Printer Options Borders Columns and enter the range name BORDCOL when prompted to "Enter Border Columns:". Quit or press [Esc] to leave the Options submenu and get back to the main Print menu.

Select Range from the main Print menu and press [F3] when prompted to "Enter Printing range:". This displays the list of available range names, as mentioned earlier; select DOC. ([F3] can be used to list the available ranges any time a range is to be entered in a command.) When back at the main Print menu, select Align, which aligns the printer at the top of the page, then select Go, which sends the data to be printed to the printer. If you have a printer attached directly to your computer, it will begin to print. If you do not have a printer available, you should be using /Print File instead of /Print Printer. Select Range again, and Lotus will highlight the range used most recently. Since you want to specify a new range, ignore the highlighted one, press F3 to get the list of ranges, and select INITREP for the initial report. This time *do not* select Align (because you are not at the top of a page); just select Go, which sends the range to be printed, and Page, which moves the print head down to the top of the next page. If you find that the printing begins in the middle of a page or that there are unanticipated blank lines in the middle of your report, you are not aligning the printer properly. Go back to the beginning of this paragraph and try again.

To print the revised report, you do not need to reset the border columns, since the same ones are to be used. Repeat the rest of the sequence, using the ranges DOC and REVREP to print the revised report. (Select Range DOC Align Go Range REVREP Go.)

## Other Print Options

Lotus has default margins set at 4 and 76 (these defaults can be changed), to leave about one-half inch of blank space at the left and right sides of a page. Sometimes, if you are very close to being able to squeeze a report onto a page, changing the margins will help. Another solution for this common dilemma is to make the global column width or some individual columns narrower. Also, if your printer will produce condensed print or if you are using wide paper, you must change the right margin to instruct Lotus to plan for a larger number of characters on a single printed row. A typical right margin setting for compressed print using 8-1/2 x 11 inch paper is 130. Margins is another useful option in the Print menu. Pg-length changes the page length for different sizes of paper or forms. Header and Footer specify what goes in headers and footers to be placed at the top or bottom of each page of multipage reports. Setup tells the printer what type size and font to use (see your lab assistant or your Lotus and printer manuals for more information on Setup).

## Text (Printing Formulas with /RFT or /PPOOC)

To check the underlying assumptions of the worksheet and to provide important documentation of the worksheet, it is useful to print out the formulas. There are two ways to do this, each with advantages and disadvantages.

The faster alternative, which lists the contents of each nonblank cell in the specified range, one cell at a time, is /Print Printer Options Other Cell-Formulas. Although the resulting linear listing does not show the relationships among cells in the worksheet as clearly as a row-by-column display does, it is the most commonly used. If disaster strikes, but you have a printout of the worksheet, you can reenter it without having to try to figure out what formulas should be where. To get a printout, select Options Other Cell-Formulas, then Quit or press [Esc] to return to the main Print menu. Select Range A1..M40. Only cells that contain entries are listed, and hidden cells are printed. Under this option, border rows and columns are not printed twice.

The worksheet formulas can be displayed in their normal row and column positions by formatting the worksheet as text. Save your worksheet before beginning this process, then use /Worksheet Erase Yes to dispose of the worksheet after the formulas have been printed. Be careful not to save the changed worksheet under the old filename, since all the column widths and range formats needed to display the report normally will be lost. Since the /Worksheet Global Format Text command affects only cells that have not been formatted using the Range Format command, the most efficient way to print out cell formulas is to reset the format of the entire section of the worksheet to be printed using /Range Format Text. If some formulas are long, as they usually are, you must also make the columns wide enough to display the whole formula. Set the global column width first, then individually set any columns that are not affected by the global (/Worksheet Column Set-Width). This is tedious, but the only option to display text in a rectangular worksheet format.

## Chapter Review

This chapter built on and reinforced what you learned in Chapter 3. You have now worked with a large subset of the Lotus spreadsheet-oriented commands and several complex @functions and have learned how to design a worksheet for modeling, viewing, and printing. Chapter 5 will teach you how to generate and print graphs, how to use some of the data-management Lotus commands, and how to write simple Lotus macros (programs) to minimize typing.

## Practice Exercises

Exercise 4-1

**Filename: 4EX1.WKS**
(Continuation of Exercise 3-1)

As the administrative services specialist for XYZ CPAs, you have calculated the first month's estimated operating costs and savings of acquiring the proposed computer system. The completed analysis is contained in the worksheet (see Exercise 3-1 for additional background and assumptions). In addition to the operating costs and savings, you have estimated the initial startup cost outlay (for site preparation, data conversion, training, etc.) at a total of $40,000. The clerical cost savings are estimated to increase at the rate of 30% per year over the next five years, because the computer system will allow the company to avoid hiring additional personnel in the automated areas. However, hardware and software costs are expected to increase at 20% per year, computer personnel salaries to increase at 15% per year, and overhead costs to increase at 10% per year for the next five years.[1]

1. Prepare a schedule showing total monthly operating costs and savings (in each of the major categories) for years 1 through 5.
2. Convert these monthly cost and savings totals to annual figures and prepare a table with six columns (for the initial outlay and each of the five years) and four rows (for costs, cost savings, net inflow or outflow, and cumulative inflow or outflow. Calculate the payback period for the system.
3. If you have already studied discounted cash flows, calculate the net present value and internal rate of return of the computer acquisition.

Your completed report should look like the one that follows.


```
Projected Monthly Operating Costs and Savings Estimates
                 for the Next Five (5) Years.

Schedule of Estimated Monthly Costs:
```

| ITEM | YEAR 1 | YEAR 2 | YEAR 3 | YEAR 4 | YEAR 5 |
|------|--------|--------|--------|--------|--------|
| Hardware Rental | $3,000 | $3,600 | $4,320 | $5,184 | $6,221 |
| PERSONNEL | 5,500 | 6,325 | 7,274 | 8,365 | 9,620 |
| Software Rental | 500 | 600 | 720 | 864 | 1,037 |
| Other Overhead | 2,000 | 2,200 | 2,420 | 2,662 | 2,928 |
| TOTALS | $11,000 | $12,725 | $14,734 | $17,075 | $19,805 |

```
================================================================

****************************************************************
***
Schedule of Estimated Monthly Savings:
```

| ITEM | YEAR 1 | YEAR 2 | YEAR 3 | YEAR 4 | YEAR 5 |
|------|--------|--------|--------|--------|--------|
| CLERICAL COSTS | $6,800 | $8,840 | $11,492 | $14,940 | $19,421 |
| INVENTORY | 4,000 | 4,400 | 4,840 | 5,324 | 5,856 |
| TOTALS | $10,800 | $13,240 | $16,332 | $20,264 | $25,278 |

```
================================================================
```

---

[1] After Barry E. Cushing and Marshall B. Romney, *Accounting Information Systems and Business Organizations*, Fourth Edition, Reading, MA: Addison-Wesley Publishing Company, 1987, 524–526.

```
****************************************************************************
***
Cash Flow Table:


                              COST        NET IN     CUMULATIVE
YEAR              COSTS       SAVINGS      (OUT)      IN (OUT)         YEAR
----------------------------------------------------------------------------
---
OUTLAY           $40,000          $0    ($40,000)    ($40,000)      OUTLAY
1                132,000     129,600      (2,400)     (42,400)        1
2                152,700     158,880       6,180      (36,220)        2
3                176,805     195,984      19,179      (17,041)        3
4                204,898     243,163      38,265       21,224         4
5               $237,664    $303,335     $65,671      $86,895         5


               4 years (or less) is the payback period.


           $29,725   is the Net Present Value


           31.25% is the Internal Rate of Return


****************************************************************************
***
```

## Reminders

1. In Year 1 of the Cost and Savings schedules, reference the cells that contain the monthly cost and savings calculations in other portions of the worksheet, and enter formulas to calculate totals. Enter formulas in Year 2 to reflect the expected increase above the levels in Year 1. Since costs and savings are expected to continue to increase annually at the same rate, copy the formulas to the columns for Years 3 through 5. Remember to put relatively constant data, such as the rates of change, in a reference area, and use absolute cell references where appropriate. Enter and copy repeating labels and change spacing as needed to make the report more readable.
2. Create formulas that reference the cost and savings totals just calculated. Create formulas to calculate the net inflow or outflow by year, and the cumulative inflow or outflow for each year. (The cumulative flow formula for the outlay year will be different from the formula for subsequent years.) Use an @VLOOKUP on the cumulative flows to calculate the payback period. The project will have paid back when the cumulative flows are greater than or equal to zero.
3. Use the @NPV and @IRR functions applied to the amounts in the Cash Flow Table.

Exercise 4-2

**Filename: 4EX2.WKS**
(Continuation of Exercise 3-2)

In the Carlton Manufacturing Company, the supervisors of three production departments (Machining, Assembly, Finishing) and one service department (Maintenance) report to the plant manager. The plant manager also makes recommendations concerning salary increments for these subordinates as well as his own staff and makes recommendations concerning equipment purchases for the departments under his control. The cost summary for the assembly department for May 1990 is included in the worksheet file and is shown in Exercise 3-2. You also have the following additional information:

Budgeted costs are based on budgeted activity of 1000 units of production. Actual number of units of production was 1100. All other departments also exceeded their budgeted activity level by exactly ten percent.

Maintenance department costs are allocated in three equal amounts to the three departments under the plant manager. All other allocations are made in four equal parts to all four departments. Budgeted and actual salaries for the four department supervisors total $7500, including $1950 for the maintenance supervisor.

Depreciation is computed on a straight-line basis. Equipment has been purchased during 1981 that was not included in the initial budget for the year.

Each cost is categorized as controllable by the assembly department supervisor (A), the plant manager (P), or neither (N) and as fixed (F) or variable with the level of activity (V).

1. Prepare a performance report for the month of May for the assembly department supervisor. Assume it is company policy for performance reports to include only controllable costs and to use the principle of flexible budgeting.
2. The total actual controllable costs from the performance reports for the machining and finishing departments and the total budgeted controllable costs for these departments according to the budgeted (rather than the actual) activity level are as follows:

| Department | Budget | Actual |
|------------|--------|--------|
| Machining  | $7500  | $8400  |
| Finishing  | 6000   | 6300   |

Using the same format and company policies, prepare a performance report for the plant manager.[2]

Your completed reports should look like the ones shown next.

```
Assembly Department
Performance Report - Controllable Costs, Flexible Budget


                                                          VARIANCE
                                                          (OVER)   VARIANCE
CONTROLLABLE                      FLEXIBLE                 UNDER    % OF
COST                              BUDGET      ACTUAL       BUDGET   BUDGET
-----------------------------------------------------------------------------
----
Direct Labor           A  V      $11,550     $12,000      ($450)    -4%
Materials Spoilage     A  V        $660        $630          30      5%
```

2   Adapted from Barry E. Cushing and Marshall B. Romney, *Accounting Information Systems*, Fifth Edition, Reading, MA: Addison-Wesley Publishing Company, 1990, 57–59. Reprinted with permission.

| | | | BUDGET | ACTUAL | VARIANCE (OVER) UNDER BUDGET | VARIANCE % OF BUDGET |
|---|---|---|---|---|---|---|
| Overtime Premium | A | V | $1,650 | $1,740 | (90) | -5% |
| Reassembly | A | V | $1,320 | $1,170 | 150 | 11% |
| Supplies | A | V | $990 | $930 | 60 | 6% |
| TOTAL | | | $16,170 | $16,470 | ($300) | -2% |

============================================================

Maintenance Department
Calculation of Variable Costs

| | | | BUDGET | ACTUAL | VARIANCE (OVER) UNDER BUDGET | VARIANCE % OF BUDGET |
|---|---|---|---|---|---|---|
| Maintenance Costs | P | F | $9,600 | $9,870 | ($270) | -3% |
| Supervisor's Salary | | F | 1,950 | 1,950 | 0 | 0% |
| Fixed Cost Allocations | P | | 1,950 | 2,040 | (90) | -5% |
| Total Variable Cost | | | $5,700 | $5,880 | ($180) | 3% |

============================================================

*********************************************************************************
****
Plant Manager
Performance Report - Controllable Costs, Flexible Budget

| CONTROLLABLE COST | | | FLEXIBLE BUDGET | ACTUAL | VARIANCE (OVER) UNDER BUDGET | VARIANCE % OF BUDGET |
|---|---|---|---|---|---|---|
| Machining Dept. | | V | $8,250 | $8,400 | ($150) | -2% |
| Assembly Dept. | | V | 16,170 | 16,470 | (300) | -2% |
| Finishing Dept. | | V | $6,600 | 6,300 | 300 | 5% |
| Maintenance Dept. | | V | $6,270 | 5,880 | 390 | 6% |
| Salary-Supervisors | | F | 7,500 | 7,500 | 0 | 0% |
| Depreciation-Equip. | P | F | 1,200 | 1,440 | (240) | -20% |
| Salary-Plant Staff | P | F | 3,000 | 3,120 | (120) | -4% |
| TOTALS | | | $48,990 | $49,110 | ($120) | 0% |

============================================================

*********************************************************************************
****

## Reminders

1. Reference only the cells in the existing Assembly Department -All Costs- Fixed Budget Performance Report that contain variable costs. Enter given amounts, or formulas, to calculate the maintenance department costs based on the information provided in the exercise. Remember to use the actual activity level to adjust from the fixed to flexible budget amounts. Reference only Budget and Actual amounts, and use formulas to calculate the variances and percent variances in all cases. Enter repeating labels and modify spacing to improve the readability of the report.
2. Reference the appropriate cells or enter given amounts to construct the Plant Manager's Performance Report. Enter formulas to total the report.

Exercise 4-3

**Filename: 4EX3.WKS**
(Continuation of Exercise 3-3)

Based on the capacity planning done for the Perry Corporation in Exercise 3-3, prepare a financial projection of the monthly total costs over the two-year period.

The monthly salary for an analyst-programmer (A-P) is $2,000. Monthly hardware rental and all other fixed costs of the present system are $10,000 and will be $15,000 after the new system is implemented. Once implemented, the new system will exactly triple throughput (i.e., work formerly taking three hours on the computer will now take one hour). Variable costs of operating both the old and the new systems total $20 per hour during both productive and nonproductive use.

Open the template provided (which is a solution to Exercise 3-3) and complete the formulas and formatting to match the report shown below and complete the report. Be sure to design your worksheet to allow "what if?" analysis with respect to any of the underlying assumptions.

1. Print a report showing the projected monthly costs for each period under these assumptions. Print the report on two pages (in two parts) with the documentation, reference area, and company /report title at the top at each page.
2. How do the results change when the variable cost changes to $18 and the system becomes four time more efficient? Print a copy of your output.
3. What would be the results if the new system hardware rental is decreased to $12,500, an A-P's salary goes up to $2,200 per month, and the system productivity goes up to 95%? Print a copy of your output.

```
Perry Corporation
Long-Range Systems Plan
January 1, 1990

Monthly Computer System Hr Use:
```

|  | ---------------MONTHS--------------- | | | |
|  | 1-6 | 7-12 | 13-18 | 19-24 |
| --- | --- | --- | --- | --- |
| Existing Systems | 400 | 440 | 484 | 532 |
| Project A | 20 | 75 | 80 | 88 |
| Project B | 30 | 30 | 100 | 150 |

```
Project C                              25        30        30       100
Project D                               0         0        20        30
---------------------------------------------------------------------------
TOTAL SYSTEM HR USE - CURRENT         475       575       714       900
                                    =======================================
TOTAL SYSTEM HR USE - NEW             475       575       238       300
                                    =======================================
ADJUSTED FOR UNPRODUCTIVE TIME        594       719       298       375
                                    =======================================
```

```
***************************************************************************
Analyst-Programmer Hours used per Month:
                                    ---------------MONTHS---------------
                                     1-6       7-12      13-18     19-24
---------------------------------------------------------------------------
Existing Systems                      200       220       242       266
Project A                             240       380       100       110
Project B                             352       400       550       120
Project C                             264       280       300       500
Project D                               0       120       380       410
Conversion                              0       176         0         0
---------------------------------------------------------------------------
TOTAL A-P HOURS REQUIRED            1,056     1,576     1,572     1,406
                                    =======================================
A-P REQUIRED (rounded)                  6         9         9         8
                                    =======================================
```

```
***************************************************************************
Financial Projection
COST CATEGORY                        '1-6      '7-12     '13-18    '19-24
---------------------------------------------------------------------------
Analyst-Programmer Salaries       $12,000   $18,000   $18,000   $16,000
Fixed System Cost                  10,000    10,000    15,000    15,000
Variable System Cost ($20/Hr)      11,875    14,375     5,950     7,500
---------------------------------------------------------------------------
TOTALS                            $33,875   $42,375   $38,950   $38,500
                                    =======================================
```

## Exercise 4-4

### Filename: 4EX4.WKS
(Continuation of Exercise 3-4)

Modify the report completed in Exercise 3-4 to calculate the additional data shown in the following report. Design the worksheet so it will be easy to use for answering what if? questions.

1. What is the effect of changing the federal tax rates to 10%, 25%, and 35% on the average employee in the organization?
2. If the FICA rate is lowered to 7% and state taxes go up to 3.25%, what is the overall effect on the employees?

```
*********************************************************************************
*****
```

| PAY WEEK | EMP | RATE | PROJ | HRS | GROSS | FED TAX | FICA | ST TAX | NET PAY |
|----------|-----|------|------|-----|-------|---------|------|--------|---------|
| 01-Jun-90 | 345 | 8.75 | 133 | 40 | 350.00 | 52.50 | 26.25 | 8.75 | 262.50 |
| 01-Jun-90 | 432 | 20.55 | 140 | 40 | 822.00 | 123.30 | 61.65 | 20.55 | 616.50 |
| 01-Jun-90 | 654 | 15.65 | 140 | 40 | 626.00 | 93.90 | 46.95 | 15.65 | 469.50 |
| 01-Jun-90 | 678 | 10.75 | 133 | 40 | 430.00 | 64.50 | 32.25 | 10.75 | 322.50 |
| 08-Jun-90 | 234 | 100.00 | 133 | 14 | 1400.00 | 462.00 | 105.00 | 35.00 | 798.00 |
| 08-Jun-90 | 345 | 8.75 | 133 | 40 | 350.00 | 52.50 | 26.25 | 8.75 | 262.50 |
| 08-Jun-90 | 432 | 20.55 | 133 | 20 | 411.00 | 61.65 | 30.82 | 10.27 | 308.25 |
| 08-Jun-90 | 432 | 20.55 | 147 | 20 | 411.00 | 61.65 | 30.82 | 10.27 | 308.25 |
| 08-Jun-90 | 567 | 80.00 | 145 | 8 | 640.00 | 211.20 | 48.00 | 16.00 | 364.80 |
| 08-Jun-90 | 654 | 15.65 | 133 | 28 | 438.20 | 65.73 | 32.86 | 10.95 | 328.65 |
| 08-Jun-90 | 654 | 15.65 | 140 | 12 | 187.80 | 28.17 | 14.08 | 4.69 | 140.85 |
| 08-Jun-90 | 678 | 10.75 | 133 | 24 | 258.00 | 38.70 | 19.35 | 6.45 | 193.50 |
| 08-Jun-90 | 678 | 10.75 | 140 | 16 | 172.00 | 25.80 | 12.90 | 4.30 | 129.00 |
| 15-Jun-90 | 345 | 8.75 | 133 | 40 | 350.00 | 52.50 | 26.25 | 8.75 | 262.50 |
| 15-Jun-90 | 432 | 20.55 | 147 | 40 | 822.00 | 123.30 | 61.65 | 20.55 | 616.50 |
| 15-Jun-90 | 654 | 15.65 | 147 | 40 | 626.00 | 93.90 | 46.95 | 15.65 | 469.50 |
| 15-Jun-90 | 657 | 75.00 | 147 | 12 | 900.00 | 297.00 | 67.50 | 22.50 | 513.00 |
| 15-Jun-90 | 678 | 10.75 | 133 | 40 | 430.00 | 64.50 | 32.25 | 10.75 | 322.50 |
| 22-Jun-90 | 234 | 100.00 | 133 | 16 | 1600.00 | 528.00 | 120.00 | 40.00 | 912.00 |
| 22-Jun-90 | 345 | 8.75 | 133 | 40 | 350.00 | 52.50 | 26.25 | 8.75 | 262.50 |
| 22-Jun-90 | 432 | 20.55 | 133 | 40 | 822.00 | 123.30 | 61.65 | 20.55 | 616.50 |
| 22-Jun-90 | 455 | 85.00 | 133 | 12 | 1020.00 | 336.60 | 76.50 | 25.50 | 581.40 |
| 22-Jun-90 | 654 | 15.65 | 151 | 40 | 626.00 | 93.90 | 46.95 | 15.65 | 469.50 |
| 22-Jun-90 | 678 | 10.75 | 133 | 40 | 430.00 | 64.50 | 32.25 | 10.75 | 322.50 |
| 29-Jun-90 | 234 | 100.00 | 150 | 6 | 600.00 | 198.00 | 45.00 | 15.00 | 342.00 |
| 29-Jun-90 | 345 | 8.75 | 150 | 40 | 350.00 | 52.50 | 26.25 | 8.75 | 262.50 |
| 29-Jun-90 | 432 | 20.55 | 151 | 40 | 822.00 | 123.30 | 61.65 | 20.55 | 616.50 |
| 29-Jun-90 | 625 | 70.00 | 151 | 6 | 420.00 | 138.60 | 31.50 | 10.50 | 239.40 |
| 29-Jun-90 | 654 | 15.65 | 151 | 40 | 626.00 | 93.90 | 46.95 | 15.65 | 469.50 |
| 29-Jun-90 | 678 | 10.75 | 151 | 40 | 430.00 | 64.50 | 32.25 | 10.75 | 322.50 |

```
-------------------------------------------------------------------------------
-----
```

| | | | | | | | | | |
|----------|-----|------|------|-----|-------|---------|------|--------|---------|
| Minimum: | | 8.75 | | 6.0 | 172.00 | 25.80 | 12.90 | 4.30 | 129.00 |
| Maximum: | | 100.00 | | 40.0 | 1600.00 | 528.00 | 120.00 | 40.00 | 912.00 |
| Average: | | 31.18 | | 29.1 | 590.67 | 128.08 | 44.30 | 14.77 | 403.52 |

```
*********************************************************************************
*****
```

# Chapter 5: Advanced Features of Lotus 1-2-3

Most of the Lotus worksheet features have been introduced in the preceding chapters. In addition to its worksheet modeling capabilities, Lotus has some basic but useful capabilities for displaying worksheet data in the form of graphs, performing some data management and statistical analysis, and writing programs using the Lotus command language embodied in the menus. This chapter introduces these three features.

## Case Setting

The controller believes that graphs may be useful in understanding the operations of the laundry department. Summary historical data on costs and activity levels for the past five years is provided in file 5CASEA.WKS and shown in Figure 5.1. You have been requested to experiment with constructing relevant graphs.

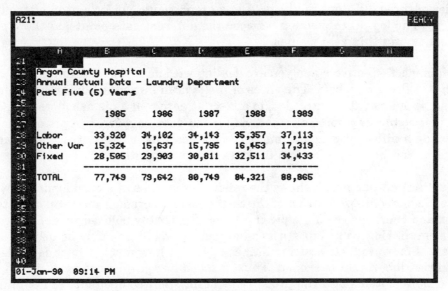

**Figure 5.1 Summary historical cost data**

## Graphics (/G)

If "a picture is worth a thousand words," then this is the right place for accountants and information systems to meet. Displaying data in the form of graphs can help users to quickly detect trends and relationships in data. When preparing a report or presentation, Lotus allows you, with relatively little additional work, to use graphs to communicate information efficiently and persuasively. Remember, if your presentation looks good, it makes you look good!

## Purposes of Different Graph Types

Lotus 1-2-3 has five different types of graphs: line, bar, XY, stacked-bar, and pie. Each plays a different role in a presentation. Selection of a graph type depends on the data you are working with and what you are trying to portray for your presentation. There are often two or more reasonably good alternative graph types to display a data set. Select your graph type carefully, so that it effectively communicates what you want it to say, based on the following guidelines.

A **line** graph displays **trend** data. Trend, or **time-series**, data are data on the same item(s) at different points in time. Any consistent time interval can be used, with months, quarters, and years used most commonly by accountants. It is often important to understand how things are changing over time. What has happened to sales over the past 10 years? What is the pattern of sales within a year; are they cyclical? The best graph for this type of information is usually a line graph, which clearly shows trends. Several related trend lines can be combined on a single graph to facilitate comparison of related factors.

A **bar** graph is sometimes used instead of a line graph for trend data; the choice is determined by the number of data points. For a large number of data points, such as six or twelve months, a line chart is most effective. A bar chart can represent four or fewer data points for each item more clearly, especially when large differences occur from point to point. Bar charts are also used to compare the levels of some attribute of different items, such as sales of three different products. A line graph would not be a good alternative, because there is no logical connection between the different data points, as there is between last year's sales and this year's sales.

A **pie** graph is most effective when you are dealing with data that contain percentages or numbers that make up a whole. The slices of the pie can be shaded differently, and a slice of the pie can be pulled out, or exploded, to attract attention. If a pie has more than eight slices, consider combining some slices, dividing the data between two pie or stacked-bar charts, or using a different graph to make the presentation clearer. Too many data items in any graph is confusing and makes the data difficult to interpret.

Like a pie, a **stacked-bar** graph shows the relative proportion of a total made up by several components. To show the proportion of the cost of a single product made up of materials, direct labor, and overhead, a single pie chart would probably be used rather than a single stacked-bar graph. However, four stacked-bar graphs would probably be used to compare the unit costs of four products and simultaneously show how much of each is made up by materials, direct labor, and overhead. Thus, stacked-bar graphs are most useful for comparing different items and the proportions of different components of the different items.

An **XY** graph shows the relationships between two amounts, such as profits and sales, or pounds of laundry and water costs. XY graphs can be used with lines drawn between the points or without lines. When done without lines, an XY graph is often referred to as a **scatter plot.**

# Generating Graphs

Your computer must have a graphics card installed for you to view the graphs discussed in this chapter. Although you can create graphs without viewing them, it is much more difficult to get them right. Graphs are created, perfected, viewed on screen, and saved for later use or printing in one set of steps, and printed in another. You must save printable graph files while in the Lotus worksheet Graph menu and then exit the worksheet and use the PrintGraph utility in the Lotus Access menu to print the graph files.

The steps used to create, view, print, and save the settings of a graph are as follows:

1. Select Graph from the main Lotus menu with /Graph.
2. Select the Type of graph.
3. Enter the Range or ranges that contain the data to be graphed.
4. View the graph.
5. Name the graph, to save the settings for later use.
6. Set any special Options that you want to use.
7. Save (/File Save) the worksheet file.
8. Save (within Graph) a printable file for printing the graph.

The steps do not need to be done in exactly this order. Users typically revisit the Options subcommand several times to make minor changes to improve the appearance of the graph. The graph may be named any time after the type and ranges have been specified. The Graphics command is /Graph; the subcommands are Type X A B C D E F Reset View Save Options Name Quit.

Appearance and readability are as important for graphs as for numerical reports. The commands for enhancing the appearance of graphs are under /Graph Options: Legend Format Titles Grid Scale Color B&W Data-Labels Quit.

Three of these commands control graph documentation. Titles (First Second X-Axis Y-Axis) lets you enter two title lines for the whole graph, one for the X-axis and one for the Y-axis. Data-Labels lets you specify a range that contains labels for the data. Clear, concise labels help readers interpret data more easily and accurately. Legend enters a brief description of the data represented by each symbol (on a line graph) or pattern (on a bar or stacked-bar graph) to help the reader interpret the graph.

The remaining commands control the appearance of the data. Format (which relates only to Line and XY graphs) displays the data points as Lines Symbols Both or Neither. Grid (Horizontal Vertical Both Clear) lets you overlay horizontal or vertical lines to help the reader identify the plots. Scale controls the scales of the X- and Y-axis. The default scale takes the difference between the high point and the low point in the data range and spreads the difference evenly over the space available. Color and B&W determine whether the graph is displayed in color (if you have a color monitor) or in black and white (or whatever other two colors your screen can display).

## Creating and Viewing a Simple Graph (/GTRV)

The first step in creating a graph is to select the appropriate type, using /Graph Type (/GT), from the five available types of Lotus graphs: Line Bar XY Stacked-Bar and Pie. Next, enter the data range(s) that contain the numbers to be displayed in the graph. Lotus provides for six data ranges, assigned as A B C D E F, plus an X range used for some graphs. The meaning of each range varies somewhat among graph types. You can view the current graph (the one most recently created or selected for use) at any time by selecting View from the Graph menu or by pressing [F10] from anywhere else in the worksheet.

A pie graph is the simplest graph to create and understand. Retrieve file 5CASEA.WKS. To create a pie graph, select /Graph Type Pie. The **A** range contains the data that determine the sizes of the pie slices, which show what percentage (of a whole pie) each data item (piece) represents. Start by graphing the 1989 laundry department costs. Select **A**. When prompted with "Enter A axis range:" enter F28..F30. To see your first graph, select View. The graph should appear on your screen and look like Figure 5.2.

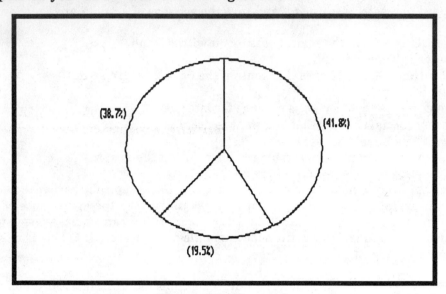

**Figure 5.2  Pie graph**

Note that although the pie graph shows the percentages represented by each slice (line item), it does not indicate which line item each slice represents. Press any key on the keyboard to return to the Graphics menu. Labels for the slices must be entered in the X range of a pie graph. To identify the years, select **X** and enter A28..A30 (which contains the line-item names). View the graph, which is now labeled with both the line-item names and the percentages.

The pie graph uses the B range to contain codes for the shading of the different slices. These codes have been entered in B17..B19. Codes 1 through 7 indicate different shading patterns. Adding 100 to any code makes Lotus explode or pull out the related pie slice. The pie is the only type of graph that uses the B range this way. All other graph types have preset shadings associated with ranges A through F. Select **B** and enter the range B17..B19. Use View to see the shadings.

To title the pie graph, use Options Titles First "Enter graph title, top line:" 1989 Actual Data ↵, Titles Second "Enter graph title, second line:" Laundry Department ↵ Quit. This is typically all that needs to be specified for a Pie graph. Use View to display the pie graph, shown in Figure 5.3.

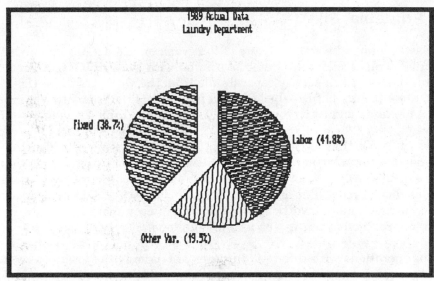

**Figure 5.3  Pie graph with options**

To review, the steps to create the pie graph of 1989 data were /Graph Type Pie A F28..F30 ↵ X
A28..A30 ↵ B G28..G30 ↵ Options Titles First 1989 Actual Data ↵ Titles Second Laundry
Department ↵ Quit. View was used several times to visually check your progress. Range
names could have been used instead of cell addresses, if ranges were named. The most
error-prone part of using the Graph command sequence is correctly identifying the data
ranges. A good rule of thumb for graphing is to make sure that you assign parallel ranges
for each variable. If the X range is a row, then the A B C D E F ranges will also be rows that
include the same columns as the X range. This gets easier with practice.

## Naming a Graph (/GN)

Naming a graph allows you to keep its settings (the type, data ranges, and options) so you
can return to view and modify it later, even though you have created other graphs in the
meantime.  /Graph Name has the subcommands Use Create Delete Reset. Create lets you
assign a name to the graph, which saves its settings so you can later Use it to view or
modify the graph. Delete gets rid of a single existing graph name, and Reset deletes all
named graphs. Enter Name Create PIE89 ↵ to name the graph you have been working on
PIE89.

The named graph exists only within the worksheet in which it was created. Once you have
created and named a graph, you must exit from the Graph menu with [Esc] or Quit and *save
the worksheet* with /File Save Replace. This saves named graphs as part of the worksheet,
so that the graphs will be available the next time you retrieve that worksheet. Save the file
now, so that the file on the disk will contain the graph settings and name, in case some
disaster befalls the worksheet in main memory. If you make changes to a named graph,
you must use Name Create again and select the old filename, to save the modifications.
Alternatively, you could assign a new name to the changed graph and thereby keep both the
original and the modified graph.

## Saving a Printable File (/GS)

The /Graph Save command saves a picture of the graph on the default disk in a file with an extension of .PIC. This .PIC file can later be printed with the PrintGraph command on the GraphProgram Disk and is a totally separate file from the worksheet file. Use /Graph Save PIE89 ↵ to create a printable file called PIE89.PIC. It is not necessary, but it is convenient and consistent to Name and Save the graph with the same graph name or a similar one.

When working on a file that only you will use, the major naming consideration is a name that you will be able to understand and distinguish. When working on a file that others will use, it is important to develop and follow standard logical naming conventions and to select filenames that at least hint at the contents. This aspect of data organization and access that accountants have traditionally dealt with is even more important in a computerized environment than it was in a manual one.

Three different operations with different purposes are naming the graph to save its settings, saving a worksheet file to save the named graphs, and saving a graph to a .PIC file for printing. If you have created a graph that you want to keep and print, you will have to do all three. This can be confusing at first, but it will become easier as you work with graphs.

## Recalculations

Once the graph has been defined, you can return to the worksheet (with Quit or [Esc]), modify the data in the ranges being graphed, and view the graph of the modified data. To illustrate this, change the value in cell F28 to 28000 and view the graph by pressing [F10]. Notice how the graph changed automatically to reflect the new data value. Reenter 37113 in cell F28, and the graph will return to the former shape. This feature is most useful for dealing with planning or projected data under different assumptions.

Another important distinction between naming a graph and saving a .PIC file of the graph is that a change in the graphed data will not change a .PIC file, but it will change the appearance of the named graph being viewed on the screen. The named graph reflects the current data in the graphed range, and a change in those data is immediately reflected in the graph. The file created with /Graph Save is just a copy of what the graph looked like at the time it was saved; thus, it is not affected by any changes made in the worksheet after it was saved. To print a copy of the graph as it appears with the changed data, you would have to save another .PIC file under a different name, which is common.

## Changing Graph Type(/GT) and Reset (/GR)

You can easily display the data used for the pie graph as a bar graph by changing the graph type with /Graph Type Bar. Using View should display the graph shown in Figure 5.4. This is not as useful as the pie graph, so it will not be named now. It is the user's responsibility to select the correct and appropriate graph for the data and the situation.

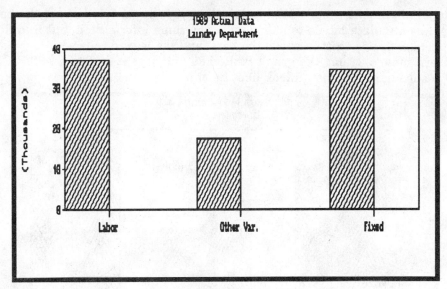

**Figure 5.4  Bar graph**

Graph settings can be reset or cleared for the entire graph or for individual ranges with /Graph Reset (Graph **X A B C D E F** Quit). Some users prefer to start each graph by resetting all the graph variables with the sequence /Graph Reset Graph, to start with a "clean slate." On the other hand, to generate a different type of graph using much of the same data and labels, you may want to reuse all the settings you can and change only what is different. Whether to reset and start from scratch or to start from an existing graph and change only what is different depends on how similar to an existing graph the new one will be.

Clear all settings with **Reset Graph** and **View** the cleared blank screen. Recall the graph with **Name Use** and select PIE89 from the list of named graphs on the bottom line of the control panel.

## Plotting More Than One Data Set

While a single set of numbers is often fairly clear and may not even need to be graphed, multiple data sets require the power of graphics to display relationships. The more types of data to be interpreted simultaneously, the more you need graphics.

A bar graph that would compare each type of cost over the five years would be useful. To construct this graph, select Type Bar, leave the A range as it is, and set the B range to the 1988 data (E28..E30), C to 1987 (D28..D30), D to 1986 (C28..C30), and E to 1985 (B28..B30). Select Option Titles First and edit the title to read 1985 through 1989 Actual Cost Data. Select Titles **X** and enter Type of Cost. Select Titles **Y** and enter Dollars. The titles have now been changed to reflect the current bar graph instead of the preceding pie graph.

Legends are useful in understanding the meanings of the different bars, so select **Options Legend A** and enter 1989 Data. Enter Legends for each of the other ranges B through E, assigning them the appropriate years, the same way that the legend for A was defined. Although Data-Labels are redundant with the Legend in this case, enter them to clarify the differences between the two. Since Data-Labels must be in a range, leave the Graph menu and copy the contents of B26..F26 to the range B38..F40, resulting in three rows of years 1985 through 1989. Select /Graph Options Data-Labels **A** F38..F40 ⏎ ⏎ **B** E38..E40 ⏎ ⏎ **C** D38..D40 ⏎ ⏎ **D** C38..C40 ⏎ ⏎ **E** B38..B40 ⏎ ⏎. The next step in the sequence accepts the default of

Center for label alignment, since data labels will always be centered above the bar. In this case, the legends and data labels tell the reader the same information, but in different ways. The data labels are written above the bars, and the legend tells what each different shading pattern means. Name the graph BAR85-89 and save it as BAR85-89.PIC. When viewed, the resulting graph should look like the one in Figure 5.5.

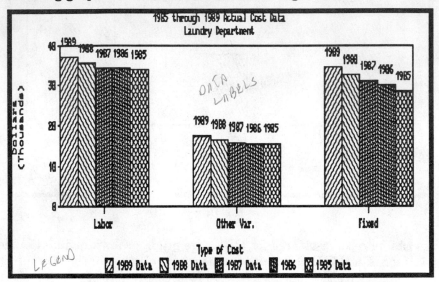

**Figure 5.5 Bar graph using options to document**

The next graph will be a line graph showing the cost trends over the past five years. This requires defining ranges that are rows instead of columns. Since this graph will be very different from the preceding ones, use /Graph Reset Graph to eliminate all the current settings, then select Type Line. Set range **X** to B26..F26, **A** to B28..F28, **B** to B29..F29, and **C** to B30..F30. Using Options Legend, set the legends to Labor (range A), Other Variable Cost (range B), and Fixed Costs (range C). Set the Titles as 1985 through 1989 Actual Costs (first title line), Laundry Department (second line), Year (X title), and Dollars (Y title). Name the graph and save a .PIC file as LINECOST. When viewed, the resulting graph should look like the one in Figure 5.6.

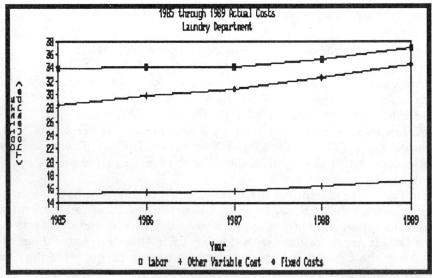

**Figure 5.6 Line graph**

Finally, create a stacked-bar graph to show the proportion made up by each type of cost for each year. The only thing you need to do is change graph Type to Stacked-Bar. Name your graph STACK and save it with the same name. Save your worksheet file (/File Save) to save the named graphs. The results should look like Figure 5.7.

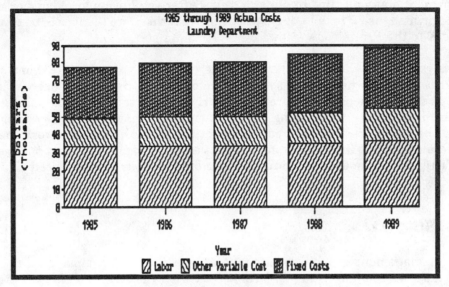

**Figure 5.7 Stacked bar graph**

## PrintGraph

Before you can print a graph, you must save it using /Graph Save, which you already have done for a number of the graphs. You must leave the Lotus worksheet with /Quit to return to the Access menu described in Chapter 3. With the GraphProgram Disk in the default drive or on the hard drive/network), select PrintGraph. The first screen (Figure 5.8), which is similar in format to the main Lotus program menu, displays all (default) options currently in effect.

```
Copyright 1986 Lotus Development Corp. All Rights Reserved. Release 2.01   MENU

Select graphs for printing
Image-Select   Settings  Go  Align  Page  Exit

  GRAPH        IMAGE OPTIONS                          HARDWARE SETUP
  IMAGES       Size                 Range Colors      Graphs Directory:
  SELECTED       Top        .395    X                   A:\
                 Left       .750    A                 Fonts Directory:
                 Width     6.500    B                   A:\
                 Height    4.691    C                 Interface:
                 Rotate     .000    D                   Parallel 1
                                    E                 Printer Type:
               Font                 F
                 1  BLOCK1                            Paper Size
                 2  BLOCK1                              Width      8.500
                                                       Length    11.000

                                                     ACTION OPTIONS
                                                       Pause: No   Eject: No
```

**Figure 5.8 PrintGraph menu**

The Image-Select command lists all .PIC files created with the Save command within graph. Since you can select several files to be printed at once, selections from this list are made differently from your previous file selections. Move through the list of files with ↑ and ↓ and use the space bar to mark each file you want to print the space bar works as a toggle, so press it a second time to unmark a file. After you have marked one or more graphs to be printed, use ↵ to tell Lotus PrintGraph that these are the files to be printed and to take you back to the PrintGraph menu.

Settings lets you change the size or the font of the graph images and rotate them, specify the types of hardware being used, and save these changes if desired. If you are working in a lab, its Lotus software is probably already properly configured; if it is not, ask the lab assistant for help. If you are working on your own machine, consult your owner's manual to complete the configuration. The remaining options (Go, Align, Page) work the same way they do under Print in the worksheet. Select all four graphs and print them using Align Go. This may take several minutes, depending on your printer speed.

# Database (/D)

Lotus' data-management capabilities are found under the Data command on the main menu. The data subcommands are Fill Table Sort Query Distribution Matrix Regression Parse.

These Lotus commands allow some basic manipulations of data in a worksheet. Lotus is not a database-management system and should not be (mis)used as one. However, Lotus 1-2-3 does perform several data-handling operations that are useful in worksheet analysis. Only a few of these commands will be used here. Before we can explore these commands, it is important to understand some new terminology. These definitions are specific to Lotus and may be used somewhat differently by other database-management systems.

- **Database:** A range of cells with the top row containing "field names," all other rows containing data records. Field names must be labels.
- **Record**: Each row of data (not including the first row of field names).
- **Field**: Each column.
- **Input range**: Usually the database (field names and records).
- **Criterion range**: Range containing criteria of items being searched for.
- **Output range**: Area to which records are copied.

## Data Fill (/DF) and Sort (/DS)

The Data Sort command sorts the records (rows) according to one or two key fields (columns). Selecting /Data Sort displays the subcommands Data-range Primary-key Secondary-key Reset Go Quit.

A data range and a primary key must be specified the first time this command is used. The data range is usually all columns of all rows in the database excluding field names. The primary key is the field (column) by which the records will be sorted. The records can be sorted in ascending (A) or descending (D) order. An optional secondary key is used to break ties in the primary key and is specified in the same manner. Subsequent sort operations will use the same range and key(s) until you specify others or Reset them.

Retrieve file 4CASEA.WKS, and save immediately as 5CASEB. Insert a new column A, set it to a width of 3, and move to A32. Since the line items do not appear to be in any logical order, the numbers 1 through 7 should be entered to the left of the line-item names to provide a way to use Sort to return them to their original order. Use /Data Fill, enter a Fill range of A32..A38 as the location to be filled with data, enter 1 for the Start value, and use ↵ to accept the defaults of 1 for the Step value and 8191 for the Stop value. The numbers 1 through 7 will be entered in the indicated range; Lotus stops when it gets to the end of the range or to the Stop value, whichever occurs first.

First, sort the items from largest to smallest ACTUAL expense. Define the data range (**not** including the field names) with /Data Sort Data-range A32..N38. Select Primary-key D32 Descending ↵. To execute the sort, select Go; your worksheet should look like Figure 5.9.

| | Argon County Hospital | | | | |
| | Performance Report - Laundry Department | | | | |
| | July - September 1990 | | | | |
| | | | | VARIANCE | |
| | | | | (OVER) | VARIANCE |
| | | | | UNDER | % OF |
| | | BUDGET | ACTUAL | BUDGET | BUDGET |
| | Patient Days | 9,500 | 11,900 | (2,400) | -25% |
| | Pounds Processed | 125,000 | 156,000 | (31,000) | -25% |
| | COSTS | | | | |
| 1 | Laundry Labor | $9,000 | $12,500 | ($3,500) | -39% |
| 6 | Allocated Admin. Costs | 4,000 | 5,000 | (1,000) | -25% |
| 5 | Supervisor's Salary | 3,150 | 3,750 | (600) | -19% |
| 3 | Water | 1,700 | 2,500 | (800) | -47% |
| 4 | Maintenance | 1,400 | 2,200 | (800) | -57% |
| 2 | Supplies | 1,100 | 1,875 | (775) | -70% |
| 7 | Equipment Depreciation | 1,200 | 1,250 | (50) | -4% |

**Figure 5.9  Sorted data**

Next, use /Data Sort Primary-Key F32 Ascending to sort the data by the size of VARIANCE in the initial report. Since all the variance values are negative, the ascending order starts with the most extreme negative variance and progresses to the largest positive variance. To break any exact ties, use ACTUAL in descending order by entering Secondary-key D32 D. Note that the tie between Maintenance and Water is broken.

## Query (/DQ)

The /Data Query commands are used to select those records (rows) from the database (input range) that meet the criteria specified in the criterion range. To illustrate this command, retrieve 5CASEC.WK1, which contains the table of doctors' charges used for the VLOOKUP in Chapter 4.

The /Data Query subcommands are Input Criterion Output Find Extract Unique Delete Reset Quit.

To search the database for an item, you need to identify at least two ranges. The input range is the database *including* field names. The criterion range is a small range used to hold the name of the field to be searched and the logical expressions used in the search. If you are using the Extract option, you also need to specify an output range to which records that meet the criterion are copied. Lotus will use as many rows as are needed below the field names to hold the output. The output range determines which fields will be copied from the input range.

Specify the /Data Query Input range as A28..H37 and the Criterion range as H17..H18. To Find the item BURN in the TREAT CODE column, enter CODE in the first row of the criterion range (H17) and BURN in the second row of the criterion range (H18). Since the criterion names must match the field names exactly, it is most accurate to copy the field name from the input range (A28) to the criterion range (H17). Labels such as BURN can be in upper- or lowercase to find a match. Execute the search by selecting /Data Query Find. The first data value to meet the criterion is highlighted, which lets you look at the record but not make any changes to it. Row 30, which contains the record for BURN, should be highlighted and the mode indicator should display FIND. Use [Esc] to return to MENU mode.

To find the records for which the hospital charge is less than $40, move the cell pointer to the top window and enter the field name CHARGE in H17 and the logical expression +G29<40 in cell H18. Note that you must exit from the Lotus Command menus entirely before you can use the [F6] key to switch between windows and change the criterion values. The result displayed in H18 is "1," signifying that Lotus evaluated the logical expression "is G29 less than 40?" and found it to be true (as opposed to false, "0"). It is easier to review the criterion if the cell contents are displayed as text, so use /Range Format Text to format H18. Use [F6] again to move the cell pointer back to the bottom window. Press [F7] to instruct Lotus to repeat the latest /Data Query operation, which was a Find. [F7] causes Lotus to perform exactly the same steps as the most recent /Data Query performed, but the records found will be different because the criterion value was changed. The first record highlighted should be row 32, DRES, with a hospital charge of 15. Continue highlighting any other records that meet the criterion by pressing ↓. When there are no more records that meet the criterion, Lotus will beep. Use ↑ to return to preceding records that meet the criterion. [Esc] returns you to MENU mode.

To construct an output range, copy the field names (A28..H28) to A41..H41. Position cell A39 in the upper left corner of the screen. Specify the output range with /Data Query Output A41..H41 followed by Extract to make Lotus copy the records that meet the same criterion into the output range, as shown in Figure 5.10.

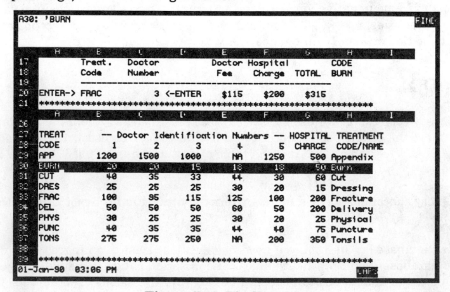

**Figure 5.10 Finding data**

/Range erase B41..C41, use [F7] to repeat the query operation. Notice that only the fields contained in the output range are copied, not the entire record.

# Macros

By now, you have probably discovered a few keystroke sequences that you keep typing over and over. A **macro** is a string of keystrokes recorded and stored in the worksheet. Essentially, a macro is a computer program made up of Lotus commands. Macros can save time and increase accuracy, *if* they are correct. They are used primarily for entering repetitious commands and designing worksheets for data entry.

You create a macro by entering the keystroke sequence as a label (') in a cell and assigning a range name to the cell that contains the macro. The name given to the macro range must start with a backslash (\) followed by one letter from A to Z. Lotus executes the macro whenever [Alt] is held down and the letter is pressed. Lotus then does exactly what it would have done if you had typed in the series of keystrokes contained in the macro, excluding the beginning label character (' " or ^).

Macros are usually kept together in a separate area of the worksheet, out of the way of the documentation and data areas. Use AA1, which is a commonly used starting point. Macros use words enclosed in curly brackets { } to represent special-purpose keys. These are listed below for your reference.

| Macro Key | Equivalent | Macro Key | Equivalent |
|---|---|---|---|
| {Up} | Up Arrow (↑) | {Bs} | Back Space [Backspace] |
| {Down} | Down Arrow (↓) | {?} | Pause for manual input and ↵ |
| {Left} | Left Arrow (←) | {Edit} | [F2] |
| {Right} | Right Arrow (→) | {Name} | [F3] |
| {PgUp} | Page Up [PgUp] | {Abs} | [F4] |
| {PgDn} | Page Down [PgDn] | {GoTo} | [F5] |
| {Home} | Beginning [Home] | {Window} | [F6] |
| {End} | End [End] | {Query} | [F7] |
| ~ | Return ↵ | {Table} | [F8] |
| {Esc} | Escape [Esc] | {Calc} | [F9] |
| {Del} | Delete [Del] | {Graph} | [F10] |

Retrieve your completed hospital performance report from Chapter 4 (4CASEA). For the first simple macro, suppose you are tired of using four key strokes every time you want to erase one cell. To enter a macro to erase a current cell using /Range Erase ↵, move to AB1 and enter a single quote (') followed by the sequence of command letters, /RE and a tilde (~). The ~ is a special character that represents ↵ in a macro. Name the cell range AB1 as macro \E with /Range Name Create \E. Move to cell W3 and enter the word GARBAGE for testing the range erase macro. To use the macro, stay at W3 and activate the macro with the key combination **[Alt] E**. The current cell, W3, will be erased. For documentation, it is a good idea to label the macro, usually in the cell immediately to the left of the first cell containing the macro. Move to cell AA1 and enter '\E, which will be displayed as \E, meaning that the entry in the cell immediately to the right is the beginning of the macro named \E.

Another procedure that is repeated often is printing. Using a macro to reset borders, margins, and ranges can be a real time saver when the worksheet is used to generate multiple reports. Since there are multiple ranges to be printed in the performance report, it is a good example for a simple print macro. The ranges you named in Chapter 4 will be used in this example.

Move to AA10 and enter '\P, as documentation, then name the range AB10 \P, for print. Enter '/PPOBCbordcol~Q in cell AB10, enter Rdoc~AG in AB11, enter Rinitrep~GP in AB12, enter Rdoc~AG in AB13 (can be copied from AB11), and enter Rrevrep~GPQ in AB14. The relevant areas of your worksheet should now look like Figure 5.11. This is the exact series of commands (if ~ is replaced by ⏎ when you are entering from the keyboard) used to print the initial and revised reports in Chapter 4. They can now be printed with a simple [Alt] P. Use it to print the reports.

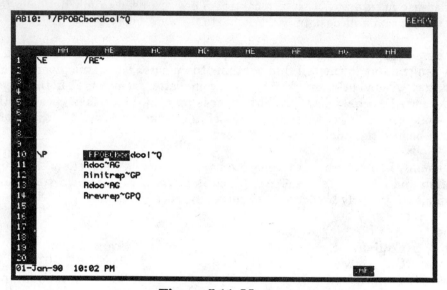

**Figure 5.11 Macros**

The macro is everything contained in AB10..AB14. Lotus assumes that the macro continues in subsequent cells below the first named one until it reaches an empty cell. Although you could have entered the entire macro in AB10, a macro is easier to read, debug, and modify if it is broken into logical segments that are placed in separate cells. The convention used here is to enter Lotus commands in capital letters and range names in lowercase letters. This is purely for the convenience of the human reader. As far as Lotus is concerned, the entire macro can be in lowercase, uppercase, or a random mixture of the two. However, designing for human use is an important aspect of good systems design, because it contributes substantially to the speed and accuracy with which the system can be developed, used, and evaluated.

A task that is repeated frequently by smart PC operators is to save one worksheet using /File Save ⏎ Replace. If you are tempted to write a macro to automate this procedure, which would be '/FS~R, remember that using it would defeat the purpose of the safety mechanism that asks you if you really want to replace the old file! Be very careful that you don't automate yourself into trouble with macros.

These are simple examples of macros, designed to give you an idea of how they are constructed, how they work, and the types of things they are useful for. Many macros are larger than the entire worksheets we have been dealing with. There are advanced macro commands (/X commands) that can be used to build complex programs in Lotus. Many books are available to help you learn to write more complex macros. However, a word of caution is in order. Although many organizations use Lotus macros extensively, the macros are difficult to debug and are often found to be riddled with errors.

# Chapter Review

You now know how to develop and print graphs, use some of the basic data-management capabilities of Lotus, and develop and use simple macros to automate repetitive command sequences. Although there is much more you could learn, especially about the Data commands and sophisticated macros, you have a basic understanding of most of what Lotus can do. If you have worked through the cases in the chapters and have successfully completed some of the practice exercises from each chapter, you are now armed with enough Lotus skills to legitimately claim to be a Lotus user.

Even more important, you are aware of how Lotus can be used in an AIS and how important AIS concepts, such as report design, backup, and recovery, apply to Lotus. With this background, you can go on to learn additional features on the job and on your own. Since new versions, with more new features, will continue to be introduced indefinitely, today's well-prepared graduates are those who have the ability to continue to learn after they leave the classroom.

# Practice Exercises

Exercise 5-1

**Filename: 5EX1.WKS**
(Continuation of Exercise 4-1)

Prepare and print graphs to display the following:
1. What percentage is each Estimated Monthly Cost item of the Total in year one? Emphasize the Overhead component and Title the graph. (Name the graph 5-1-1 and save the printable graph file as 5-1-1.PIC.)
2. Show the trends of the
   a.   Estimated Monthly Costs for each of the four items over the next five years (5-1-2A)
   b.   four Estimated Monthly Costs items side by side for each of the five years (5-1-2B)
   c.   four Estimated Monthly Costs items one on top of the other for each of the five years (5-1-2C)

   Each graph is different and would be used for different purposes. When would you use each graph?
3. Plot the relationship of the cash flow for savings against costs for each of the five years (5-1-3).

Prepare and print the database to display the following:
4. The Monthly Cost Savings for Clerical Costs in alphabetical order by type of Clerk
5. The Monthly Cost Savings for Clerical Costs from largest to smallest Total Savings

**Reminders**

1. Design a pie graph using H31..H34 as the A range and labels G31..G34 as the X range. Put code values (adding 100 to explode Overhead) in the B range C15..C18. Document the graph with titles.
2. a.  Build a line graph with H31..L31 as the A range (other ranges parallel A) and H29..L29 as the labels in the X range. Document with legend, titles for the graph, and both the X-axis and the Y-axis.
     b.  Convert to bar graph.
     c.  Convert to stacked-bar graph.
     d.  Create a stacked-bar graph using H44..L44 as the A range, label axis, title, and show legend.
3. Design an XY graph with I57..I61 (Savings) as the A range and H57..H61 (Costs) as the X range. From Options, select Grid Both.
4. Select A46..D48 as the data range and column A as the primary key sorted in ascending order.
5. Select column D as the primary key and sort in descending order.

Exercise 5-2

**Filename: 5EX2.WKS**
(Continuation of Exercise 4-2)

Prepare and print graphs to display the following:
1. the Variance (Over) Under Budget for the Assembly Department for each of the Controllable Costs (Name and save the graph and .PIC file as 5-2-1.)
2. Use a bar graph to compare the Budget and Actual Fixed Costs of the Plant Manager (5-2-2)
3. the relative size of Actual costs for the Assembly Department, with Overtime Premium exploded (5-2-3)

Prepare and print the database to display the following:
4. the Assembly Department performance report All Costs sorted alphabetically by line items within the variable and fixed cost categories
5. the Assembly Department performance report All Costs sorted in descending order by Variance % of Budget and then Budget Cost
6. the Assembly Department performance report All Costs sorted in ascending order by Variance (Over) Under Budget

Prepare and use a macro to do the following:
7. shorten the time it takes to change the "Variance % of Budget" to an absolute number

**Reminders:**

1. Design a bar graph using data F56..F60 as the A range and labels A56..A60 as the X range. Document the graph with titles.
2. Build a bar graph with D89..D95 as the A range and E89..E95 as the B range. Document the graph with appropriate titles, and edit the labels in column A to improve graph appearance.
3. Create a pie using E57..E61 as the A range and explode Overtime Premium by adding 100 to the code.

4. Using Data Sort, select A32..G43 as the data range and sort using column C as the primary key in ascending order and column A as the secondary key in descending order.
5. Select column G as the primary key and column D as the secondary key, both in descending order.
6. Select column F as the primary key used in ascending order.
7. Macro \A will be {EDIT} {HOME} @ABS({END}). Run the macro for each cell in the range.

Exercise 5-3

**Filename: 5EX3.WKS**
(Continuation of Exercise 4-3)

See Exercises 3-3 and 4-3 for additional background information.

Prepare graphic printouts to support the following reports:
1. a trend line of the average monthly analyst-programmer hours over the two years for each project (A to D) (Name the graph and save the printable graph file as 5-3-1.)
2. a bar chart that compares fixed System, Variable System, and Analyst costs over the two years (5-3-2)
3. Convert the bar chart of the previous question to a stacked-bar graph (5-3-3)
4. a pie graph of Monthly Computer System Use for months 19–24, with the Existing Systems section exploded (5-3-4)

Use the /Data commands to do the following:
5. write down the sequence of commands and print the results.
6. find Fixed System Cost in the Financial Projection section.
7. extract all columns of analyst-programmer hours with more than 250 in months 7-12.
8. sort analyst-programmer hours in ascending order for months 7-12.

Create and print copies of macros to do the following:
9. eliminate the extra formatting character and change the cells to right-justify on the line entitled COST CATEGORY. Use graphs named 5-3-2 and 5-3-3 to see that the label changes are reflected in the graphs.
10. automate printing the two-page report required in Exercise 4-3.

9 '/ Range Label Right A.67 A.693

Exercise 5-4

**Filename: 5EX4.WKS**
(Continuation of Exercise 4-4)

1 RN

'/ PPAG ~

See Exercises 3-4 and 4-4 for additional background information.

Prepare graphic output to support the reports.
1. Use a bar graph to show the relationship among the three taxes for the four employes paid for the week ending June 1, 1990. There should be four bars (one for each employee) in three groups (one for each type of tax). (Name the graph and save the printable graph file as 5-4-1.)

2. Use a stacked-bar graph to display the total of the three taxes paid by each emplyee for the week ending June 22, 1990. There should be six bars, each with three parts (one for each type of tax). (5-4-2)
3. Display with a pie graph the proportion represented by net pay and each of the taxes for the average employee. Explode the net pay. (5-4-3)

Use the Database commands to perform the following manipulations and print:
4. sort by Employee number and Hours, both in Ascending order
5. extract into an output range below the current averages, the Employees' records with pay rates greater than $20 and hours equal to 20
6. extract only Employee number, pay rate, gross, and net for employees working 20 or more hours

Design a macro to do the following:
7. make Employee a four character code and add a zero (0) as the first character of each of the current employee numbers. Run the macro, then print the macro and the file

# Chapter 6: Integrating Lotus 1-2-3 with Other Software

Accountants often need to transfer data from one computer file or application to another. Lotus allows data to be transferred among worksheet files and to or from other applications, including dBASE, with relative ease. This chapter discusses the reasons for transferring data among different applications and several ways to transfer data into Lotus from other applications, out of Lotus to other applications, and among files within Lotus.

## Case Setting

While working on the next year's budget, the controller found that it would be useful to be able to transfer data among Lotus files and asked you to investigate how to do it. The controller also realized that the Actual data entered in the performance report had been taken from hard-copy reports generated by the hospital's expense transaction-processing system. You have also been assigned to investigate whether the hospital information systems (IS) department could generate electronic reports that could be read by Lotus, to avoid reentering the data manually.

## Common Reasons to Transfer Data

Data that are already in one Lotus worksheet file are often needed in other Lotus worksheet files. The same data may be used in several different reports, or data may need to be consolidated. There are several File commands that let you save or retrieve only portions of a file. This allows you to deal with either values or formulas and add values to or subtract values from the current worksheet.

As useful and flexible as Lotus is, it cannot do everything. Sometimes another type of software, such as a database-management system, word processor, or graphics package is more appropriate for performing tasks or operations on data that already exist within a Lotus file. Also, other types of application systems may need to use data that are already in Lotus files. This is common in organizations with departments that used to provide data manually to the centralized IS department, but now generate the data using Lotus. Many software packages can convert Lotus files for their own use; most can use a data file in a common format, such as ASCII, which Lotus can produce.

It is even more common for data in the transaction-processing or other systems to require further analysis that is best done using an electronic spreadsheet. Data from transaction-processing systems often must be combined, recombined, or summarized for reports and presentations. This requires data to be transferred from the other applications into a Lotus worksheet.

Unfortunately, much data transfer is currently done manually, by reentering data into each application in which they are used. Transferring data among computer files is an excellent candidate for automation, since it involves machine-readable data at both ends of the transfer process and is structured and repetitive. Substantial benefits are likely to result from automating data transfer, which when done manually is time consuming and highly susceptible to human error and circumvents existing input controls. If data must be transferred often, it is usually worth making the computer perform the conversion rather than retyping the data. Only if the need to transfer data occurs rarely and the amount of data involved is small, does it make sense to perform the conversion manually.

It is extremely frustrating to get a computer-generated hard-copy report from an IS department and have to waste your time reentering the data into a Lotus worksheet. With a bit of cooperation on the part of the IS department, they probably can generate a file that Lotus can use. Although this requires some effort by the IS department, it will be compensated for by the time savings in user departments and may even save the IS department time in the long run by decreasing the demand for special hard-copy reports. This latter benefit can help to persuade IS to provide a machine-readable file.

There is usually a tradeoff between using multiple types of specialized software and using a single package that does many things adequately but none or only one of them spectacularly. For example, Lotus has excellent electronic spreadsheet capabilities, but only adequate graphic and database capabilities. While these capabilities meet the needs of many users much of the time, they do not meet the needs of all users all the time. The costs of using two different applications are the time, effort, and resources required to transfer data among the applications and the added dangers of data loss or contamination in doing so. As an accountant and manager, it will be your job to decide when the benefits exceed the added costs of using different applications to perform different operations on a set of data.

In general, integration is becoming easier, faster, and more automated. Many software packages now provide good import and export capabilities, and a wider variety of features seems to be incorporated in each new version. Integrated packages that do several types of tasks well, such as Lotus Symphony®, Ashton-Tate Framework®, and Microsoft Works®, are becoming more common. The trend toward ease and automation is expected to continue until data transfer is simple and highly automated.

In spite of this progress, human decisions about and intervention in the integration process will continue to be necessary for the foreseeable future. A human user will have to tell the computer how and when to perform the data conversion, even when the computer performs the actual translation process itself. The remainder of this chapter explains how to use the various Lotus options for data transfer.

# Data Exchange among Lotus Files

The Lotus File commands transfer data among different Lotus worksheets. They allow you to save part of the current worksheet in a separate file on disk or to bring part or all of a worksheet on a disk into the current worksheet file. It is possible to transfer formulas or current values that result from the formulas, or to add or subtract values. You can use /File Extract, /File Combine, or both to accomplish these tasks.

## File Extract (/FX)

The /File Xtract command saves a specified part of the current worksheet in memory to a .WK? file on disk. You can make Xtract save either the standard form of the worksheet with all the formulas intact or just the current values of the calculations. In either case, the resulting file is a worksheet file, and all the print options, ranges, and other settings are saved as they would be by saving the worksheet using /File Save. Using /File Xtract to save formulas is essentially the same as using /File Save to save a file under a new name, except that it is possible to save only part of the worksheet instead of all of it. It is important to make sure that none of the formulas in the extracted range references cells outside the extracted range.

To save only part of a worksheet with the formulas intact, use /File Xtract Formulas. Retrieve file 6CASE.WKS. To extract the formulas in the range A16..E36, select the commands /File Xtract Formulas, enter the extract filename 6-FXF, and enter the extract range A16..E36. This copies the contents of the cells in A16..E36 of the current worksheet into cells A1..E21 of the worksheet file 6-FXF. The documentation section of the current worksheet will not be included in 6-FXF.WKS. Now retrieve 6-FXF to see the results. Note that the formulas are retained in columns D, E, and row 21. Print cells D9..E21 using the Options Other Cell-Formulas.

To see the difference between the Formulas and the Values options of Xtract, retrieve 6CASE.WKS again and select /File Xtract Values. Enter the extract filename 6-FXV, and again enter the extract range A16..E36. This copies the values from the cells in A16..E36 of the current worksheet into cells A1..F20 of the worksheet file 6-FXV. Again, the documentation section of the current worksheet will not be included in 6-FXV.WKS. Retrieve 6-FXV to see the results and check that there are values instead of formulas in columns D and E. Print cells D9..E21 of this file using the Options Other Cell-Formulas and compare the printout to the one from 6-FXF.

It can be useful to extract the values of the final budget from a budget worksheet, once the budget has been approved. Complex models are commonly used during the process of setting the budget, but once the final budget is agreed upon, only the budget values are carried forward into the types of performance reports discussed in preceding chapters.

## File Combine (/FC)

The File Combine command brings all or part of an existing worksheet from a disk file into the current worksheet. The data are brought in so that the current location of the cell pointer becomes the upper left corner of the range of the combined data. /File Combine offers three choices of how the data will be combined. Data from the incoming file can be copied over (Copy), added to (Add), or subtracted (Subtract) from the values in the current cells. Next, you must choose whether to bring in only part of a file (Named-Range) or the whole file (Entire-File). Lotus 1-2-3 version 2 or higher will allow part of a worksheet to be combined using either a named range in the file from which it is being brought in or the cell addresses of the range. When an entire file is combined, it is frequently a file that was previously extracted from another larger file. None of the worksheet settings of the incoming file (not even the name of a range being combined) are brought in to the current file.

/File Combine Copy replaces the cell entries in the current worksheet with the contents of the corresponding cells of the incoming worksheet. The exception is that blank cells in the incoming file do not replace occupied cells in the current file. /File Combine Copy brings in labels, numbers, and formulas and copies them over any existing cell entries in the current worksheet. Save your file before using /File Combine Copy and check the results carefully before saving the combined file.

When combining multiple files, keep the file with the most ranges and nondefault settings as the base into which the others are combined. Use /File Combine Copy Entire-File to bring the related pieces of a project into the base file.

/File Combine Add adds the value of any number or formula in the incoming worksheet to any corresponding number or empty cell. If the corresponding cell in the current worksheet contains a label or formula, it is not affected by /File Combine Add. Label entries are not brought in when /File Combine Add is used. /File Combine Subtract works the same way as Add, except that values are subtracted instead of added.

The different effects of Copy and Add are illustrated by the following examples. Starting with a blank worksheet (/Worksheet Erase Yes), select /File Combine Add Entire-File 6CASE. Nothing appears in A1 because label cell entries in 6CASE are not brought in by /File Combine. Go to E29, to see that cells that contain formulas in 6CASE contain numbers in the current worksheet. Now move to C41 and select /File Combine Copy Entire-File 6CASE. This time, a label appears in C41 because all the cell entries in 6CASE are brought in. Cell contents that are at A1 in 6CASE now are at C41 in the current worksheet, and the contents of the other cells are shifted down and to the right by the same amount. Numbers, labels, and formulas, along with their individually set formats, are copied into the current worksheet; column width settings and ranges are not. Move around the worksheet, which occupies cells A1..G76, to make sure you understand what has been brought in by the Combine commands.

A common use for /File Combine Add is to consolidate several worksheets, for example, to combine all the different department budgets to prepare the budget for the entire hospital. Retrieve file 6CASE.WKS and use /Range Name Create to see that there are two new ranges in the file. Cell C36 has been named TOTACT and cell B36 has been named TOTBUDG. Retrieve 6CONSOL, which is designed to contain the quarterly budget and actual figures for all the departments of the hospital. Quarterly figures for the emergency room and the lab have been entered. Move to cell B26, the cell for the laundry department's budget figure for the quarter. Select /File Combine Add Named/Specified-Range, "Enter the range name or coordinates:" TOTBUDG, and select file 6CASE.WKS as the file to combine (Figure 6.1).

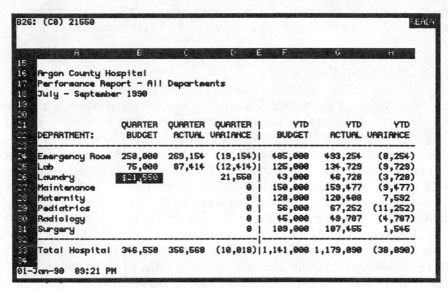

**Figure 6.1  Results of file combine**

The total original budget for the laundry department for the quarter ($21,550) appears in cell B26. Move to C26 and use a similar command sequence to bring in the actual amount (TOTACT) of the quarter for the laundry department. The amount $29,075 should appear. The amounts brought in carry the currency format with them.

The YTD (year to date) amounts for the laundry department have not yet been updated. Move to cell F26, which contains 43,000, and repeat the sequence of commands to add the TOTBUDG amount from 6CASE to the current amount. Lotus changes the amount to $64,550, by adding the 21,550 from the TOTBUDG range in 6CASE to the existing 43,000 budget (the year-to-date budget as of the end of the prior quarter) in the YTD column. Perform similar commands to add the quarter actual to the YTD ACTUAL for the laundry department. The resulting amount in G26 should be $75,803. Do *not* save the modified file.

Once you have successfully completed these steps, retrieve the original 6CONSOL.WKS file again. The entries in cells B36 and B38 are two macros, named \B (for budget) and \A (for actual), that will perform the same two series of commands you just performed manually. To use the macros, move to cell B26 and press [Alt] B to add the laundry budget amount. Also use the \B macro to add the budget amount to the prior quarter year-to-date amount in F26 and use the \A macro to add the actual amount to cells C26 and G26. It is common to develop macros to automate the process of integrating files.

## Exchanging Data with Other Software

There has been a significant increase in recent years in the ability of application programs to share files. The emphasis on increased flexibility and connectivity has forced most software manufactures to expand the ability of their software to transfer data to and from other programs. Lotus uses /File Import to bring into a worksheet data that are in standard text (ASCII) format. These data may have been generated by a DBMS, a word processor, or one of many other types of programs. The /Print File option is used to create output from a Lotus worksheet that can then be imported into a DBMS, a word processor, or another program in a similar manner. The /Translate utility, which is in the Lotus

Access menu, provides additional options for converting data from other programs into Lotus file format, from Lotus into other file formats, and between other formats.

## File Import (/FI)

/File Import is used to bring a text (ASCII) file into an active worksheet. Files being imported must have the extension .PRN and can be specified as either text or numbers. A file imported using the Text option is brought in as a column of labels, with each entire row of the imported file being placed in a single cell. A file containing both labels and numbers is brought in using Numbers if it is in the proper format. A label item in the file being imported using the Numbers option must be enclosed in quotes (" ") and numbers must be separated by commas or spaces. Each item in a row in the incoming file is placed in a separate cell of the Lotus worksheet row. dBASE can create files in the needed format using the COPY TO *filename* DELIMITED command. The merge capability of a word processor may be used to create a file containing the needed punctuation and spacing, or the file can simply be edited. Use the text out, or ASCII, option of a word processor to create a .PRN file, to avoid the special formatting characters that a word processor normally places in files when they are saved.

The file 6FEENM.PRN is an ASCII file created by a word processor. The file contains both text and numbers and is properly formatted to be imported into Lotus using File Import Numbers. You can view this file on your screen by selecting /System and entering TYPE B:6FEENM.PRN at the DOS prompt. Using PRINT instead of TYPE will print a hard copy of the file. After the file is displayed on the screen, as shown in Figure 6.2, and printed if you wish, enter EXIT to return to Lotus. Version 1 of Lotus 1-2-3 will require that you exit Lotus completely in order to enter commands at the DOS prompt.

```
B:\>TYPE B:6-FEE-NM.PRN
"CODE" 1 2 3 4 5 "CHARGE" "NAME"
"APP" 1200 1500 1000 "NA" 1250 500 "Appendix"
"BURN" 20 20 15 18 18 50 "Burn"
"CUT" 40 35 33 44 30 60 "Cut"
"DRES" 25 25 25 30 20 15 "Dressing"
"FRAC" 100 95 115 125 100 200 "Fracture"
"DEL" 50 50 50 60 50 200 "Delivery"
"PHYS" 30 25 25 30 20 25 "Physical"
"PUNC" 40 35 35 44 40 75 "Puncture"
"TONS" 275 275 250 "NA" 200 350 "Tonsils"

B:\>_
```

**Figure 6.2  ASCII file to be imported (6FEENM.PRN)**

Beginning with a blank worksheet, select /File Import Numbers 6FEENM.PRN. The resulting .WK? file is one that could be used as the basis for the file used in the data-management examples in Chapter 5. Although it was necessary to change the NA LABEL entries to @NA functions and to do other minor cleanup, you can see that importing was much faster than reentering the data file. Save the worksheet as 6FEE.WK?

A file that contains the same data as 6FEENM.PRN (but not the needed quotes around labels) is continued in 6FEETX.PRN. You can also view it on the screen by following the process you used to view 6FEENM.PRN. If data in a .PRN file are arranged in columns, you can import the file as text and use /Data Parse to convert the column of long labels into several columns of labels and numbers. (/Data Parse is not available for version 1 of Lotus 1-2-3.) Select /File Import Text 6FEETX.PRN. The imported file will appear as shown in Figure 6.3.

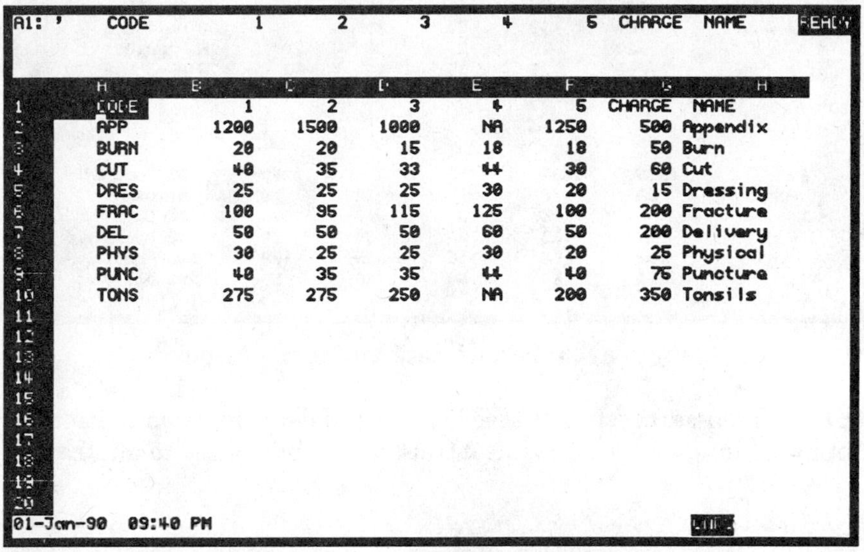

**Figure 6.3  Imported ASCII file (6FEETX.PRN)**

Look at the cell-contents line to see that all the data are contained in long labels in column A. There is nothing in column B or the columns to the right of B.

Move to A2, the first row of the data. Select /Data Parse Format-Line Create. Lotus uses the first row of data to create a format line, which determines how the long labels in column A will be broken up and entered into individual cells. Although you could type the format line yourself as a LABEL entry, it is easier to let Lotus do it. The | at the beginning of the cell-contents line tells Lotus that the entry is a format line. This is a label-definition character, like the comma used to begin a label entry, which tells Lotus what kind of label the cell contains. The remaining characters in the format line can be L (label), V (value), D (date), T (time), S (skip), > (continue the field), or * (undefined character). Select Format-Line Edit and use the arrow keys, [Backspace], and [Del] to modify the format line Lotus created. Note that Lotus switches automatically to overstrike mode for editing; return to Insert mode, if necessary, by pressing [Ins]. Edit the format line until it contains the following:

|****L>>>********V>>>****V>>>****V>>>****V>>>****V>>>*L>>>>>>>.

Press ↵ when you have completed editing the line. Select Input-Column and define the entire column of labels (A2..A11) as the input column. It is typical to place the output range a few rows below the end of the labels so you can move easily between the original and the parsed data to check the results. Select Output-Range, specify the output range as A15, and select Go. The data should appear in individual cells beginning with A15, as shown in Figure 6.4.

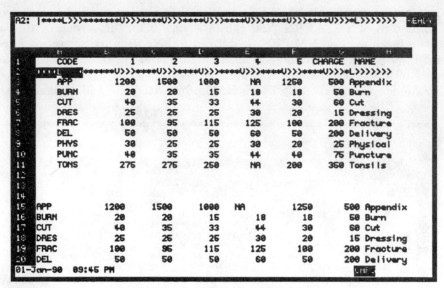

**Figure 6.4  Parsed data and format line**

Once the data have been successfully parsed, you can delete the rows containing the format line and the input column, or you can /File Xtract the output range to another file.

## Print File (/PF)

As discussed in Chapter 3, /Print File saves a text or printable ASCII file to disk. This is useful not only when a printer is not currently available, but also when you want to include the worksheet output in a report, a letter, or other document being composed on a word processor.

The controller needs to incorporate the laundry department performance report into a word-processing document. To create this file, retrieve 6CASE, select /Print File, and enter the print filename 6CASE.PRN. (If the file 6CASE.PRN already existed, you would be able to select it from the list of PRN files and be asked if you wanted to Replace or Cancel.) Specify the print range as A16..E36 and select Options Other Unformatted Quit Align Go Quit. When you leave the Print menu, the drive light should indicate activity, as the file 6CASE.PRN is written on the disk. Select /System and enter DIR B:*.PRN to see a list of all the .PRN files on the disk. Enter TYPE B:6CASE.PRN to see the text file displayed on the screen. This file can now be used in a word-processing package. Using the Unformatted option in the Print menu eliminates formatting codes, such as page breaks and margins, that could cause problems for the program that will try to read the file. Enter EXIT to return to Lotus.

If the values in the worksheet change, a new copy of the file must be printed and imported into the word-processing document or other file, or the file must be edited to incorporate the same changes that were made in the worksheet file. While not technically complex, this process is tedious and prone to errors of omission (forgetting to update one or more of the files), especially when it is done under time constraints. The next step in integrated software is to allow the Lotus file and the word-processing file to be linked so that a change in the Lotus worksheet will automatically update values in the word-processing document. This capability is currently available in integrated software packages such as Symphony, Framework, and Works.

## Translate (from the Lotus Access Menu)

If you want to import files from any one of a number of popular PC application packages, Lotus may be able to translate the file for you. Translate is found in the Lotus Access menu, along with PrintGraph. Translate is not available in the Student Edition of Lotus 1-2-3. Consult your Lotus manual for information on using Translate with version 1. Translate is a set of utility programs for translating or converting files among common PC software formats, including Lotus.

The hospital's list of fees is an example of the type of file that might be exported to a database-management system (DBMS). The files that are exported to a DBMS must be in the form required by the package they are being exported to. In general, transaction files (such as sales) or reference files (such as price lists) are usually good candidates for exporting to a database. Although you could create a .PRN file with Lotus and then import that file into dBASE, it is much easier to use Translate to create a file in a format that can be directly read by dBASE.

Return to the Lotus Access menu by selecting /Quit Yes and select Translate. (If you entered Lotus using the command 123 instead of LOTUS, reenter Lotus by entering LOTUS at the DOS prompt. The first menu will be the Access menu.) When the Translate utility screen shown in Figure 6.5 appears, select translate **FROM 1-2-3, release 2** (or the version you are working with) and then select translate **TO dBASE III.**

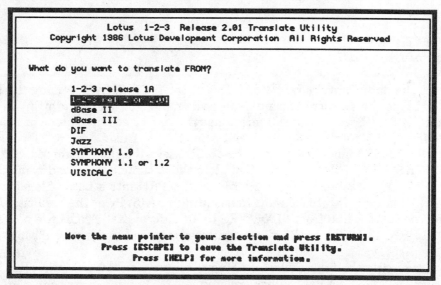

**Figure 6.5 Translate utility screen**

The next set of instructions tells you what the file can and must contain to be successfully translated from Lotus to dBASE. Read these instructions and follow the directions at the bottom of the screen. When you return to the Translate screen, read the directions at the bottom of the screen to see that you press [Esc] to edit the source-file specifications. If the source file lists a drive other than the one that contains your Lotus files, press [Esc] and change the source-file specifications to the correct drive. Select file 6FEE.WKS as the source file and press return to accept the suggestion of 6FEE.DBF as the name of the destination file. Select entire Worksheet and Yes to continue with the translation. When the translation is complete, press [Esc] to return to the first Translate screen. You can now continue to translate other files. When you are done translating files, press [Esc] and respond Yes when asked "Do you want to leave Translate?" You will be returned to the Lotus Access menu, from which you can exit to the DOS prompt or return to the worksheet.

## Chapter Review

This chapter has introduced you to numerous ways to transfer data among Lotus files and between Lotus and other application software. There is usually more than one way to accomplish any transfer task. How you accomplish a specific data transfer task depends on which application software the data is being transferred to and from. With practice, you will find acceptable ways to transfer data among the application software you use frequently. If a specific type of data will need to be transferred many times, it is useful to develop standard data transfer procedures to ensure the consistency of the results. It is even more efficient and effective to automate the task with macros or programs. Part III will introduce you to dBASE, a powerful DBMS from which data is frequently transferred to Lotus 1-2-3.

## Practice Exercises

Exercise 6-1

**Filename: 6EX1.WKS**
(Continuation of Exercise 5-1)

1. Extract the data from the range A21..E39 of the file 6EX1.WKS using the Formulas option. Place the extracted formulas in a file named 6-FXF-1 and print the worksheet 6-FKF using the cell formulas option. Extract the values of range G51..K61 to a file named 6-FXV-1 and print 6-FXV-1 using the cell formulas option.
2. Open 6EX1A and place the cursor at A45. Retrieve the range named COMP from file 6EX1.WKS using /File Combine. Complete the documentation and print the report.
3. With a blank worksheet, import the file 6EX1B.PRN into a Lotus file as text and parse the long labels into columns to be output at A15. Print the resulting Lotus file.
4. Output cells A43..E50 from 6EX1.WKS to an unformatted ASCII file named 6EX1C.PRN. Print the file on the computer screen and make a hard copy of the screen display.
5. If you are using the full version of Lotus 1-2-3 (version 2.0 or higher) use Translate to convert the file 6-FXV-1 that you created in part 1 of this exercise to a dBASE III PLUS format. To prepare the file for translation, delete rows 1-6, and insert a new first row of labels that conform to dBASE requirements (YEAR, COST, SAVINGS, NET, CUM).
6. If you are using the full version of Lotus 1-2-3 (version 2.0 or higher) use Translate to convert the file (6EX1D from dBASE to Lotus 1-2-3. Print the resulting Lotus 1-2-3 file.

**Reminders**

1. /File Retrieve 6EX1.WKS and /File Xtract Formulas 6-FXF-1 A21..E39. /File Retrieve 6-FXF-1 /Print Printer Range [Esc] [Home] A1..E19 Options Other Cell-Formulas Quit Align Go Page Quit. Follow similar steps for values.

2. /File Retrieve 6EX1A.WKS [F5] A45 and /File Combine Add Named/Specified-Range COMP 6EX1.WKS.
3. /File Import Text 6EX1B.PRN and move to A6: /Data Parse Format-Line Create Input-Column A6..A11 Output-Range A15 Go.
4. /Print /File 6EX1.PRN Range A43..E50 Go Quit /System TYPE B: 6EX1.PRN. Exit to return to Lotus.
5. /File Retrieve 6-FXV-1. /Worksheet Delete Row A1..A6 /Worksheet Insert Row A1..A1. Enter column headings and save with /File Save Replace /Quit Yes Translate FROM? 1-2-3, release 2 TO? dBase III. Press [Esc] and change the drive to the one that contains the files to be translated. Select 6-FXV-1 and accept the default destination name. Translate the entire worksheet and proceed with translation.
6. Translate FROM? dBase III TO? 1-2-3, release 2, file 6EX1D, accept default destination.

Exercise 6-2

**Filename: 6EX2.WKS**
(Continuation of Exercise 5-2)

1. Extract the data values from the range A21..G45 of the file 6EX2.WKS. Place the extracted formulas in a file named 6-FXF-2.WKS and print the cell formulas. Extract the values of range A49..G63 to a file named 6-FXV-2.WKS and print 6-FXV-2 using the cell formulas option.
2. Retrieve 6EX2A, and /File Combine add, the range named TOTAL FIXED into cell B36 and the range named DATE into cell A36, from 6EX2.WKS. Complete the documentation and print the report.
3. Import the file 6EX2B.PRN into an empty Lotus file as text and parse the long labels into columns to be output at A15. Document and print the import file.
4. Create a printable file from 6EX2.WKS with cells A67..G78. Print the file on the computer screen and make a hard copy of the screen display.

**Reminders**

1. /File Retrieve 6EX2.WKS and /File Xtract Formulas 6-FXF-2 A21..G45 /File Retrieve 6-FXF-2 /Print Printer Range A1..G25. Options Other Cell-Formulas Quit Align Go Page Quit. Follow similar steps to extract and print values.
2. /File Retrieve move to cell B36 and /File Combine Add Named/Specified-Range TOTAL FIXED 6EX2.WKS. Move to A36 and /File Combine Copy Named /Specified Range DATE 6EX2.WKS.
3. /File Import 6EX2B.PRN and move to A2: /Data Parse Format-Line Create Input-Column A2..A7 Output-Range A10 Go.
4. /Print File 6EX2.PRN Range A67..G78 Go Quit /System TYPE B: 6EX2.PRN.

Exercise 6-3

**Filename: 6EX3.WKS**
(Continuation of Exercise 5-3)

1. Extract the formulas of range A7..E44 from the file 6EX3.WKS. Place the extracted data in 6-FXF-3.WKS and print the cell formulas. Follow similar procedures to extract the values of range A63..E71 to 6-FXV-3.WKS and print the cell formulas.

2. Using 6EX3A, retrieve with /File Combine, from the file 6EX3.WKS, the range named TOTAL COST for cell address B31. Complete the documentation for the long-range development plan and print the report.
3. Import the file 6EX3B.PRN into a Lotus file as text and parse the long labels into columns to be output at A10. Document and print the import file.
4. Create a printable file from 6EX3.WKS with cells A47..E61. Print the file on the computer screen and make a hard copy of the screen display.


Exercise 6-4

**Filename: 6EX4.WKS**
(Continuation of Exercise 5-4)

1. From the file 6EX4.WKS, extract the formulas of range A5..J28. Place the extracted formulas in 6-FXF-4.WKS and print the cell formulas. Follow similar procedures to extract the values of range A47..J57 to 6-FXV-4.WKS and print the cell formulas.
2. Using 6EX4A, retrieve with /File Combine, from the file 6EX4.WKS, the range named HEADING for A24 and PROJECT2 for B38. Complete the documentation and print the report.
3. Import the file 6EX4B.PRN into a Lotus file as text and parse the long labels into columns to be output at A12. Document and print the import file.
4. Create a printable file from 6EX4.WKS with cells A17..J27. Print the file on the computer screen and make a hard copy of the screen display.

# PART III: dBASE III PLUS

dBASE III PLUS is the most widely used relational database software for IBM-compatible microcomputers. The next four chapters will instruct you on the use of dBASE III PLUS to improve your efficiency as an accountant. You will learn to create, modify, display, and list the records of a database.

The use of database management systems (DBMS) software is growing among accountants and managers. It allows users to meet many of their needs for ad hoc reports without waiting for the IS department to provide them. DBMS software is also used to develop transactions processing systems for small businesses, and for departmental computing. It is increasingly important for accountants to be able to work with a DBMS. dBASE III PLUS is the most widely used relational DBMS for IBM compatible microcomputers.

Unlike a spreadsheet, a DBMS requires the user to specify the structure of the data files before any data can be entered. Chapter 7 covers creating dBASE data file structures, entering data, changing data and saving data. It will show you how to create and populate a database using dBASE. Chapter 8 covers retrieving data to assist in decision making; Chapter 9 organizes data for reporting and programming; and Chapter 10 describes the linking of multiple files to develop an accounting system.

Part III should provide you with a solid foundation of dBASE skills, and an understanding of the sorts of tasks for which a DBMS is appropriate. Although this book could not cover all aspects and features of dBASE, it will provide you with a level of knowledge sufficient to use dBASE to perform many tasks. As your needs outgrow your current level of knowledge, you should be able to continue your learning process by using reference manuals and other resources.

# Chapter 7: Getting Started with dBASE III PLUS

**Database management systems** (DBMS) are as important to accounting as electronic spreadsheets, even though spreadsheets are the most popular end-user software for mathematical modeling and analysis. Accountants are very involved in designing and auditing **transaction-processing systems** (TPS), which gather, record, and store the basic daily accounting transactions of an organization. A **fourth-generation language** (4GL) is a computer language that contains, among other things, a DBMS, a programming language, a natural language interface or query language, and a report generator. dBASE contains all of these. With increasing frequency, information systems (IS) professionals use 4GLs to program transaction processing and other systems, instead of using a procedural language such as COBOL. Managers and accountants are beginning to use 4GLs to answer ad hoc queries and to generate special reports.

## Case Setting

Argon County Hospital has many patients, each of whom can have multiple charges for each day. The seasonal overload typically results in the manual billing process falling far behind in getting bills out and in mischarging several patients. To remedy this situation, the controller is considering using a DBMS to automate the billing process. The controller and others in the hospital are so pleased with the usefulness of Lotus that you have been asked to investigate a specific DBMS, dBASE III PLUS.

To investigate using dBASE for a new application, you would typically use only a sample of the actual data. The data file for billings would have to contain information on the charges for each item provided to each patient on each day. The billing clerk was delighted to provide you with a sample of the billing data on two patients for two days, with four different types of items, as shown below.

| Patient Number | Item | Amount Charged | Charge Date | Bill |
|---|---|---|---|---|
| 1111 | Room | 100.00 | 01/01/90 | Y |
| 1111 | DrFee | 75.50 | 01/01/90 | Y |
| 1111 | Drugs | 15.25 | 01/01/90 | Y |
| 1111 | Room | 100.00 | 01/02/90 | N |
| 1111 | Other | 45.00 | 01/02/90 | N |
| 1234 | Drugs | 25.95 | 01/02/90 | N |
| 1234 | Other | 25.00 | 01/02/90 | N |

The first step in automating the billing process using dBASE is to create a file structure, enter the sample data, correct the data, and save the file. Once the data are entered, they can be easily retrieved in many ways to support managerial decision making and control (Chapter 8 addresses using the data in this manner). Generating a specialized output form such as an invoice requires reorganizing the data and writing a program to display the data in the desired format (these topics are the subject of Chapter 9). Chapter 10 addresses using data from multiple files to add data from a patient master file to the invoice and transferring data among dBASE and other software. The combination of these activities is required to develop an automated transactions-processing and management information system.

## Starting dBASE

To start dBASE III PLUS, your computer must be at the operating system level (DOS prompt). If you are on a network or a PC with a hard drive that has dBASE on it, just enter DBASE at the DOS prompt or select dBASE from the menu, if your computer has one. If you are working with a computer system that requires you to load the program from a floppy disk, insert the dBASE System Disk 1 into the A drive. At the A> prompt, enter DBASE. (Remember that "enter" means to type the indicated characters and press ⏎.)

The first dBASE screen will be the copyright screen, which tells you to press ⏎ to assent to the agreement displayed on the screen and begin dBASE. When you press ⏎, you are entering into a software license agreement, or contract, with Ashton-Tate, and you are legally accountable for violations of that contract.

When you press ⏎, a second screen may appear with the instructions "Insert System Disk 2 and press ENTER" at the bottom of the screen. If it does, place the dBASE System Disk 2 in drive A and press ⏎. The next screen should be either the Assistant menu or a screen that tells you to "Type a command (or ASSIST) and press the ENTER key (⏎)." If you see the latter screen, enter ASSIST or press [F2]. The Assistant menu displays a series of options at the top of the screen (Figure 7.1).

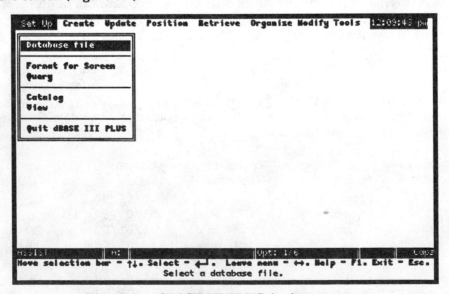

**Figure 7.1  dBASE III PLUS Assistant menu**

# Screen Tour

This section explains how to interact with dBASE, the meaning of the messages on the Assistant screen, how to enter commands, and how to get help. Each area of the screen tells you something about what dBASE is doing and the status of your work.

## Giving dBASE Instructions

There are three ways you can tell dBASE III PLUS what to do: use the **Assistant**, type commands at the **dot prompt**, and run **programs**. The Assistant, or **Assist menu**, is the dBASE menu system, similar to the Command menu of Lotus 1-2-3. The advantages of menus are that new users can quickly learn to use the software without learning an entire command language and that programming experience is not necessary to use the software. It is the most user-friendly way of interacting with dBASE.

The Assistant is emphasized in the following chapters. [Esc] is used to leave the Assistant and get to the dot prompt. Since it is easy to accidentally press [Esc] one extra time when backing out of commands, you will sometimes find yourself at the dot prompt when you do not want to be there. To return to the Assistant from the dot prompt, type ASSIST or press [F2]. Press [Esc] now to leave the Assistant and go to the dot prompt.

The **dot prompt**, which is a period (.) displayed in the lower left corner of the screen, indicates that dBASE is ready for you to enter a command by typing instructions and pressing ↵. This requires you to learn the dBASE language and rules. Whenever you issue a command using the Assistant, the equivalent dot prompt command is automatically displayed on the screen. Many features of dBASE are not available through the Assistant, and the dot prompt commands must be used to access those features.

Using a **program** requires you to create a file that contains a series of dBASE commands, which can then be run by entering only one command at the dot prompt. This is similar to Lotus macros or to using a programming language such as BASIC. The advantages of programming, once the program has been written and debugged, are speed and accuracy. The cost is that in order to write programs you must understand both programming and the dBASE language. Any dBASE command that can be entered at the dot prompt can also be included in a dBASE program. (Programs are introduced in Chapter 9.)

A relatively painless way to learn the dBASE command language is to watch the Action line at the lower left corner of the screen, where dBASE displays the dot prompt command equivalent of the Assist menu command sequence you enter. The only problem with this is that sometimes the last part of the command is not visible, because it executes too quickly after the last Assist menu selection is made. Now, press [F2] or type ASSIST ↵ to return to the Assistant.

## Using [Esc]

As in Lotus, [Esc] is used to back out of unwanted commands, so it is still generally a good rule to press [Esc] when you are in trouble. However, dBASE may require a different key to be pressed to recover from certain types of errors. If errors occur, dBASE will tell you what to do, so *read your screen carefully*. When you are entering or editing data, [Esc] will terminate editing without saving your changes. Users sometimes press [Esc] instead of the proper dBASE sequence of [Ctrl] [End] to save changes and are surprised when the changes they have made are not saved.

## Assistant Messages and Commands

The **status bar** (in reverse video near the bottom of the screen) displays the current mode (ASSIST), the current disk drive (A:), the database file in use (blank, since none is in use), the current database record or menu option in use (Opt: 1/6), and whether Insert mode (Ins), and Caps Lock (Caps) are on. The **navigation line** (just below the status bar) reminds you how to move between menus and submenu options. The **message line** (at the very bottom of the screen) displays a brief explanation of what the highlighted menu option will do if selected. A *clock* is displayed in the upper right corner of the screen.

The Assist menu lists a number of options across the top of the screen, somewhat like the Lotus Command menu. However, the dBASE **submenus** pull down vertically below the highlighted command, instead of being displayed horizontally one line below it. As you move to different options, notice that some subcommands (**Set Up** and **Create**) are brighter than others (**Update** and **Position**). The commands that are dimmer are not available until a database file is in use. They cannot be highlighted using the arrow keys because you have not yet told dBASE to make a new database file or to use an existing one.

You select an option from the menu by using the directional arrows or by typing the first letter of the option to highlight it. Only the Main menu options can be accessed by typing the first letter; pulldown commands must be accessed with the arrow keys. After you select highlighted commands by pressing ↵, additional submenus are often be displayed at the sides of the pulldown menus.

One of the first things to do in a dBASE session is to set the default drive as the one with your Student Data Disk in it. Enter your first command by highlighting **Tools Set Drive** and pressing ↵. Notice what is happening on the **action line** immediately above the status bar. The action line displays the dot prompt command generated by your Assist menu selections, which is SET DEFAULT TO. (See Figure 7.2.)

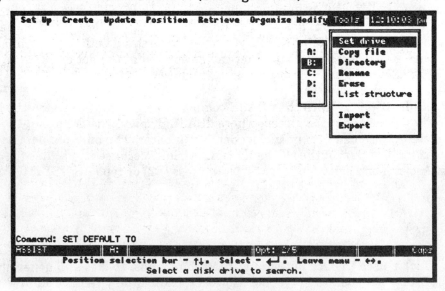

**Figure 7.2 Setting the default drive**

Watch the action line to learn the dot prompt commands when you enter Assistant commands from the menus. Next, use the arrow keys to highlight the drive that contains your data disk and press ↵. The drive you select appears in the second section of the status line. We will use drive B, so <B:> appears in the second section of the status line. If you are working on a computer with a single floppy drive, you may need to use the A drive instead. The drive you selected is now the default drive, where dBASE will look for and save files, unless you explicitly instruct it to use a different drive.

## F Keys and Help

The only function key that works from anywhere in dBASE is [F1], the **help** key. Get help with any item on the Assist menu by highlighting the item and pressing [F1] for context-sensitive help. If you make a mistake entering a command at the dot prompt, dBASE offers you help. Responding to the dBASE prompt "Do you want some help? (Y/N)" with Y displays a screen explaining the correct use of the command. If a dot prompt command does not work, look for the question mark (?) above the action line. The question mark is placed above the location where dBASE thinks the problem is. One common mistake new users often make is to enter a hyphen (-) instead of an underline (_) character in a field name. Misspellings, typos, and punctuation are other common errors. You can also get help at the dot prompt by entering HELP or pressing [F1].

Unlike Lotus, dBASE lets you control what the function keys [F2] through [F10] do. These function keys can be used only when you are at the dot prompt. The [F1] cannot be reset to anything other than Help. Using [F2] returns you to the Assistant from the dot prompt.

Use [Esc] to get to the dot prompt and enter DISPLAY STATUS. The first screen you see indicates that the default disk drive is A:. It also provides information about the files in use, if any files are active. Press any key to continue, as instructed, to see the settings of the dBASE options and the commands that the function keys [F2] through [F10] will enter. [F6] is usually set to Display Status. Press [F6] now to see that it does exactly the same thing that entering DISPLAY STATUS would do.

# Developing a New Data File

A relational database is a set of files, each consisting of a series of **records** (rows) and **fields** (columns). In the data file you are about to create, each record represents an individual charge to a patient, and each field represents a piece of information about the charge. In relational database terminology, the files are referred to as **tables**, the records as **entities**, and the fields as **attributes**.

Before creating a database, you must determine what data are needed. Design begins with consideration of the information outputs the system will produce, which determines what data must be included. Each patient's bill must include the patient identification number, the item being charged, the amount of the charge, the date of the charge, and if the patient has been billed for the service.

## Creating a Data File Structure

To create a dBASE file, you must specify the filename, the name, type, width, and number of decimals of each field for the structure. dBASE filenames must be legitimate DOS filenames. They will automatically be given a .DBF file extension by dBASE. A file **structure** in dBASE consists of the field names, the field types, the maximum number of characters (field width), and the number of decimal places each field can contain. Field names are restricted to 10 characters, and can contain only the letters A through Z, numbers 0 through 9, and the underscore (_). dBASE increases data-entry accuracy by accepting only the specified type and number of characters allowed for a field. The characteristics of the different types of data fields are as follows.

| Field | Description |
|---|---|
| Character | alphanumeric (number, letter, special character) |
| Date | any legitimate date, entered in MM/DD/YY format |
| Logical | Y (yes) or N (no); T (true) or F (false) |
| Memo | up to 4096 characters |
| Numeric | numbers and a decimal point (.) |

As a general rule, use a character field unless you need to calculate with the data, because character fields are the most flexible and easiest to manipulate and index. Use the minimum number of fields and field sizes for efficient storage and retrieval.

To create a new database file, select **Create Database file B:** and enter the filename CHARGES when prompted with "Enter the name of the file:" (Figure 7.3).

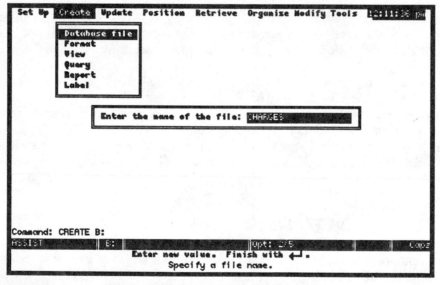

**Figure 7.3 Creating a database file**

The navigation line says "Enter new value. Finish with ↵". The message line displays "Specify a file name", which tells you that the new value to be entered should be a filename. dBASE provides a lot of help if you *read the screen*.

Pressing ↵ will take you to the Create screen, which is the first of several special dBASE screens you will use. See Figure 7.4 for an example of the Create screen after the field specifications have been entered. Several of the special screens display a **control panel** at the top of the screen. The control panel tells you how to move around the screen using various cursor-control keys; how to insert and delete characters, words, and fields; how to leave the CREATE process and save your work; or how to abort without saving your work. The control panel uses the caret (^) as a symbol for the [Ctrl] key, which is a fairly common convention. For example, ^End means press the [End] key while holding down the [Ctrl] key to save your material and return to the Assist menu. The status bar now indicates that you are in Create mode using drive B:, that CHARGES is the name of the file being created, and that the pointer is in field 1 of one.

You decided that the CHARGES file should contain the following fields:

| Data Description | Field Name | Type | Width | Dec |
|---|---|---|---|---|
| Patient ID number | PAT_NUM | Character | 4 | |
| Item being charged | ITEM | Character | 5 | |
| Amount of charge | AMT_CHARG | Numeric | 9 | 2 |
| Date of the charge | CHARG_DATE | Date | 8 | |
| Billed for service? | BILL | Logical | 1 | |

The navigation line tells you to enter the field name, and the message line reminds you what characters can be used in field names. Type in PAT_NUM and press ↵. The field name is displayed in uppercase even if you enter it in lowercase. The cursor moves to the Type area, where the default is Character. Press C or use ↵ to accept the default. Enter 4 in the Width area to complete the first field and move to the Field Name area for the second field. The area for the number of decimal places (Dec) is skipped because it is used only for numeric fields, and field 1 is Character.

Enter the second field the same way. Set the width of the third (numeric) field to 9 and Dec places to 2. The field width is set automatically to 8 if the field type is Date (field 4) and to 1 if the field is Logical (field 5). You will hear a beep and the cursor will jump to the next highlighted area when one area is filled (CHARG_DATE). When you are finished, if you entered the field specifications correctly, your screen should look like Figure 7.4. If you made a mistake, use the arrow keys to move to the incorrect field specification and edit or reenter the correct data.

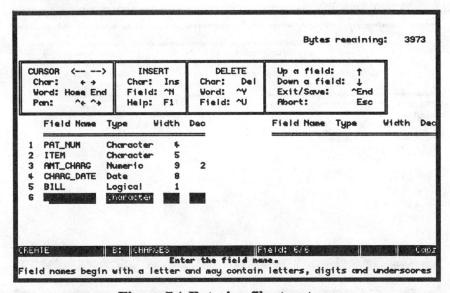

**Figure 7.4 Entering file structure**

Pressing ↵ at the beginning of an empty Field Name tells dBASE to exit from Create mode and to save the file structure. Holding down [Ctrl] and pressing [End] also tells dBASE to exit from Create mode and to save the file structure. You can use [Ctrl] [End] to exit and save with the cursor positioned anywhere on the screen.

After you have defined all five fields, exit from Create mode. Press ↵ instead of typing a field name in field 6. Any time you press ↵ at the beginning of an empty Field Name area, the message line prompts you to "Press ENTER to confirm. Any other key to resume." This prompt gives you another chance to continue entering field specifications, in case you accidentally issued the instructions to save and exit. Press ↵ now to confirm that you want to exit and save. dBASE puts the file structure information on the disk and asks if you want to "Input data records now? (Y/N)." Although you could enter data immediately, type N to return to the Assistant.

## Data Entry: Update APPEND

Any time you want to add records to an existing data file, select **Update Append** to get the Data Entry screen. The Data Entry screen looks like the one shown in Figure 7.5, except that there are no data in the highlighted field areas. The Data Entry screen also displays a control panel at the top of the screen. Below the control panel are the field names on the left followed by highlighted areas reflecting the width of each field and the location of the decimal point in numeric fields. The status line indicates that you are in APPEND mode, using drive B, and positioned at record None.

When you start entering data and reach the end of a field, dBASE beeps and sends you to the next field automatically. If the data does not fill the field, press ↵ to advance to the next field. When the last field of a record is completed, a new blank record is displayed. Numeric data are automatically right-justified. If the number has only zeros following the decimal point, they do not need to be typed, but will be inserted for you. While you are typing, the numbers start at the left edge of the field; they will right-justify when you press the decimal point or ↵. When entering dates, you must enter numbers in all six places reserved for the date characters. Put a zero (0) place holder before any year or month or day less than 10. Enter the data listed in the table on page 129. The Data Entry screen for the first record should look like Figure 7.5 before entering **Y** in the BILL field.

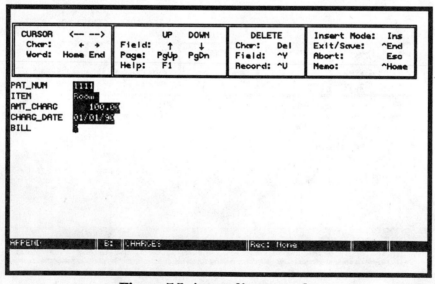

**Figure 7.5 Appending records**

After entering record 7, you come to a blank record. Press ↵ to leave APPEND mode and return to the Assistant. Any time you press ↵ at the beginning of a new blank record, dBASE assumes you have finished entering data and returns you to the Assist menu. If this happens by accident before you are done entering the data, select **Update Append** to continue adding records where you left off. Another way to leave Append is to use [Ctrl] [End] (hold down [Ctrl] and press [End]) to save your changes and leave dBASE. Pressing ↵ at the beginning of a blank data entry area and using [Ctrl] [End] are two common ways of leaving dBASE entry and editing screens, such as Append, Create, and Edit.

To add data on another patient, select **Update Append**. A blank record appears on the screen, with record number EOF/7. EOF stands for end of file and is the location immediately following the last data record in the file. Enter the two records below.

```
PAT_NUM      ITEM        AMT_CHARG     CHARG_DATE     BILL
2222         Room          100.00      01/02/90       N
2222         DrFee         125.00      01/02/90       N
```

Now that all the records have been entered, it is important that you check the accuracy of your work. A famous computing acronym is GIGO, which stands for "garbage in, garbage out." If incorrect data or instructions are entered, the output will also be incorrect. Computers can do the simplest types of error checking, such as making sure that only legitimate dates are entered in date fields, but human intelligence is still required to detect errors related to content, logic, and meaning.

In addition to checking for content errors, pay special attention to spelling, spacing, punctuation, and lower/upper case in checking your data entry. Correcting any errors now will save you grief later, when you are trying to retrieve data. If you try to find a record that contains the entry Room in the ITEM field, but you tell dBASE to look for ROOM in the ITEM field, dBASE will not find a match. There are functions that let dBASE find less exactly specified entries, but this requires more complex commands.

## Displaying Data (LIST)

Once data have been entered in the computer, they can be displayed on screen or printed on paper. A hard-copy printout can be used for control, to check accuracy, as an audit trail, for documentation and as one form of backup to the electronic media. Hard copy is also used to share or transfer information to other individuals, departments, or organizations for decision making and control.

dBASE has a number of ways of letting you see data, the simplest of which is **List**. Display the data you have entered on screen, so you can check its accuracy, by using **Retrieve List Execute the command N**. The equivalent dot prompt command is LIST. The data should appear on the screen as shown in Figure 7.6.

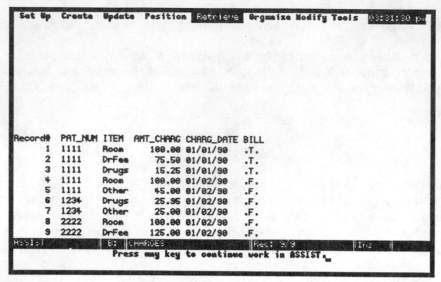

Set Up  Create  Update  Position  Retrieve  Organize  Modify  Tools          03:31:30 pm

| Record# | PAT_NUM | ITEM  | AMT_CHARG | CHARG_DATE | BILL |
|---------|---------|-------|-----------|------------|------|
| 1       | 1111    | Room  | 100.00    | 01/01/90   | .T.  |
| 2       | 1111    | DrFee | 75.50     | 01/01/90   | .T.  |
| 3       | 1111    | Drugs | 15.25     | 01/01/90   | .T.  |
| 4       | 1111    | Room  | 100.00    | 01/02/90   | .F.  |
| 5       | 1111    | Other | 45.00     | 01/02/90   | .F.  |
| 6       | 1234    | Drugs | 25.95     | 01/02/90   | .F.  |
| 7       | 1234    | Other | 25.00     | 01/02/90   | .F.  |
| 8       | 2222    | Room  | 100.00    | 01/02/90   | .F.  |
| 9       | 2222    | DrFee | 125.00    | 01/02/90   | .F.  |

Assist          B: CHARGES          Rec: 9/9          Ins

Press any key to continue work in ASSIST.

Figure 7.6 List records

The only difference between what you entered and the screen display is that dBASE stores and displays logical data as T/F rather than Y/N.

Printing a hard copy using **List** is the same as displaying data on screen, except for the final step of responding Y to the prompt "Direct the output to the printer? [Y/N]." If you have a printer available, print the data now by repeating the same command sequence and responding Y to the final question. The equivalent dot prompt command is LIST TO PRINT. The output from most other commands is sent to the printer in the same manner.

# Leaving dBASE (QUIT)

When you have finished your work in dBASE, it is important that you exit using the QUIT command to close all open files and save them. This is a good place to quit dBASE and take a break. Even if you plan to continue immediately, practice this process now by highlighting **Set Up**, moving the pointer to **Quit dBASE III PLUS**, and pressing ⏎. The equivalent dot prompt command is QUIT. This also saves all your work on the disk and returns you to the operating system level DOS prompt. Use DIR B:CH*.DBF at the DOS prompt to make sure the CHARGES.DBF file is on your disk. Reload dBASE when you are ready to continue.

# Using and Changing a Database

The purpose of creating computerized files and entering data in them is to be able to use and change those data more easily and efficiently than could be done in a manual system. dBASE makes it easy to access data, change data, and even to change the structure of the data file.

## Using an Existing Database (Set Up, USE)

Once a dBASE file is saved on disk, it can be opened for use by selecting **Set Up Database file**, selecting the drive containing the file (B:), and selecting the filename from the list of files (CHARGES.DBF). This is shown in Figure 7.7.

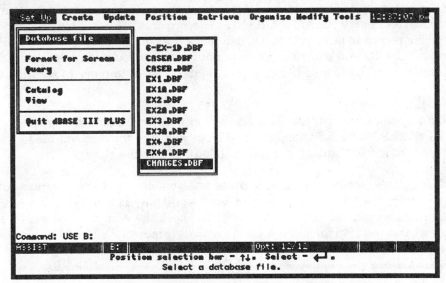

**Figure 7.7  Opening a database file**

As you enter the commands, the action line displays the dot prompt command as USE B: CHARGES. This means that if you were at the dot prompt (.), you would enter the command USE B: CHARGES to open the database. For now, respond to the question "Is the file indexed? (Y/N)" by typing N. dBASE appears to return to exactly where it was when you first loaded it. However, you can tell that the CHARGES.DBF file has been successfully prepared for use by the fact that the filename, CHARGES, is now displayed on the middle section of the status line.

## Moving the Record Pointer with Position Goto

The record pointer indicates the **current record**, much as the cell pointer indicates the active cell in Lotus. The current record number is displayed on the status line, along with the total number of records in the file. Since you just opened the data file, the record pointer is at the top, or beginning, of the file (BOF). The display Rec: 1/9 in the fourth block of the status line means that record number 1 is the current record and that there are a total of 9 records in the file.

You can move the record pointer to different records in the file by selecting **Position Goto Record**, followed by one of three options. Selecting the **BOTTOM** option moves the record pointer to the bottom of, or the last record in, the file. **TOP** moves the record pointer to the top, or the first record at the beginning, of the file. **RECORD**, followed by a record number, moves to the specified record.

Select **Position Goto Record RECORD** 4. Notice that the current position of the record pointer in the action line becomes 4/9. The dot prompt command would be GOTO 4. Use **Position Goto Record BOTTOM** to move you to the last record in the file, 9/9. The dot prompt command would be GOTO BOTTOM. Enter the command sequence again and select **TOP** to move the record pointer back to 1/9 at the beginning of the file.

## Editing (EDIT and BROWSE)

In checking the accuracy of the entered data against the relevant source documents, you found that the correct entry for AMT_CHARG in record 6 should be 22.95. Since you know the number of the record to be changed, you can move the pointer to it by selecting **Position Goto Record RECORD** and entering the record number 6. If you had not positioned the record pointer at record 6 before editing, you could use [PgDn] to move to record 6 in EDIT mode.

Correct the data by selecting **Update Edit** and edit or reenter the data to change AMT_CHARG to 22.95. The Edit mode screen looks just like the Append mode screen after data are entered. Exit from editing with [Ctrl] [End] to save the change.

Instead of viewing one record at a time, **Browse** lets you view and edit a screen full of records arranged in rows and columns. The Browse display is similar to an electronic spreadsheet, although you cannot use formulas. To check the edit you just made, select **Update Browse** and use [PgUp] to show all the records (Figure 7.8). Use either **Browse** or **Edit** to correct any other errors in the data.

```
┌─────────────────────────────────────────────────────────────────────────────┐
│ ┌──────────────────────┬────────────────────┬────────────────┬─────────────┐ │
│ │ CURSOR   <─── ───>    │        UP   DOWN   │ DELETE         │ Insert Mode: Ins │
│ │ Char:     ←    →      │ Record:  ↑     ↓   │ Char:    Del   │ Exit:      ^End │
│ │ Field: Home End       │ Page:  PgUp  PgDn  │ Field:   ^Y    │ Abort:      Esc │
│ │ Pan:       ^← ^→      │ Help:   F1         │ Record:  ^U    │ Set Options: ^Home │
│ └──────────────────────┴────────────────────┴────────────────┴─────────────┘ │
│ PAT_NUM ITEM- AMT_CHARG CHARG_DATE BILL                                       │
│ 1111    Room    100.00  01/01/90   N                                          │
│ 1111    DrFee    75.50  01/01/90   Y                                          │
│ 1111    Drugs    15.25  01/01/90   Y                                          │
│ 1111    Room    100.00  01/02/90   N                                          │
│ 1111    Other    45.00  01/02/90   N                                          │
│ 1234    Drugs    22.95  01/02/90   N                                          │
│ 1234    Other    25.00  01/02/90   N                                          │
│ 2222    Room    100.00  01/02/90   N                                          │
│ 2222    DrFee   125.00  01/02/90   N                                          │
│                                                                               │
│ BROWSE          │ B: │CHARGES           │Rec: 1/9                             │
│                            View and edit fields.                              │
└─────────────────────────────────────────────────────────────────────────────┘
```

**Figure 7.8 Browse**

## Removing Records (DELETE, PACK, RECALL, ZAP)

dBASE has a two-step sequence to remove records under **Update**. Records to be removed are first marked using the Delete command. This is a logical deletion only, because the record is marked with an asterisk (*) but is not yet physically deleted. The Pack command physically removes the marked records from the file.

In reviewing the data with the billing supervisor, you discovered that record number 5 (a charge of 45.00 on 01/02/90 to patient number 1111 for Other) was an incorrect charge and should be deleted. Go to record 5 and select **Update Delete Execute the command.** Records can also be marked for deletion using [Ctrl] U in either Browse or Edit mode. This works as a toggle, so using ^U a second time "unmarks" the record. (New dBASE users often accidentally enter blank records in their data files. If you have any blank records, delete them now.)

Records marked for deletion are indicated by an * next to the record number. One way to see which records are marked for deletion is to list or display all records on the screen and see which ones are marked. Of course, a hard copy makes this easier to view. In BROWSE and EDIT mode, Del is displayed in the lower right corner on the status line when the current record has been marked for deletion. It is a good idea to check to make sure only the proper records are marked before packing the data.

If a record has been marked for deletion but has not yet been physically deleted, the record can be undeleted with the RECALL command. If you want to undelete a record, move the record pointer to the record and issue the recall command with **Update Recall** or use the [Ctrl] U in EDIT or BROWSE mode.

Once you have satisfied yourself that only the records you want to delete are marked for deletion, select **Update Pack**. When dBASE has finished packing the file, list the records again. There should now be no records marked for deletion, and the file should contain fewer records than it did before you packed it.

The ZAP command erases all the records in the file. If you ever need to save the file structure but remove all records, use Zap. Be very careful using the ZAP and PACK commands. If these commands are used incorrectly, you may lose data you did not intend to delete.

## Saving  (USE)

Each time you select **Set Up Database file**, dBASE closes the currently open file by saving any changes on the disk and then opens the new file for use. Even if the same file is **SET UP**, dBASE will close and then reopen it. This is how to save the changes on the disk using dBASE. Entering USE at the dot prompt, not followed by a filename, closes the open file and saves it to disk. Entering USE CHARGES at the dot prompt *closes* CHARGES, *saves* it to disk, and *opens* it for use again. QUIT also closes and saves all open files before exiting dBASE.

Explicitly including a Save option on the Set Up menu would be more user friendly. The lack of this option is a weakness in the design of the dBASE III PLUS user interface. It is important for accountants to be able to evaluate the quality of the user interface, as well as internal controls and other aspects of systems design.

## Tools

The **Tools** menu provides the capability to perform several DOS commands (change the default drive and copy, list, rename, and erase files) and list the structure of an open file. It also lets you import data from and export data to another software package, PFS File. Transferring data to and from other types of software is covered in Chapter 10.

## DOS Commands

You have already used Tools to change the default drive. Selecting **Tools Directory B: .dbf Database Files** lists all the .DBF files on the B: drive. This is the same as using the command DIR B:*.DBF at the DOS prompt. If you are unsure what kind of file you are searching for, use a wild card (*) to display **All Files** on the disk. Select **Tools Directory B: .dbf Database Files** (Figure 7.9).

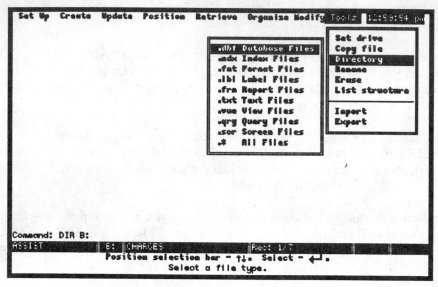

**Figure 7.9  Tools directory for listing files**

The **Copy file, Rename,** and **Erase** subcommands under **Tools** perform the same tasks that they do at the DOS prompt, but the dBASE Assistant provides additional prompts to tell you what to enter. Erase is the same as Delete.

**Copy file** is used to make backup files. Since a file cannot be copied while it is open, you must close a file you have been working with before you can copy it. [Esc] to the dot prompt, enter USE to close all files, and press [F2] to return to Assist. To make a backup copy with a different file name on the same disk, select **Tools Copy file B: CHARGES.DBF B: ,** and enter CHARGBAK.DBF when prompted. Use **Tools Directory** to see that the file named CHARGBAK.DBF is now on your disk. If the file name you are looking for does not appear on a file list, use [PgDn] to see additional file names. To make a backup copy with the same file name on a different disk, see Chapter 2.

## Listing File Structures

View the structure of the database in use by selecting **Tools List structure N.** The structure listing tells you the drive (B:) and the filename (CHARGES.DBF); the number of records (9); the date of the last update; the number, name, type, width, and decimals of each field; and the total width of the record. The total record width is one character more than the sum of the individual field widths, because dBASE uses one additional character to mark records for deletion, as will be discussed in Chapter 8. The date of the last update is the system date when the file was last saved. If the system date was incorrect, this date will also be wrong. After viewing the screen shown in Figure 7.10, press any key to return to the Assist menu.

```
Set Up  Create  Update  Position  Retrieve  Organize  Modify  Tools  04:03:05 PM




Structure for database: B:CHARGES.dbf
Number of data records:          8
Date of last update   : 01/01/90
Field  Field Name  Type      Width    Dec
    1   PAT_NUM     Character    4
    2   ITEM        Character    5
    3   AMT_CHARG   Numeric      9       2
    4   CHARG_DATE  Date         8
    5   BILL        Logical      1
** Total **                     28
ASSIST              E: CHARGES                Rec: 1/8
          Press any key to continue work in ASSIST._
```

Figure 7.10  List structure for CHARGES

## Changing File Structure (MODIFY)

You sometimes need to change the structure of a data file because a field is not large enough, additional data fields are needed, or a different field name is preferred. As the special assistant to the controller for the hospital, you asked for input on the design and contents of the database. Accounts Receivable suggested that a width of 10 was a better size for the AMT_CHARG field, to allow sufficient space for totals on reports. To implement the suggestion, select **Modify Database file**, and the same screen used to **Create** the initial file structure appears. Move down to field 3 (AMT_CHARG), use ↵ twice to move to the Width specification, and enter 10. To exit MODIFY STRUCTURE mode and save the changes, use [Ctrl] [End] ↵. A new field can be added by using [Ctrl] N, and a field can be deleted by using [Ctrl] U.

You cannot change both a field name and a field width in the same structure modification session. If you have both these types of changes to make, do one first, use [Ctrl] [End] to save the changes, and then use Modify Structure again to make the other set of changes. If you find you have to make many changes to your file structure, consult your dBASE manual for further information.

## Chapter Review

This chapter introduced the fundamental skills of using dBASE to create and enter data into a file structure. Unlike spreadsheets, the structure of a database file must be set before data can be entered. You should now be comfortable using the dBASE Assist menu, and have some idea of what the dot prompt commands are for the activities you have performed. You should be familiar with the Create, Browse, Edit, and Append mode screens and how to make and save changes using them. You know how to quit dBASE and reuse an existing data file when you enter dBASE with **Set Up**. Although you already know how to get a simple listing of all your data on the screen or printer, the next chapter will teach you how to get more sophisticated output from the data in a dBASE file.

# Practice Exercises

The practice exercises at the the ends of Chapters 7 through 10 are designed to improve your dBASE skills while reinforcing your knowledge and understanding of accounting systems and applications.

Reminders are provided for some of the exercises, to help you remember what kinds of things need to be done to complete the exercise. First try to complete the work without using the reminders. Your work environment usually will not provide reminders, so you don't want to become dependent on them. They are intended as a way to check your work and to help you learn.

Finally, be sure to capitalize, space, and punctuate the fields and data correctly. dBASE is case sensitive, and you will have problems if you are inconsistent or sloppy. If you need help, remember to consult the control panel and read the screen.

Exercise 7-1

The Darwin Department Store is developing a computerized cash receipts and accounts receivable system. Receipts of customer payments on account will be entered daily in a Cash Receipts transaction file.[1]

1. Create a Cash Receipts file that contains the customer account number, the date of the receipt, the check number, and the amount received. Name the file CASHREC.DBF and use the structure shown below.

| Field Name | Field Description | Field Contents | Width | Decimal Places |
|---|---|---|---|---|
| CUST | Customer number | 0001-2000 | 4 | |
| DATE_RECD | Date check recorded | Month/Day/Year | 8 | |
| CHECK | Check number used | 101-99999 | 5 | |
| AMOUNT | Amount of check | Dollars and Cents | 8 | 2 |

2. Enter the following data.

| CUST | DATE_RECD | CHECK | AMOUNT |
|---|---|---|---|
| 0023 | 02/01/90 | 4332 | 123.45 |
| 1076 | 02/01/90 | 11023 | 87.89 |
| 0155 | 02/01/90 | 766 | 236.78 |
| 0976 | 02/02/90 | 7867 | 63.61 |
| 0056 | 02/02/90 | 784 | 233.90 |

3. Print a hard copy of the file structure and a hard copy of the data.
4. Add the following records to CASHREC.DBF.

| | | | |
|---|---|---|---|
| 0076 | 02/02/90 | 434 | 333.33 |

---

[1] After Barry E. Cushing and Marshall B. Romney, *Accounting Information Systems*, Fifth Edition, Reading, MA: Addison-Wesley Publishing Company, 1990, 827–829.

    0467           02/02/90          567           66.66

5. Check the data, edit incorrect entries, and change the DATE_RECD of record 4 to 02/01/90 and CHECK of record 3 to 768. Print all records.
6. Make a copy of CASHREC.DBF named CASHREC2.DBF.
7. Add a new field, CREDIT, to the end of the file CASHREC2.DBF. Make the field Numeric, six characters wide, and no decimal places. Print a hard copy of the revised CASHREC2.DBF file structure and all records.
8. Mark records 2 and 5 in CASHREC2.DBF for deletion, physically remove the records from the file, and print the remaining records.

### Reminders

1. Select **Create Database file** to create CASHREC.DBF.
2. Use **Update Append** and enter data.
3. Select **Tools List Structure Y** and **Retrieve List Execute Y** to print.
4. Use **Update Append** to enter data.
5. Use **Update Browse** or **Edit** to change the data, then **Retrieve List Execute Y** to print.
6. First [Esc] to the dot prompt and enter USE to close CASHREC.DBF. Enter ASSIST or press [F2] to return to the Assistant and select **Tools Copy B:CASHREC.DBF B: CASHREC2.DBF.** (The dot prompt equivalent command is COPY FILE CASHREC.DBF TO CASHREC2.DBF.) You could also Quit dBASE and use the DOS command COPY CASHREC.DBF B: CASHREC2.DBF.
7. Open the new file with **Set Up Database file B:CASHREC2.DBF** N. Select **Modify Database file**, move to field 5, and enter the field name, type, width, and decimals. Select **Tools List Structure Y** and **Retrieve List Execute Y** to print.
8. Select **Update Browse** or **Edit** to mark records 2 and 5 with [Ctrl] U. Use **Retrieve List Execute** to check that correct records are marked, then **Update Pack** and **Retrieve List Execute Y** to print.

Exercise 7-2

The Moose Wings Co-operative Flight Club owns several airplanes and gliders. It serves less than 2,000 members, who are numbered sequentially from the founder, Tom Eagle (0001), to the newest member, Jacques Noveau (1368). Members rent the flying machines by the quarter hour, and all planes must be returned on the same day. The club wants to use a PC and dBASE to record usage and bill members weekly for the flights taken. For each flight taken, the following data are entered.[2]

---

2   After SMAC Examination in Barry E. Cushing and Marshall B. Romney, *Accounting Information Systems*, Fifth Edition, Reading, MA: Addison-Wesley Publishing Company, 1990, 561–562.

| Field Name | Field Description | Field Contents | Width | Decimal Places |
|---|---|---|---|---|
| MEMB | Member number | 0001-1368 | 4 | |
| DATE | Date of flight | Month/Day/Year | 8 | |
| PLANE | Plane used | G, C, P, or L* | 1 | |
| T_OFF | Time of takeoff | Hour Minute | 4 | |
| T_AIR | Time in the air | Hours | 5 | 2 |

*G = Glider; C = Cessna; P = Piper Cub; L = Lear

The following data contains a flight record for each plane on April 1, 1990.

| MEMBER NUMBER | DATE OF FLIGHT | PLANE USED | TIME OF TAKEOFF | TIME IN THE AIR |
|---|---|---|---|---|
| 1234 | 04/01/90 | C | 625 | 2.75 |
| 1111 | 04/10/90 | G | 943 | 6.00 |
| 1210 | 04/01/90 | P | 859 | 1.50 |
| 0023 | 04/01/90 | L | 1342 | 4.75 |

1. Create a database file named FLIGHTS.DBF with the structure shown above and enter the four records.
2. Print file structure and all records of FLIGHTS.DBF.
3. Add the following records.

| 0126 | 04/01/90 | C | 1229 | 0.75 |
|---|---|---|---|---|
| 0999 | 04/01/90 | P | 1401 | 1.25 |

4. Check the data, edit the incorrect entries, and change the T_AIR for record 3 and 6 to 1.75.
5. Make a copy of the FLIGHTS.DBF and name it FLIGHTS2.DBF.
6. Modify the file structure of FLIGHTS2.DBF by changing PLANE to PL and list the file structure and all records to get a hard-copy printout of FLIGHTS2.DBF.
7. Mark records 1 and 4 in FLIGHTS2.DBF for deletion, physically remove the records from the file, and print the remaining records.

## Reminders

1. **Create** a new **Database** file named FLIGHTS.DBF and enter the records using **Update Append.**
2. Select **Tools List Structure Y** and **Retrieve List Execute Y** to print.
3. Use **Update Append** to add more records.
4. Use **Update Edit** or **Browse** to correct records that have incorrect data (records 2, 3, and 6). **Retrieve List Y** will print the records.
5. First [Esc] to the dot prompt. Enter USE to close FLIGHTS.DBF. Enter ASSIST or press [F2]. Select **Tools Copy B:FLIGHTS2.DBF B: FLIGHTS2.DBF.**
6. Select **Set Up Database File** FLIGHTS2.DBF. **Modify Database file** and make the indicated change. Select **Tools List Structure Y** and **Retrieve List Execute Y** to print.
7. Select **Update Browse** or **Edit** to mark records 1 and 4 with [Ctrl] U. Use **Retrieve List Execute** to check that correct records are marked, then **Update Pack** and **Retrieve List Execute Y** to print.

Exercise 7-3

The Appalachian Manufacturing Company creates wood products using wood, glue, and stain in its production process. They would like to use their PC and dBASE to manage their raw materials inventory and have decided to start by creating a Raw Materials Inventory file with the following structure and sample data:

**Structure**

| Field Name | Field Type | Width | Decimal Places |
|---|---|---|---|
| CODE | C | 3 | |
| DESCRIPT | C | 13 | |
| U COST | N | 8 | 2 |
| QUAN | N | 6 | |
| UNIT | C | 4 | |
| UP_DATE | D | 8 | |

**Data**

| UNIT CODE | INVENTORY DESCRIPTION | UNIT COST | QUANTITY | UNIT OF MEASURE | LAST UP_DATE |
|---|---|---|---|---|---|
| WPA | Pine Grade A | 2.75 | 64 | BdFt | 09/07/90 |
| SLA | Stain Light | 4.27 | 23 | Qrt | 09/21/90 |
| WPB | Pine Grade B | 2.47 | 77 | BdFt | 09/14/90 |
| GWA | Wood Glue | 4.99 | 14 | Qrt | 09/21/90 |
| WOA | Oak Grade A | 3.80 | 151 | BdFt | 09/21/90 |

CODE consists of the product group (Wood, Stain, Glue), the type (Pine, Oak, Birch, Light, Medium, Dark), and the quality or grade (A = best, B = other).

1. Enter the structure and data in a file named PRODUCT.DBF.
2. Print the file structure and records of PRODUCT.DBF.
3. Add the following records to PRODUCT.DBF.

| SDA | Stain Dark | 4.38 | 9 | Qrt | 09/21/90 |
|---|---|---|---|---|---|
| WBA | Birch Grade A | 4.50 | 65 | BdFt | 09/21/90 |

4. Correct any data-entry errors and change the UP_DATE of record 6 to 08/31/90.
5. Make a copy of the PRODUCT.DBF and name it PRODUCT2.DBF.
6. Change the width of U_COST to six characters wide with two decimal places and print out a copy of the file structure for PRODUCT2.DBF with all records.
7. Mark records 2 and 7 in PRODUCT2.DBF for deletion, physically remove the records from the file, and print the remaining records.

Exercise 7-4

The R & D Consulting firm, which specializes in developing and installing accounting information systems, needs a database to track project times and costs and to compute salaries. Both full-time staff and part-time consultants may work on several projects each week. All hours for the week are posted on the last day of the week by employee number and project. Enter the following material in dBASE and provide the printouts requested.

1. Create JOB.DBF with the following suggested structure and sample data.

**Structure**

| Field Name | Field Type | Width | Decimal Places |
|------------|-----------|-------|----------------|
| EMPL | C | 3 | |
| P_RATE | N | 6 | 2 |
| PROJ | C | 4 | |
| P_PERIOD | D | 8 | |
| HRS | N | 2 | |
| END | L | 1 | |

**Data**

| EMPL | P_RATE | PROJ | P_PERIOD | HRS | END |
|------|--------|------|----------|-----|-----|
| 345 | 8.35 | 133 | 06/01/90 | 40 | N |
| 432 | 20.55 | 140 | 06/01/90 | 40 | Y |
| 654 | 15.65 | 140 | 06/01/90 | 40 | Y |
| 678 | 10.75 | 133 | 06/01/90 | 40 | N |
| 234 | 100.00 | 133 | 06/08/90 | 14 | N |

2. Print the file structure and records of JOB.DBF.
3. Add the following records

| | | | | | |
|------|--------|------|----------|-----|-----|
| 345 | 8.75 | 133 | 06/08/90 | 40 | N |
| 432 | 20.55 | 133 | 06/08/90 | 20 | N |

4. Check and correct the file with the following information:
   - Employee 345 got a raise to $8.75 per hour.
   - Project 140 was not finished.
5. Make a copy of the JOB.DBF and name it JOB2.DBF.
6. Modify the JOB2.DBF file structure by changing P_PERIOD to PAY_WEEK and print a copy of the structure and all records.
7. Mark records 4 and 5 in PRODUCT2.DBF for deletion, physically remove the records from the file, and print the remaining records.

# Chapter 8: Accessing Data with dBASE III PLUS

This chapter deals with retrieving, displaying, and manipulating the data that you learned how to enter in Chapter 7. Managers use programs like dBASE primarily to access and develop reports from the data on their operations without having to go through the IS department. Electronic searches and reorganization of data are much faster than equivalent manual operations and much more accurate if the search is specified correctly. Software such as dBASE lets users harness the power of a database without having to deal with how the computer physically stores and organizes data. The user needs to understand only the logical structure and contents of the database to use it effectively.

## Case Setting

Now that the patient charges have been entered in the data file, the controller has asked you to investigate how dBASE can be used to analyze the data. The controller is interested in listing the billings by item, date, patient, and amount. In addition, summary statistics such as the number of items, totals, and averages by subgroup would be useful. The file CASEA.DBF on the Student Data Disk is an expanded version of the CHARGES file from Chapter 7; it contains the 31 records shown in the table below.

| | | | | |
|---|---|---|---|---|
| 1234 | Room | 125.00 | 01/02/90 | F |
| 2222 | Room | 100.00 | 01/03/90 | F |
| 1111 | DrFee | 75.50 | 01/03/90 | F |
| 2234 | DrFee | 99.99 | 01/03/90 | F |
| 1111 | Room | 100.00 | 01/01/90 | T |
| 1111 | Drugs | 49.99 | 01/03/90 | F |
| 2222 | Other | 0.99 | 01/03/90 | F |
| 1234 | DrFee | 150.50 | 01/01/90 | T |
| 2222 | Drugs | 12.95 | 01/03/90 | F |
| 1111 | Drugs | 15.25 | 01/01/90 | T |
| 2234 | Room | 100.00 | 01/03/90 | F |
| 2222 | Room | 100.00 | 01/02/90 | F |
| 1234 | Drugs | 14.95 | 01/03/90 | F |
| 1111 | DrFee | 75.50 | 01/01/90 | T |
| 2234 | Other | 49.99 | 01/03/90 | F |
| 1234 | Room | 125.00 | 01/03/90 | F |
| 2222 | Other | 49.99 | 01/03/90 | F |
| 1234 | Drugs | 65.25 | 01/01/90 | T |
| 2222 | DrFee | 125.00 | 01/02/90 | F |
| 1111 | Other | 45.00 | 01/02/90 | F |

| 1234 | DrFee | 150.50 | 01/03/90 | F |
|------|-------|--------|----------|---|
| 1111 | Room  | 100.00 | 01/03/90 | F |
| 2222 | DrFee | 125.00 | 01/03/90 | F |
| 2234 | Drugs |  50.00 | 01/03/90 | F |
| 1234 | Room  | 125.00 | 01/01/90 | T |
| 1111 | Drugs |  50.01 | 01/03/90 | F |
| 2222 | Other |   0.05 | 01/03/90 | F |
| 1111 | Other |  50.00 | 01/03/90 | F |
| 2243 | Room  | 125.00 | 01/03/90 | F |
| 1234 | Drugs |  22.95 | 01/02/90 | F |
| 1111 | Room  | 100.00 | 01/02/90 | F |

# Displaying Selected Data Using Retrieve

In Chapter 7, you sent all the records in the data file to both the screen and the printer using **Retrieve List Execute the command**. Normally, users want to display or process only part of the data. One way this is done in dBASE is by specifying fields, search conditions, and scopes using subcommands of **Retrieve**.

The first level of subcommands of the Retrieve menu option determines the format for displaying records or the calculations to be performed. The first four **Retrieve** subcommands (**List, Display, Report,** and **Label**) display the record contents. The last three Retrieve subcommands (**Sum, Average,** and **Count**) calculate statistics for the records. Each Retrieve option can be applied to all records by immediately selecting **Execute the command** (hereafter, **Execute**).

Each Retrieve option can also be applied to a subset of the records or fields using the subcommands **Specify scope, Construct a field list, Build a search condition,** and **Build a scope condition**. Limiting the records processed in this manner lets you see only the information you need. "Information overload" comes from too much data being presented to a user. Both stress and time can be saved by limiting data listings, to let users concentrate on the information relevant to their decisions.

After you have selected an item on a dBASE submenu, it changes from high intensity to low intensity if it is no longer available for selection. dBASE turns off the options that can not be used. Available options are indicated with high intensity, and you can use the arrow keys to highlight them. Press the left or right arrow (← or →) to leave the active submenu when you are finished making selections from it.

To retrieve data, a file must have been opened with **Set Up** (from the Assistant) or **USE** (from the dot prompt). When you enter dBASE, first set the default drive with **Tools Set drive B:**, then open the data file with **Set Up Database file B: CASEA.DBF N**. Remember to watch the action line to learn the dot prompt commands.

## Displaying Data with LIST and DISPLAY

The List and Display subcommands of **Retrieve** both show the contents of records on the screen, but there are a few important differences between them. **List** provides the opportunity to send the listing to the printer as well as to the screen. **Display** sends output only to the computer screen; it cannot be sent to the printer using the Assist menu, although **Display** can send output to the printer using the dot prompt commands. The default scope for **List** is all records. When there are too many records to fit on one screen, **List** causes them to continue scrolling by without pausing. Use [Ctrl] S to stop the scrolling at any time; press any key to let it continue. After the listing is complete, press any key to return to the Assist menu. The default for **Display** is the current record instead of all records, so selecting **Retrieve Display Execute** displays only the single record at which the pointer is located.

## Specify Scope and Build a Scope Condition

**Specify scope** limits the number of records processed by reference to their position in the database. The options on the scope submenu are **ALL** the records; the **NEXT** specified number of records, including and following the current record; a specified **RECORD** number; and the **REST** of the records from the record pointer to the EOF. Selecting **Retrieve Display Specify scope ALL Execute** results in one full screen of records and a prompt that tells you to "Press any key to continue...." **Display** pauses after each screen of records for easier viewing.

It is common to want to view only the first few or next several records in a file. To view only the first 10 records, move to the **TOP** (beginning) of the file and select **Retrieve List Specify scope NEXT 10 Execute N** (Figure 8.1). The dot prompt command is LIST NEXT 10. The first 10 records are now displayed on the screen with field names across the top of the records.

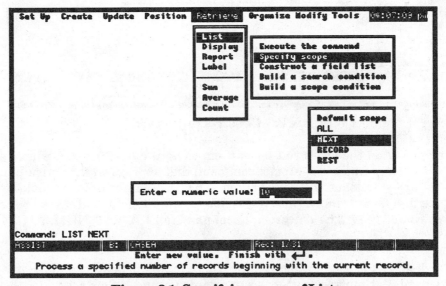

Figure 8.1  Specifying scope of List

When you return to the Assist menu, notice that the record pointer is on record 10 of 31. The records listed with NEXT begin with the current record. To see this, select **Retrieve List Specify scope NEXT 5 Execute N**. Records 10 through 14 are displayed. To display records 11 through 15, move to record 11 using **Position Goto record RECORD 11**, then issue the command to list the next five records. You could also move among records in EDIT or BROWSE mode.

**Build a scope condition** is used to construct a command containing WHILE, so that records are listed or processed only as long as the specified condition is met. The combinations of logical conditions available for use with **Build a scope condition** are the same as those available with **Build a search condition**, as discussed below. **Build a scope condition** (WHILE) is most useful when the records are organized in a logical order and is primarily used in programming. These topics are covered in the next chapter.

## Construct a Field List

**Retrieve List Execute** displays all fields of all records in order of record number. To display only selected fields and to change the order in which fields are listed, select **Construct a field list** from the Retrieve List submenu. dBASE displays a menu of the field names for you to select from. Use the arrow keys to move to the desired field and press ↵ to select the field for display. To show only patient numbers, amounts charged, and items, in that order, select PAT_NUM, then move to AMT_CHARG and select it. Finally, move to ITEM (Figure 8.2) and select it.

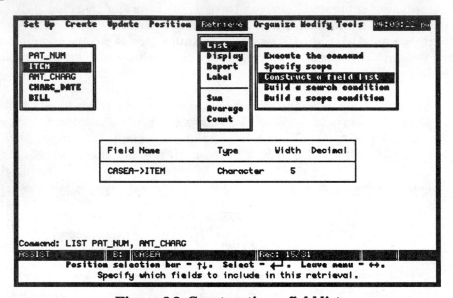

**Figure 8.2  Constructing a field list**

Fields are displayed in the order you select them using the Assist menu, which is also the order they are entered in the dot prompt command that appears on the action line. Press a side arrow (← or →) to leave the active submenu when you are finished making selections from it. Notice that **Construct a field list** is now in low intensity and cannot be selected again. Select **Execute N**. The dot prompt command is LIST PAT_NUM, AMT_CHARG, ITEM.

**Construct a field list** is useful when you want to print all the fields of a file that is too wide to print on one page. Dot-matrix printers wrap records around if they are wider than a page, making them difficult to read. Laser printers sometimes do not even wrap the records, they just don't print the fields that are beyond the right margin of the page. To print on two pages, use **List**, select those fields you want to be printed on the first page, and send them to the printer. Then use **List** again and select the fields you want to be printed on the second page and send them to the printer.

## Build a Search Condition (FOR)

Perhaps the most common way to limit data is to work with only those records that meet a specific condition. Unusually large or small amounts are often considered to be exceptions that warrant closer examination. They can be output in an exception report by using a condition that displays only the data less than or greater than a specified cutoff amount. It is also common to limit the records to those for a certain date, month, item, product line, salesperson, or similar condition. Any time an accountant or manager wants to focus on a logically defined subset of the data, a search condition is likely to be appropriate.

To make dBASE act only on the records that meet certain criteria, specify the conditions that the records must meet with **Build a search condition.** Criteria are specified by conditional expressions, which are combinations of field names or constants and logical operators. Multiple expressions can be combined using .AND. and .OR.

## Logical Operators

The dBASE logical operators specify a relationship between two items. This relationship is expressed with **< >** or **=** . Combinations of these logical operators can be created. For example, to list all charges greater than or equal to (>=) 125.00, select **Retrieve List Build a search condition AMT_CHARG** and dBASE will display the logical operators (Figure 8.3).

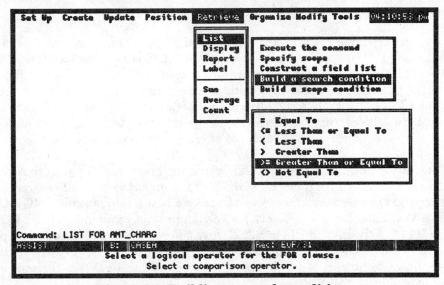

**Figure 8.3  Building a search condition**

Complete the search by selecting **>= 125 No more conditions Execute.** In the future, we will shorten **No more conditions** to **No more**, and we may also abbreviate other commands. Print the list and check to make sure that the numbers of the records listed are 1, 8, 16, 19, 19, 21, 21, 23, 25, and 29. All fields of the records that meet your criteria of charges of 125.00 or more should be displayed. The dot prompt command is LIST FOR AMT_CHARG >= 125.

Desk-check your data to make sure the output is accurate! The computer does exactly what you tell it to do. If the wrong commands or data are entered, the wrong information will come out (remember: GIGO!). Make it a habit to check your output for accuracy. No records with amounts less than 125.00 should be listed, but all records with amounts of 125.00 or more should be listed. If you are not sure about a search condition, create **test data** to determine whether the search is functioning properly.

List only the charges to patient 1111 by selecting **Retrieve List Build a search condition PAT_NUM = 1111 No more Execute.** Print the list and check to make sure record numbers 3, 5, 6, 10, 14, 20, 22, 26, 28, and 31 are listed. The dot prompt command is LIST FOR PAT_NUM='1111'.

## Using .AND. and .OR. to Combine Expressions

These logical operators become even more powerful when you combine search conditions using .AND. and .OR. After you select **Retrieve List Build a search condition** and enter a logical condition, **Combine with .AND.** and **Combine with .OR.** appear, along with the option for **No more conditions**. The combination of two logical expressions with .AND. is an exclusive relationship that decreases the number of records selected. The combination of two logical expressions with .OR. is an inclusive relationship that increases the number of records selected.

To list only the charges of 125 or more to patient 1111, select **Retrieve List Build search AMT_CHARG >= 125 .AND. Build search PAT_NUM = 1111 No more Execute**. Any record selected must have both a patient number of 1111 and a charge of 125 or more. The dot prompt command is LIST FOR AMT_CHARG >= 125 .AND. PAT_NUM = '1111'. The list should contain records 2, 9, 12, and 16.

List all the charges of 125 or more to any patient and all the charges to patient 1111 of any amount by selecting **Retrieve List Build search AMT_CHARG >= 125 .OR. Build search PAT_NUM = 1111 No more Execute**. Any record should be listed that meets either the criterion that the patient number is 1111 or that the amount charged is 125 or more. The dot prompt command is LIST FOR AMT_CHARG >= 125 .OR. PAT_NUM = '1111'. Check to make sure that only the correct records are listed by referring to the table on pages 149–150, and figuring out which records meet each set of criteria. There should be 11 records listed.

To list the records for patients 1111 and 2222, you must also use .OR., even though such a request often uses "and" in common English. What is meant is "list all the records that are for either patient 1111 or patient 2222." Select **Retrieve List Build search PAT_NUM = 1111 .OR. PAT_NUM = 2222. No more Execute**. The dot prompt command is LIST FOR PAT_NUM = '1111' .OR. PAT_NUM = '2222'. Any time you are trying to list or process more than one value (such as 1111 and 2222) for a single field (PAT_NUM), the connector must be .OR., because no record can have both values (1111 .AND. 2222) simultaneously. Eighteen records should be listed.

## Precedence and Parentheses

Multiple conditions can be quite complex, with many more than two criteria. To make sure they are executed as you wish, it is a good idea to use parentheses, just as you do in mathematical formulas, to ensure that the expressions are evaluated in the proper order. Parentheses can be entered only in dot prompt commands. For example, suppose you want to list just the doctors' fees for patients 1111 and 2222. You know that there must be an .OR. between the two patient numbers, so you won't be confused by that. However, selecting **Retrieve List Build search ITEM = DrFee .AND. PAT_NUM = 1111 .OR. PAT_NUM = 2222 No more Execute** will not result in the listing you want; it will contain the doctors' fees for patient 1111 and *all* items for patient 2222. If there are no parentheses, dBASE evaluates .AND. operators first, then .OR. operators. The dot prompt command was LIST FOR ITEM = 'DrFee' .AND. PAT_NUM = '1111' .OR. PAT_NUM = '2222'. Modifying this command slightly by adding strategically located parentheses so that it becomes LIST FOR ITEM = 'DrFee' .AND. (PAT_NUM = '1111' .OR. PAT_NUM = '2222') will give the desired listing.

Although the parentheses cannot be entered from the Assistant, the same results can be obtained by using the command sequence **Retrieve List Build search ITEM = DrFee .AND. PAT_NUM = 1111 .OR. ITEM = DrFee .AND. PAT_NUM = 2222 No more Execute**. This works because both sets of logical expressions connected by .AND. are evaluated first, and the results are combined using the .OR. only after all the .AND. combinations are evaluated. The results should be records 3, 14, 19, and 23.

If there are several criteria in a search condition, and both .AND. and .OR. are required, use parentheses to control the order of evaluation. If you are performing statistical calculations, it is a good idea to list the records using the same search condition, so you can visually verify and test that the selected records are the ones you intend to process. The preceding example illustrates how valuable it would be to automate (program) a complex command sequence once you have figured out what the correct command sequence is.

## Combining Several Modifiers Simultaneously

Several modifiers can be used together in a single command. The most common combination of modifiers limits both the fields and the records to be displayed. Frequently, this allows the data of interest to be displayed on a single page, rather than on the many pages that would be required if all the data were output. This combination uses **Construct a field list** to limit the number or fields shown and to **Build a search condition** to limit the records shown to those that meet the criteria of interest. Select **Retrieve List Build a search condition PAT_NUM = 1111 No more Construct a field list PAT_NUM AMT_CHARG ITEM → Execute N** to generate the list shown in Figure 8.4. The dot prompt command is LIST FOR PAT_NUM = '1111' PAT_NUM, AMT_CHARG, ITEM.

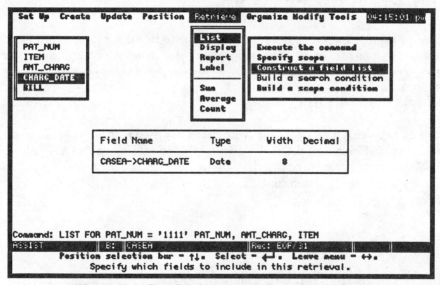

Figure 8.4 Combining a search and field list

## Statistics: Sum, Average, Count

Although the strength of a database is its ability to store, search, organize, and retrieve data, dBASE also has limited computational abilities, just as Lotus has limited data-management capabilities. dBASE has three arithmetic functions to sum, average, and count numerical data. To calculate the total for all charges, select **Retrieve Sum Execute**. The results displayed on the screen indicate that 31 records were summed and that the sum of the AMT_CHARG field is 2379.36. Selecting **Average Execute** indicates that 20 records were averaged and that the average of the AMT_CHARG field is 76.75. Selecting **Count**

**Execute** indicates that 31 records were counted. The equivalent dot prompt commands are SUM, AVERAGE, and COUNT. The results cannot be sent to the printer using the Assistant or TO PRINT at the dot prompt. Sum or average the numbers in your head or use a calculator to desk-check the dBASE calculations.

Any of the Scope, Search, and Field modifiers are used the same way they were applied to the List command. Select **Retrieve Average Build a search condition PAT_NUM = 1111 N Construct a field list** AMT_CHARG → **Execute**. The equivalent dot prompt command is AVERAGE AMT_CHARG FOR PAT_NUM = '1111'. The 10 records for patient number 1111 have an average amount charged of 66.12. It is not necessary to construct a field list if you want to **Sum** or **Average** all the numeric fields. **Construct a field list** is not available for use with **Count**.

# Dot Prompt Operations

You have already seen a number of situations where it is either convenient or necessary to use the dot prompt to enter dBASE commands. Although using the dot prompt requires that you remember dBASE commands and syntax, it provides power and flexibility. This section introduces a number of other useful dot prompt features.

# Using Dot Prompt Commands

There are a number of things it is necessary to know to use dot prompt commands effectively, as well as several tips that make using dot prompt commands easier.

### Command Abbreviations

It is necessary to type only the first four characters of any dot prompt command. For example, LOCA is sufficient for LOCATE, and ASSI is sufficient for ASSIST. This applies only to dBASE command words, not to field names, which must be spelled out completely. The dBASE command words (such as USE, FOR, WHILE, LIST, DISPLAY) cannot be used as field names.

### Reusing (↑) and Editing Dot Prompt Commands

It is possible to issue any Assist instruction with the dot prompt. In fact, several commands can be issued only from the dot prompt, such as the substring search. The dot prompt command level is more flexible and sometimes faster than the menu level, but it is not as user friendly when you are initially entering a command.

It is easy to reuse dot prompt commands. dBASE stores the last 20 commands in memory for you. (The number can be changed; the default is 20.) Recall prior commands, one at a time, by pressing ↑. Pressing the up arrow again continues to list each preceding command. The ↓ allows you to move back down through the sequence of commands. Once the desired command is displayed, you can edit it by using the arrow keys, [Del], [Ins], and [Backspace] and by typing in characters. Once the command is modified, press ↵ to tell dBASE to execute it.

It is sometimes convenient to use the Assistant to select field names and to structure the basic command, to escape to the dot prompt, to use ↑ to recall the command, and to edit it to add things that cannot be entered within Assist. This minimizes the need for remembering and typing field names, command syntax, and structure. The longer and more complex the command, the more useful this facility is.

## Quotation Marks Required for Characters

The dot prompt command to list the records for patient number 1111 is LIST FOR PAT_NUM = '1111'. Note that dot prompt commands require string or character values to be enclosed in single quotation marks (' '). The Assistant automatically enters the quotation marks for you in any Character field; at the dot prompt, you must type them in. Enter the dot prompt command, and the result should be the 10 records for patient number 1111 printed to the screen.

## Printing

Adding the phrase TO PRINT to any dot prompt LIST command and to many other commands sends the output to the printer. Use the last dot prompt command with the ↑ and edit it to read LIST FOR PAT_NUM = '1111' TO PRINT. The results of the LIST command have now been sent to the printer.

You can also use the command SET PRINT ON to cause everything (both commands and output) displayed on the screen to be sent to the printer. Everything will continue to be sent to the printer until you enter the command SET PRINT OFF. This can be a good way to keep a record of your work, but it will also generate a lot of garbage if you make many mistakes.

## ? (As Calculator and Data Display)

The ? makes a convenient calculator and a quick way to display the value of various fields of the current record. It asks dBASE to supply the value of the expression that follows it. If you enter ? 30*45 at the dot prompt, you are asking dBASE, "What is the product of 30 times 45?" dBASE answers by displaying 1350. Entering ? ITEM causes dBASE to respond by displaying the contents of the ITEM field of the current record. If dBASE is at EOF, there is no value to be displayed, so move to a different record to test the ? command.

## ! to Run DOS Commands from within dBASE

Entering an ! at the dot prompt, followed by a DOS command, executes that DOS command. Although there are also equivalents for several DOS commands in dBASE (as discussed under **Tools**), the ! lets you use many other DOS commands from within dBASE. Chapter 2 provides additional discussion of DOS commands. Enter ! DIR B:*.DBF to get a listing of all the database files on your Student Data Disk. If you get an error message instead of a directory listing, there is probably not a copy of DOS on your disk. If no copy of DOS is available, you will not be able to use the ! command.

## Expressions

In addition to displaying or performing calculations on the contents of single fields, dBASE allows you to display or process expressions. An **expression** is a data specification that can include fields, constants, memory variables, and functions. An expression is used in a command just as a field name would be. Expressions are used in subsequent chapters to construct index files and to display data in reports. A single field name is the simplest form of expression. Expressions cannot be included in lists through the Assistant; they must be entered from the dot prompt.

For example, it is possible to see how much would have been charged for each item if the amounts charged were 10% higher by using an expression that multiplies the current amount charged by 110%. The following procedures use the Assistant to develop the basic command structure and then edit the dot prompt command to include the expression. Press [F2] to return to the Assistant and go to the top of the file with **Position Goto Record TOP**. Select **Retrieve Display Specify scope NEXT 6 Construct a field list PAT_NUM AMT_CHARG ITEM** → **Execute N**. Then [Esc] to the dot prompt, press ↑ twice to display the GOTO TOP command, and press ↵ to execute it again. Press ↑ twice again to display the dot prompt command DISPLAY NEXT 6 PAT_NUM, AMT_CHARG, ITEM, which is the last command sequence you entered using the Assistant. Modify it slightly to add the expression by pressing [End] six times to position the cursor at the end of the command after ITEM, then enter a comma (,) followed by a space and the expression AMT_CHARG*1.1. The command and output are shown in Figure 8.5. The AMT_CHARG*1.1 column shows how much would have been charged if all charges were 10% higher.

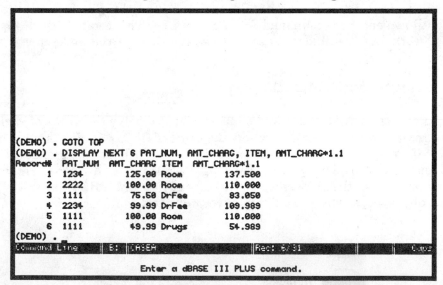

```
(DEMO) . GOTO TOP
(DEMO) . DISPLAY NEXT 6 PAT_NUM, AMT_CHARG, ITEM, AMT_CHARG*1.1
Record#  PAT_NUM  AMT_CHARG ITEM  AMT_CHARG*1.1
      1  1234       125.00 Room       137.500
      2  2222       100.00 Room       110.000
      3  1111        75.50 DrFee       83.050
      4  2234        99.99 DrFee      109.989
      5  1111       100.00 Room       110.000
      6  1111        49.99 Drugs       54.989
(DEMO) .
Command Line        E: CASEA              Rec: 6/31               Caps

                    Enter a dBASE III PLUS command.
```

**Figure 8.5  Displaying expression results**

## Using .NOT.

The .NOT. operator, which can be used only from the dot prompt, selects all records that do not meet the specified condition. Note that .NOT. is different from **Not equal to** (<>). Using the Assist menu, you can search only for an entry of T (True) in a Logical field. Return to the Assistant and select the command sequence **Retrieve List Build search BILL No more Execute** to list all records for which BILL contains .T.. The dot prompt command is LIST FOR BILL. You cannot search for an entry of F (False) in a Logical field using the Assist menu. However, from the dot prompt, all the .F. (False) entries can be listed by using LIST FOR .NOT. BILL. The .NOT. can also be applied to very complex combinations of logical conditions by enclosing the conditions within parentheses and putting .NOT. in front of the entire set. There is often more than one way to specify the same search condition. For example, the command LIST FOR PAT_NUM <> '1111' .AND. PAT_NUM <> '2222' does the same thing as the command LIST FOR .NOT. (PAT_NUM = '1111' .OR. PAT_NUM = '2222'). These commands result in a list that contains 13 records.

## Substring Search

If you can recall only part of the contents of the field you want to locate, the substring function uses a dollar sign ($) to search for the desired set of characters (string). To list the charges for items that contain the letters Dr, at the dot prompt enter LIST FOR 'Dr'$ITEM. This tells dBASE to list the records in which the characters Dr are found (next to each other and in that order) anywhere within the PAT_NUM field. This command should result in the 10 records for Drugs and DrFee. To list the records for all patient numbers that contain 23 (1234 and 2234), enter LIST FOR '23'$PAT_NUM. This type of search is useful if a state abbreviation is embedded in an address field or to search for all items that use a common unit of measurement (such as gallons) in an inventory listing.

## Functions

dBASE has many useful functions. They generally have the form FUNCTION(*arguments*), that is, the function name is followed immediately by parentheses that enclose the arguments. As with Lotus, different functions can contain different types and numbers of arguments. Some functions have no arguments. Although functions can be incorporated into some Assist commands, they are used most frequently with dot prompt commands and programs.

The UPPER(*character expression*) function can be useful if the contents of fields might be in lowercase, uppercase, or mixed case. The statement LIST FOR UPPER(ITEM) = 'DRFEE' results in a list of all records that contain DrFee in the ITEM field. Essentially, this command makes dBASE convert all the ITEM values to uppercase before it compares them to the search string expression. This is a way of getting around dBASE's sensitivity to upper- and lowercase letters. The LOWER(*character expression*) function works the same for lowercase. Other functions will be introduced as needed.

A good way to review the records marked for deletion involves the use of another dBASE function, DELETED(). The dot prompt command LIST FOR DELETED() causes only the records marked for deletion to be listed.

The CTOD(*character expression*) function converts a character string (C) to a date (D) value and the DTOC(*date expression*) function converts a date (D) value to a character string (C). These functions are important when constructing expressions that contain both a character and a date field. An expression can contain only data of the same type (numeric, character, date, or logical). Typically, date fields are converted to character strings to combine them with character data. To see this work, list the results of an expression that combines the item with the date of charge with LIST ITEM + DTOC(CHARG_DATE).

## Set Commands

A number of aspects of how dBASE operates can be controlled by Set commands. An existing index file can be put into use (activated) by the command SET INDEX TO <*name of existing index file*>. (SET PRINT ON and SET PRINT OFF, which control whether output is sent to the printer or not, were discussed previously.)

Enter SET at the dot prompt to make the Set menu appear, which puts you in SET mode. There are seven headings in the Set menu:

| Heading | Meaning |
|---------|---------|
| OPTIONS | set various environment parameters |
| SCREEN | select characteristics of screen display |
| KEYS | reprogram the function keys |
| DISK | select default drive or search path |
| FILES | select Alternate, Format, or Index files |
| MARGIN | enter left margin or width for memo fields |
| DECIMALS | enter minimum number of decimal places |

For example, the Bell option determines whether dBASE will beep at you. Setting the History option ON is what makes dBASE remember and allow you to repeat dot prompt commands using the ↑.

Change the default drive to B: by selecting DISK and pressing ↵ until B is displayed, then use the arrow keys to move to a different menu item. This is the same as setting the default drive to B: by selecting **Tools Set drive B:**. The dot prompt equivalent is SET DEFAULT TO B, as you have already seen. Use [Esc] to leave the Set menu when you have finished changing settings.

You can issue any Set command from the dot prompt by typing the full command. Some extended options, such as changing the number of commands that History remembers, can be used only from the dot prompt. Since the defaults are chosen to be the most commonly used settings, you should need to change settings only occasionally. Settings can also be set automatically when you enter dBASE by using a CONFIG.DB file. See the dBASE manual or use the dBASE on-line Help facility for more information on how the Set commands work.

# Updating Data

Updating is the process of keeping data current by adding, removing, and changing data as necessary to keep them complete and accurate. Databases can quickly become large and unwieldy, because it is easy to add to them but difficult to remember to clean them out. Maintaining current, accurate, reliable data demands that you remove data that are no longer valid or current. It is also common to have systematic changes to data in databases, such as an across-the-board pay raise or price increase of 5%. Although it is possible to individually edit each record, it is also possible to systematically modify the values of many records at once.

## Positioning the Record Pointer: SKIP and LOCATE

The **Position** option is used to move the pointer around the data file, which is important when you are updating data. The **Goto Record** option is used to locate the top, the bottom, or a specific record, as discussed previously. **Skip** moves the record pointer forward or backward in the file from its current position. The distance and direction the record pointer moves is determined by the number (positive or negative) that follows **Skip**. Since the default for **Skip** is 1, to move to the next record, just enter SKIP at the dot prompt. In the Assistant, select **Position Skip** 1. To move forward five records at a time from your current location, the dot prompt command is SKIP 5, and the Assistant selection is **Position Skip** 5. To move back three records, use SKIP –3 or **Position Skip** –3.

**Position Locate** is used with the same type of logical search conditions that were used in the Retrieve menu. It finds the first record in the file that meets the specified criteria; the search always starts at the top of the file. **Continue** is used to find subsequent records that meet the conditions of the Locate command. **Locate Build Search PAT_NUM = 1234 No more Execute** moves the record pointer to the first occurrence of patient number 1234 (record 5). **Continue** moves you to record 6. The End of LOCATE scope message means dBASE has reached the last record in the file without finding another occurrence of a record that meets the specified criteria.

## Systematic Data Changes (REPLACE)

**Update Replace** can be used to make systematic changes to a data file. You need to indicate what field to replace, what it is to be replaced with, and in which records the field is to be replaced. If an item description is changed that affects many records, Replace would probably be used. It is also used when a numeric field is changed in some systematic way, such as a 10% across-the-board price increase.

The controller prefers the term Misc (for Miscellaneous), instead of Other, in the ITEM field. Select **Update Replace ITEM** Misc **Build Search ITEM** = Other. The dot prompt equivalent is REPLACE ITEM WITH 'Misc' FOR ITEM='Other'. A message tells you that five records were replaced. Remember, to check that a command will act on the set of records you want it to, use LIST first with the same modifiers to see that the displayed records are really the ones you want to replace.

## Chapter Review

This chapter has examined several basic tools for accessing and retrieving data that are stored in a dBASE data file. Commands such as LIST, DISPLAY COUNT, SUM, and AVERAGE are used by accountants and managers to answer ad hoc queries that require either record listings or summary statistics. Among the most important capabilities are those that allow selective display and processing of data by specifying the fields to be acted on, and the conditions or scope of the records to be displayed. Complex record specifications can be developed by combining several logical conditions, and data can be manipulated and combined using functions and numeric or character operators. The next chapter builds on these topics to address organizing data, generating reports, and writing programs using dBASE.

# Practice Exercises

To complete the following exercises, use the data that have already been entered for you. Access the data by retrieving the indicated files with the Assistant **Set Up** or dot prompt command USE. When answering the questions, write down the sequence of your commands and print your output where possible. Under reminders, the record numbers have been included to help check your answers. You can also check your answers by manually performing the required operations on the list of records provided with each exercise. Focus your attention on the process needed to derive the answers rather than the answers to the problems themselves.

Exercise 8-1

**Filename: EX1.DBF**
(Continuation of Exercise 7-1)

The Darwin Department Store needs to be able to answer several questions by querying the Cash Receipts data file. The Cash Receipts file (EX1.DBF), which contains the records listed below, is an expanded version of the CASHREC.DBF you created in Exercise 7-1.

| Record# | CUST | DATE_RECD | CHECK | AMOUNT |
|--------:|------|-----------|------:|-------:|
| 1 | 0023 | 02/01/90 | 4332 | 123.45 |
| 2 | 0576 | 02/01/90 | 11023 | 487.89 |
| 3 | 0155 | 02/01/90 | 766 | 236.78 |
| 4 | 0453 | 02/02/90 | 7867 | 452.91 |
| 5 | 0051 | 02/02/90 | 784 | 233.90 |
| 6 | 0076 | 02/05/90 | 433 | 137.83 |
| 7 | 0353 | 02/09/90 | 524 | 65.49 |
| 8 | 0105 | 02/14/90 | 109 | 32.65 |
| 9 | 0122 | 02/19/90 | 201 | 13.46 |
| 10 | 0431 | 02/22/90 | 394 | 46.79 |
| 11 | 0206 | 02/23/90 | 342 | 36.98 |
| 12 | 0096 | 02/23/90 | 651 | 22.67 |
| 13 | 0231 | 02/26/90 | 259 | 14.78 |
| 14 | 0353 | 02/26/90 | 577 | 38.24 |
| 15 | 0322 | 02/26/90 | 420 | 54.87 |
| 16 | 0354 | 02/26/90 | 625 | 89.23 |
| 17 | 0256 | 02/26/90 | 189 | 25.89 |
| 18 | 0048 | 02/27/90 | 369 | 48.15 |
| 19 | 0004 | 02/27/90 | 227 | 78.42 |
| 20 | 0061 | 02/27/90 | 159 | 26.59 |
| 21 | 0084 | 02/27/90 | 475 | 57.24 |
| 22 | 0604 | 02/27/90 | 852 | 19.48 |
| 23 | 0576 | 02/28/90 | 11184 | 598.54 |
| 24 | 0240 | 02/28/90 | 688 | 68.24 |
| 25 | 0051 | 02/28/90 | 803 | 168.75 |
| 26 | 0541 | 02/28/90 | 246 | 59.26 |
| 27 | 0076 | 02/28/90 | 452 | 84.37 |
| 28 | 0155 | 02/28/90 | 727 | 158.46 |
| 29 | 0023 | 02/28/90 | 4377 | 239.15 |

```
        30      0453    02/28/90            7951        581.08
```

1. List all records for payment received on 2/2/90.
2. Display the records with payments of more than $57.24 but less than or equal to $236.78.
3. List only the CUST and AMOUNT fields of the records with payments of $75 or less.
4. Average all transactions for the last three days of the month (2/26 to 2/28/90).
5. Count the number of records with payments less than $50.
6. Locate the date 2/27/90 and continue until all records have been located for that date.
7. Sum the receipts for the month.
8. Go to record 15 and list only CHECK for the next five records.
9. List records with a payment of less than $150 on 2/01 and 2/28.

## Reminders

1. USE EX1.DBF and LIST FOR DTOC(DATE_RECD) = '02/02/90' (2 records)
2. DISPLAY FOR AMOUNT > 57.24 .AND. AMOUNT <= 236.78 (12 records)
3. LIST CUST, AMOUNT FOR AMOUNT < 75 (16 records)
4. AVERAGE FOR DTOC(DATE_RECD) >= '02/26/90' .AND. DTOC(DATE_RECD) <= '02/28/90' (18 records, average 133.93)
5. COUNT FOR AMOUNT < 50 (11 records)
6. LOCATE FOR DTOC(DATE_RECD) >= '02/27/90' and CONTINUE (5 records)
7. SUM (4301.54)
8. GOTO 15 and LIST NEXT 5 CHECK
9. LIST FOR AMOUNT<150 .AND. (CTOD('02/01/90') =DATE_RECD .OR. CTOD('02/28/90') =DATE_RECD) (4 records)

Exercise 8-2

**Filename: EX2.DBF**
(Continuation of Exercise 7-2)

Moose Wings has now entered the corrected data listed below in file EX2.DBF. The club president would like you to use dBASE to get the following information from the data file.

| Record# | MEMB | DATE | PL | T_OFF | T_AIR |
|---|---|---|---|---|---|
| 1 | 1234 | 04/01/90 | C | 625 | 2.75 |
| 2 | 1111 | 04/01/90 | G | 943 | 6.00 |
| 3 | 1210 | 04/01/90 | P | 859 | 1.75 |
| 4 | 0023 | 04/01/90 | L | 1342 | 4.75 |
| 5 | 0126 | 04/01/90 | C | 1229 | 0.75 |
| 6 | 0999 | 04/01/90 | P | 1401 | 1.75 |
| 7 | 0519 | 04/02/90 | L | 723 | 3.00 |
| 8 | 0465 | 04/02/90 | C | 1156 | 0.75 |
| 9 | 1357 | 04/02/90 | P | 1328 | 2.00 |
| 10 | 0759 | 04/03/90 | L | 1235 | 2.50 |
| 11 | 0948 | 04/03/90 | C | 1508 | 1.00 |
| 12 | 1234 | 04/04/90 | P | 1012 | 1.75 |
| 13 | 0546 | 04/04/90 | C | 1008 | 2.75 |
| 14 | 0023 | 04/04/90 | L | 1156 | 5.25 |
| 15 | 1027 | 04/05/90 | G | 1206 | 2.00 |
| 16 | 1117 | 04/05/90 | P | 815 | 1.75 |
| 17 | 0023 | 04/05/90 | L | 1324 | 1.00 |

| 18 | 0214 | 04/06/90 | C | 916  | 1.00 |
|----|------|----------|---|------|------|
| 19 | 1210 | 04/06/90 | P | 1234 | 1.00 |
| 20 | 0126 | 04/06/90 | C | 1152 | 2.00 |
| 21 | 0857 | 04/06/90 | L | 1030 | 2.50 |
| 22 | 1186 | 04/07/90 | C | 1511 | 2.50 |
| 23 | 0368 | 04/07/90 | P | 846  | 1.75 |
| 24 | 1288 | 04/07/90 | C | 637  | 2.75 |
| 25 | 0051 | 04/07/90 | P | 1201 | 1.00 |
| 26 | 0126 | 04/07/90 | C | 1014 | 0.50 |
| 27 | 0684 | 04/07/90 | G | 1020 | 4.00 |
| 28 | 1224 | 04/07/90 | P | 1528 | 2.00 |
| 29 | 1368 | 04/07/90 | C | 1121 | 0.50 |
| 30 | 0519 | 04/07/90 | L | 1203 | 2.75 |

1. List the records that have flight times of more than two and a half hours.
2. List all flights taken by member number 23.
3. Create a flight log that lists the DATE, T_OFF, and MEMB for the last day of the week (4/07/90).
4. Count the flights by Cessna and Piper Cub planes.
5. List all of the flights by the Lear lasting two and one half hours or more during the last half of the week (4/4 to 4/7/90).
6. Average the takeoff times and air time for the entire week.
7. Go to record 9 and list only MEMB for the next four records.

## Reminders

1. USE EX2.DBF and LIST FOR T_AIR > 2.5 (9 records)
2. LIST for MEMB = '0023' (3 records)
3. LIST (Construct field) DATE, T_OFF, and MEMB (Build Search) DATE = 4/07/90 (9 records)
4. Count for PL = C or PL = P (20 records)
5. LIST FOR PL = 'L' .AND. T_AIR >= 2.5 .AND. DTOC(DATE) >= '04/03/90' (3 records)
6. AVERAGE (1109, 2.19)
7. GOTO 9 and LIST NEXT 4 MEMB

Exercise 8-3

**Filename: EX3.DBF**
(Continuation of Exercise 7-3)

| Record# | COD | DESCRIPT     | U_COST | QUAN | UNIT | UP_DATE  |
|---------|-----|--------------|--------|------|------|----------|
| 1       | WPA | Pine Grade A | 2.75   | 64   | BdFt | 09/07/90 |
| 2       | SLA | Stain Light  | 4.27   | 23   | Qrt  | 09/21/90 |
| 3       | WPB | Pine Grade B | 2.47   | 77   | BdFt | 09/14/90 |
| 4       | GWA | Wood Glue    | 4.99   | 14   | Qrt  | 09/21/90 |
| 5       | WOA | Oak Grade A  | 3.80   | 151  | BdFt | 09/21/90 |
| 6       | SDA | Stain Dark   | 4.38   | 9    | Qrt  | 08/31/90 |
| 7       | WBA | Birch Grade A| 4.50   | 65   | BdFt | 09/21/90 |
| 8       | WBB | Birch Grade B| 4.45   | 94   | BdFt | 09/14/90 |
| 9       | WOB | Oak Grade B  | 3.60   | 120  | BdFt | 09/14/90 |
| 10      | WPC | Pine Grade C | 2.18   | 252  | BdFt | 09/21/90 |

```
        11   SMA     Stain Medium    4.15     15    Qrt      09/07/90
```

1. Open EX3.DBF and list all records with an UPDATE of 09/21/90.
2. Display the records with U_COST of more than $2.18 but less than or equal to $4.45.
3. List only the DESCRIPT and U_COST fields of the records with quantities of 100 or less.
4. Average the wood inventory for the third week (09/21/90).
5. Count the number of records with unit costs greater than $4.
6. Locate all the records for oak wood.
7. Sum the liquid measures for the inventory.
8. Go to record 4 and list only UPDATE for the next five records.
9. List the records with unit costs greater than $2.75 in the first (9/7) and third (9/21) weeks of September 1990.


Exercise 8-4

**Filename: EX4.DBF**
(Continuation of Exercise 7-4)

| Record# | EMPL | P_RATE | PROJ | PAY_WEEK | HRS | END |
|---------|------|--------|------|----------|-----|-----|
| 1 | 345 | 8.75 | 133 | 06/01/90 | 40 | .F. |
| 2 | 432 | 20.55 | 140 | 06/01/90 | 40 | .F. |
| 3 | 654 | 15.65 | 140 | 06/01/90 | 40 | .F. |
| 4 | 678 | 10.75 | 133 | 06/01/90 | 40 | .F. |
| 5 | 234 | 100.00 | 133 | 06/08/90 | 14 | .F. |
| 6 | 345 | 8.75 | 133 | 06/08/90 | 40 | .F. |
| 7 | 432 | 20.55 | 133 | 06/08/90 | 20 | .F. |
| 8 | 432 | 20.55 | 147 | 06/08/90 | 20 | .F. |
| 9 | 567 | 80.00 | 145 | 06/08/90 | 8 | .T. |
| 10 | 654 | 15.65 | 133 | 06/08/90 | 28 | .F. |
| 11 | 654 | 15.65 | 140 | 06/08/90 | 12 | .T. |
| 12 | 678 | 10.75 | 133 | 06/08/90 | 24 | .F. |
| 13 | 678 | 10.75 | 140 | 06/08/90 | 16 | .T. |
| 14 | 345 | 8.75 | 133 | 06/15/90 | 40 | .F. |
| 15 | 432 | 20.55 | 147 | 06/15/90 | 40 | .T. |
| 16 | 654 | 15.65 | 147 | 06/15/90 | 40 | .T. |
| 17 | 657 | 75.00 | 147 | 06/15/90 | 12 | .T. |
| 18 | 678 | 10.75 | 133 | 06/15/90 | 40 | .F. |
| 19 | 234 | 100.00 | 133 | 06/22/90 | 16 | .T. |
| 20 | 345 | 8.75 | 133 | 06/22/90 | 40 | .T. |
| 21 | 432 | 20.55 | 133 | 06/22/90 | 40 | .T. |
| 22 | 455 | 85.00 | 133 | 06/22/90 | 12 | .T. |
| 23 | 654 | 15.65 | 151 | 06/22/90 | 40 | .F. |
| 24 | 678 | 10.75 | 133 | 06/22/90 | 40 | .T. |
| 25 | 234 | 100.00 | 150 | 06/29/90 | 6 | .F. |
| 26 | 345 | 8.75 | 150 | 06/29/90 | 40 | .T. |
| 27 | 432 | 20.55 | 151 | 06/29/90 | 40 | .T. |
| 28 | 625 | 70.00 | 151 | 06/29/90 | 6 | .T. |
| 29 | 654 | 15.65 | 151 | 06/29/90 | 40 | .T. |
| 30 | 678 | 10.75 | 151 | 06/29/90 | 40 | .T. |

1. List all records of employees working full time (40 hours) on a project.
2. Display the records of employees with P_RATE of $80 or more but less than $100.

3. List only the PROJ and EMPL fields of the records with 12 hours or less.
4. Average the pay rate for the first week (ending 6/8/90).
5. Count the number of employees that worked on project 133 the week it ended.
6. Locate for date 6/15/90 and continue until all records have been located for that date.
7. Sum the hours for the month of June to date.
8. Go to record 12 and list only HRS for the next three records.
9. List records with hours of < 40 for the PAY_WEEK ending the second (6/8) and fourth (6/22) weeks of June 1990.

# Chapter 9: Advanced Features of dBASE III PLUS

This chapter introduces reorganizing data using indexes and sorts, producing reports with the dBASE report generator, and programming to automate execution of dBASE commands. Data organization and report generation are important to end users of all types. Although end users do not typically write complex programs, it is convenient for them to automate the execution of repetitive commands by writing simple programs. Accountants also need to review and understand programs in order to evaluate the internal control systems.

## Case Setting

The hospital staff and management are pleased with the dBASE application developed so far and would like to have several additional capabilities. The controller wants to be able to see the charges organized in different orders. It would also be useful to have reports showing subtotals and totals for the various types of charges, dates, and patients. The controller would like the reporting system to be menu-based, so reports can be generated by clerical personnel. dBASE will also be used to generate invoices for patient billing.

## Reorganizing Data

It is common to need to organize data according to the values of the data in various fields. At one time, it might be useful to have data in alphabetical order by name, and at another time to have data in numeric order by amount of charge. One of the major features of a DBMS is the ability to organize and reorganize data in many different orders quickly and easily. A fast, flexible, efficient DBMS lets an accountant do more work in less time. There are two ways to reorganize data: **Index** and **Sort**. The use of indexes are the primary means of data organization in dBASE and other relational DBMS.

### Using an Index

The Index command *logically* reorders the records in a data file without *physically* moving the records. An index file is a separate file (with the extension .NDX) that indicates the order of each record in the logically reorganized data file. An index file has only two fields, the index key field (in ascending order) and the record number field. An index file takes much less disk space than a database file. There can be several indexes related to each data file. An index can be activated when the file is initially opened or after

167

the file is open. An index must be active to incorporate the effects of changes made to the related data file.

## Single-Field Indexes

An index is constructed on an index key expression, which consists of one or more field names. The simplest and most common type of index key expression is a single field name. The records appear to be organized in alphabetical, numeric, or date order based on the values in the field specified as the index key. Logical and memo fields cannot be used in index key expressions.

An important field to index for the hospital case would be the patient number. The CASEA.DBF file in the following table shows the record number and the values in the PAT_NUM field for the first five records of the CASEA.DBF file in physical order. When this file is indexed on PAT_NUM, the first five **logical** records are those shown under PAT.NDX. One field of the index file would be the PAT_NUM; the other field would be the record number.

|  |  |  |  |  |
|---|---|---|---|---|
| **CASEA.DBF** | | | **PAT.NDX** | |
| Record# | PAT_NUM | | PAT_NUM | Record# |
| 1 | 1234 | | 1111 | 3 |
| 2 | 2222 | | 1111 | 5 |
| 3 | 1111 | | 1111 | 6 |
| 4 | 2234 | | 1111 | 10 |
| 5 | 1111 | | 1111 | 14 |

**DBF and NDX files**

dBASE looks for PAT_NUM 1111 in the PAT.NDX index file to find that additional data related to patient 1111 are stored in record 3 of CASEA.DBF.

You are now going to index the CASEA.DBF file on PAT_NUM and name the index file PAT.NDX. Index files can be named with any legitimate DOS filename, but it is most useful to name them in ways that indicate what DBF files and key expressions they relate to. To create the index file, select **Set Up B:** CASEA.DBF **N** to open the file without an index and then select **Organize Index.** dBASE displays the message and the prompt "The index key can be any character, numeric, or date expression involving one, or more fields in the database file. It is usually a single field. **Enter an index key expression:**".

There are two ways to enter the index key expression. You can always type in the expression if you remember the field names or have a hard copy of the file structure to refer to. As an alternative, pressing [F10] at this point causes dBASE to display a list of the field names at the left side of the screen. The field name, type, width, and decimals of the highlighted field are also displayed below the index key expression prompt. As usual with a dBASE menu, you use the arrow keys to move to the field you want to select and press ◡ to select it. (Figure 9.1)

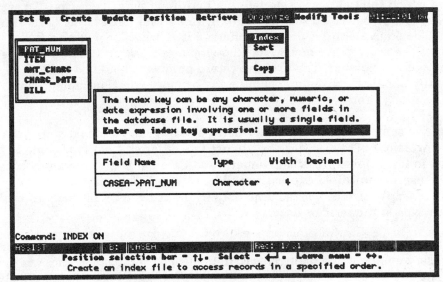

**Figure 9.1 Creating an index**

Since **PAT_NUM** is the first field, it is already highlighted. Select it with ↵ to place it in the index key expression area, then press ↵ again to tell dBASE that the index key expression is complete. Select the **B:** drive and enter **PAT** as the index filename when prompted to "Enter a file name (consisting of up to 8 letters or digits) followed by a period and a file name extension(consisting of up to 3 letters or digits.) **Enter the name of the file:**". The equivalent dot prompt command is INDEX ON PAT_NUM TO B:PAT. Note that you have to specify both the index key expression and the name of the index file. The field name could also be used as the index filename.

dBASE automatically adds the **.NDX** file extension and displays "100% indexed 31 Records indexed" at the bottom of the screen to tell you the indexing is complete and how many records were indexed. The index that determines the order the data appear in is called the Master index. When a new index is created, it becomes the Master index. List all the records to see that they now appear in order of patient number. The first five records should be in the order shown in the table on page 168. Notice that the record numbers in the first column are no longer in their physical order.

## Multifield Indexes

A multifield index key expression concatenates (combines) fields to create an index. An index of both patient number and item would let you generate lists grouped by patient, with all the charges grouped together by item for each patient. To organize the records by item within patient numbers, you need to use a multifield index key expression. To index CASEA.DBF using both PAT_NUM and ITEM on the B drive with the index filename PAT-ITEM.NDX, select **Organize Index PAT_NUM + ITEM ↵ B: PAT-ITEM**. The [F10] key can be used to display a menu of field names. The + sign used to concatenate fields must be typed in. Where possible, a hyphen will be used in .NDX filenames to separate the abbreviations of the field names that were combined in the index key expression. Note that the hyphen (–) used in these filenames is different from the underscore (_) used in field names. The equivalent dot prompt command is INDEX ON PAT_NUM + ITEM TO B:PAT-ITEM. List the records to see the new alphabetical ordering of items within patient. The first five record numbers should be 3, 14, 6, 10, and 26.

The order in which the fields are selected in a multifield index is crucial. To see why the order is so important, select **Organize Index** ITEM + PAT_NUM ⏎ B: ITEM-PAT and list the records. The equivalent dot prompt command is INDEX ON ITEM + PAT_NUM TO B:ITEM-PAT. The records are now grouped by item, and within the item groups are organized by patient number. The first five record numbers should be 3, 14, 8, 21, and 19. Think carefully about which field should be the primary (first) grouping, which field should be secondary, and so on.

Only data of the same type (character, numeric, or date) can be concatenated to make multifield expressions. Thus, if you want to use two different field types, one or more must be converted to form the expression. Numeric and date fields are commonly converted to character for use in multifield expressions. When these functions are used, only the data in the .NDX index file are converted. The data in the .DBF data file remain in their original data type of numeric or date.

The STR() function converts numeric data to character data. The STR() function has three arguments: the numeric value to be converted, the length of the string into which it is to be converted, and the number of decimal places to be used, which is optional. dBASE adds leading zeros as necessary to preserve the order. To index CASEA.DBF on patient number (character) and amount charged (numeric), the dot prompt command would be INDEX ON PAT_NUM + STR(AMT_CHARG,6,2) TO B:PAT-AMT. Enter this command at the dot prompt. List the records to see that they are organized in ascending order of amount charged within patient number by entering LIST at the dot prompt. The first five record numbers should be 10, 20, 6, 28, and 26. The equivalent Assist command sequence would be **Organize Index** PAT_NUM + STR(AMT_CHARG,6,2) ⏎ B: PAT-AMT. Although [F10] can be still used to enter the field names, the function name, parentheses, and other function arguments must be typed.

The DTOC() function converts date type data to character type data. To index the CASEA.DBF file on patient number (character) and charge date (date), the command is INDEX ON PAT_NUM + DTOC(CHARG_DATE) TO B:PAT-DATE. Display the records to confirm the indexing. The first five record numbers should be 5, 10, 14, 20, and 31. The equivalent Assist command sequence is **Organize Index** PAT_NUM + DTOC(CHARG_DATE) ⏎ B: PAT-DATE.

More than two fields can be concatenated. To group the records first by patient, within patient by date, and within date by item, use INDEX ON PAT_NUM + DTOC(CHARG_DATE) + ITEM TO B:PA-DA-IT. The equivalent Assist command sequence would be **Organize Index** PAT_NUM + DTOC(CHARG_DATE) + ITEM ⏎ B: PA-DA-IT. List the records to confirm that the grouping is correct. The first five record numbers should be 14, 10, 5, 20, and 31.

You can see that naming the index files becomes more difficult as the number of fields in the index key expression increases. If there are several complex indexes associated with a file, it is a good idea to maintain a separate listing of the index names and the fields from which each file is constructed. This is part of the data dictionary associated with the database and is an integral part of the systems documentation needed to support effective use, audit, and evaluation of the information system.

## Using Indexes with Set Up

So far, you have always responded **No** to the last question in the **Set Up** command sequence, **Is the file indexed? [Y/N]**. Now that you have created several indexes for the billings file

(CASEA.DBF), you can activate them when you set up the file by responding **Yes** to this question.

Use **Set Up** now and respond **Y**. A list of the index (.NDX) files on the disk is displayed. Select PAT.NDX first. Remember that if there are too many files to fit on the screen at one time, you may need to use ↓ or [PgDn] to see the rest of the files. The first index file you select is marked as the Master file to indicate that it will determine the order in which the records are displayed. The other index files can be opened in any order you wish; the order is indicated by numbers displayed to the right of the index filenames. Up to seven index files can be open at once. Also select the index files PAT-DATE, PAT-ITEM, and PAT-AMT. Do not select the ITEM-PAT or PA-DA-IT index files. (See Figure 9.2.)

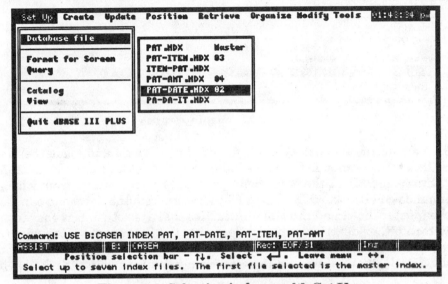

Figure 9.2 Selecting indexes with Set Up

Use ← or → to leave the menu and to indicate that the set up is complete. The dot prompt command is USE B: CASEA INDEX PAT, PAT-DATE, PAT-ITEM, PAT-AMT.


## Update/Reindex

Indexes are automatically updated by the DBMS when you change the data, *if* the database file was opened using the index. However, if the .DBF file is changed with any index that is not active, the changes will not be reflected in that index file. For example, if you changed CASEA now, the active indexes (PAT, PAT-DATE, PAT-ITEM, and PAT-AMT) would be updated to be consistent with the changes, but the index files that are not currently active (ITEM-PAT and PA-DA-IT) would not be updated. If data are changed without some index files being active, open the data file with those index files active and use the command REINDEX (available only from the dot prompt). All active index files will be updated. REINDEX uses the same index key expression initially used to create the index to recreate the index file. It is necessary to use REINDEX if you have more than seven index files related to a single data file, since only seven index files can be active at one time.

From the dot prompt the Display Status command or [F6] shows what index files are active at any time and their related index key expressions (Figure 9.3). The status is continued on a second screen, which you can see by pressing ↵.

```
(DEMO) . display status

Currently Selected Database:
Select area:  1, Database in Use: B:CASEA.dbf    Alias: CASEA
    Master index file:  B:PAT.ndx   Key: PAT_NUM
          Index file:  B:PAT-DATE.ndx  Key: PAT_NUM+DTOC(CHARG_DATE)
          Index file:  B:PAT-ITEM.ndx  Key: PAT_NUM+ITEM
          Index file:  B:PAT-AMT.ndx  Key: PAT_NUM+STR(AMT_CHARG,6,2)

File search path:
Default disk drive: B:
Print destination:  PRN:
Margin =     0
Current work area =    1

Press any key to continue...
Command Line      B:   CASEA                     Rec: 11/31            Ins
                      Enter a dBASE III PLUS command.
```

**Figure 9.3 Display status**

After a data file is open, an existing index file can be activated and made the Master index with the Set Index to command. To set the index to ITEM-PAT, enter SET INDEX TO ITEM-PAT. Entering SET at the dot prompt provides a menu system from which many of the Set commands can be issued. Selecting **Files Index** from the Set menu can also be used to change the Master index and the other index files that are active. It is easy to accidentally turn off, or deactivate, index files using the Set menu, so it is wise to display status after you use the Set menu. This book will use only the dot prompt Set commands. Consult your dBASE manual for additional information about using the Set menu.

## Physically Sorting Records

The Sort command physically rearranges records based on the value in one or more fields of a database. The records are copied into a new file in the sorted order. If the data are not organized in any logical order originally, it is virtually impossible to return the records to their original order after they have been sorted. To process the records in any different order, they would have to be sorted again, or indexed. Records can be sorted in ascending or descending order and without regard to case. The primary sort key is the first field to be sorted; other fields are referred to as secondary keys. Logical and memo fields cannot be sorted. In general, you should use **Sort** sparingly. Indexing is much faster, the index files take up much less disk storage space than sorted files, and the data exist in only one .DBF file.

The most useful way to sort the billing file (CASEA.DBF) would be by date and within date by patient number. To sort the records this way and place the sorted records in a new data file named DATE-PAT.DBF, select **Organize Sort CHARG_DATE PAT_NUM B:** DATE-PAT. The equivalent dot prompt command is SORT ON CHARG_DATE, PAT_NUM TO B:DATE-PAT. Open the new sorted file (DATE-PAT) and list the records. The first 18 records (all charges for January 1, 1990) of the sorted DATE-PAT.DBF are shown in Figure 9.4.

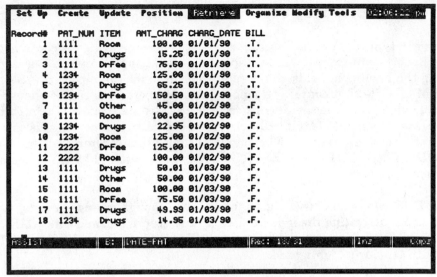

Figure 9.4  Physically sorted file

The data are still in their original order in CASEA.DBF, with the same record numbers. CASEA.DBF has not been changed in any way by the sort. The record numbers in DATE-PAT.DBF have been changed, so there is no cross-reference or audit trail between DATE-PAT.DBF and CASEA.DBF. If data are changed or a record is added to the DATE-PAT file, the entire database must be resorted to maintain the order, which does not happen automatically.

To see the difference between indexing and sorting, index CASEA.DBF using the command INDEX ON DTOC(CHARG_DATE) + PAT_NUM TO B:DATE-PAT. Even though the records are grouped using the same key fields in both cases, they are not necessarily displayed in the same order. The first six records of the indexed CASEA.DBF file are records 5, 10, 14, 8, 18, and 25.

If you appended a record for patient 1111 on 1/2/90, it would be displayed in proper logical order in the indexed file. If the same record was added to the sorted DATE-PAT.DBF file, it would appear at the end of the file. A new sorted file would have to be created to put the new record in its proper order.

Close the file with Use and select **Tools** to erase the DATE-PAT.DBF file, since we will work only with CASEA.DBF. When you are sure that a file is no longer needed, it is best to delete it from the disk. Leaving it on the disk makes it harder to keep track of the files, and it is likely that you will accidentally use the wrong file at some point.

# Generating Reports Using dBASE

Displaying data on the computer screen to answer questions from patients and hospital personnel is known as performing an **ad hoc query**. It is also useful for the end-user accountant or manager to be able to generate ad hoc reports, without waiting for the IS department. Detail reports are very much like the listings you have already produced, except that they provide for more complete documentation, more control over the formatting, and can include totals and subtotals of numeric fields. Summary reports omit the detail and include only subtotals and totals.

## Creating a Simple Report Form (.FRM)

Ad hoc reports are typically produced using a report generator, which is contained in dBASE in the Report commands. **Create Report** makes a template, which is a standardized form specifying the headings, fields, and format to be used for the report. dBASE gives the extension .FRM to a file that contains a report form. A report form can be changed using **Modify Report**, which uses the same screen interface as **Create Report**. The report form or template is activated by using **Retrieve Report**, and the desired data subset is specified using search conditions and scopes. The equivalent dot prompt commands are CREATE REPORT, MODIFY REPORT, and REPORT FORM, each followed by the name of the file containing the report form.

Select CASEA.DBF and open it without an index. Even though an index exists, you can open the file without activating the index. Select **Create Report B:** and enter CASEA-A as the name of the .FRM file to be created. The screen will change to CREATE REPORT mode (Figure 9.5), with **Options** highlighted.

### Report Headings and Printing Options

The Options submenu lets you enter the heading for the report (Page title) and control how the report will be printed. Select **Page Title** with ↵ and enter the data shown in Figure 9.5 in the box provided.

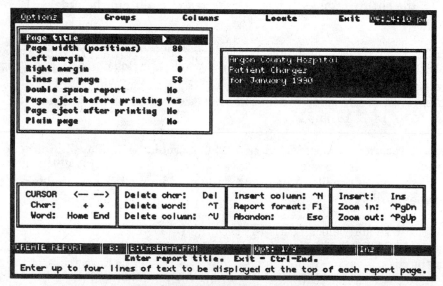

**Figure 9.5  Creating a report**

When the report is displayed (on the screen or on paper), the report title will be centered. When the report title is entered correctly, save it and return to the Options screen by pressing ↵ on the last line of the Title entry box or with [Ctrl] [End].

Changing some of the items on the Create Report screen works somewhat differently from using other dBASE menus. Use the arrow keys to highlight **Left margin**. Press ↵ to select that option, which is indicated by the appearance of ➤ next to the current setting. Change the value of the left margin setting by typing 6 and pressing ↵ to enter it. The setting for **Left margin** is now 6, and the selection indicator ➤ has disappeared. Instead of typing the new value, you can press ↑ to increase the value of the setting or ↓ to decrease the value.

When the desired value appears, press ↵ to enter it. Next, move to highlight **Page eject before printing**. For this option, pressing ↵ acts as a toggle to switch the value between Yes and No. Set **Page eject before printing** to **No** and **Page eject after printing** to **Yes**.

## Defining Column Contents

**Columns** lets you specify what data are to be shown, the column heading, the width, and whether to total numeric data in each column of the report. The current column is indicated in the fourth (location) block of the status line and is column 1 the first time you highlight **Columns**. You enter the expression that specifies the data to be displayed in the column by using the **Contents** option. The expression to be entered in **Contents** can contain a single field or a combinations of fields. This is the same type of expression used as an index key expression, with the same rules for punctuation and combining different field types to form expressions. Most report columns contain a single field.

Press ↵ to select **Contents**, and the selection indicator (➤) appears. To enter the field PAT_NUM as the contents of the first column, either type in PAT_NUM or press [F10] to display the field names and select PAT_NUM from the list. When PAT_NUM appears on the Contents line, press ↵ to tell dBASE that the expression for column 1 is completed. (Figure 9.6).

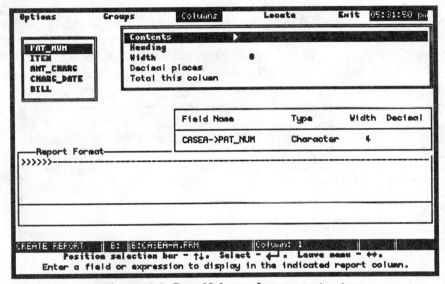

**Figure 9.6 Specifying column contents**

The Report Format box in the lower portion of the screen now shows you that the left margin is six characters wide by displaying six greater-than signs (>>>>>>) and that the first column is four characters wide by displaying four Xs (XXXX). The number on the **Width** line of the Columns menu also tells you that the column width is set at 4. The field width is used unless you change **Width**.

Move down to **Heading**, press ↵ to select it, and a box appears in the right middle of the screen where you can enter the column heading to be displayed on the report above the data in column 1. The heading is for human convenience and should contain an appropriate description of the column contents. Remember to look at the navigation and message lines for assistance. Press ↓ or ↵ twice to move to the third line of the column heading box, enter Patient on the third line, enter Number on the last line, and use ↵ or [Ctrl] [End] to save the entry. Appearing on the **Heading** line of the Columns menu will be ;;Patient;Number (the semicolon indicates a ⌐). The heading appears in the Report Format box as it will be displayed in the report.

Note that **Width** has changed to 7. This happened because the heading is seven characters wide. dBASE uses the larger of the field and the heading width. You can also widen the column even more by entering a larger value on the **Width** selection line. Neither the **Decimal places** nor **Total this column** line can be accessed now. They are available only for columns that have numeric contents, whereas PAT_NUM is a character field. This completes the definition of the first column.

Press [PgDn] to move to a column menu for the next column. You can tell that you are in a column menu for column 2 because Column: 2 appears in the fourth block of the status line. Enter the following report specifications in the indicated columns:

| Column: | Contents | Heading | Width | Dec | Total |
|---|---|---|---|---|---|
| 1 | PAT_NUM | ;;Patient;Number | 7 | | |
| 2 | ITEM | ;;;Item | 6 | | |
| 3 | AMT_CHARG | ;;Charged;Amount | 10 | 2 | Yes |
| 4 | CHARG_DATE | ;;Date;Charged | 9 | | |
| 5 | BILL | ;;Bill;Sent | 5 | | |

Invalid field names and certain other types of errors get a beep and error message from dBASE, followed by a message telling you what to do to continue. The defaults for numeric fields are to total the column and to use the same number of decimals used in the field definition. When the report specifications are complete, save them by selecting **Exit Save**. The completed report specifications screen should look like Figure 9.7.

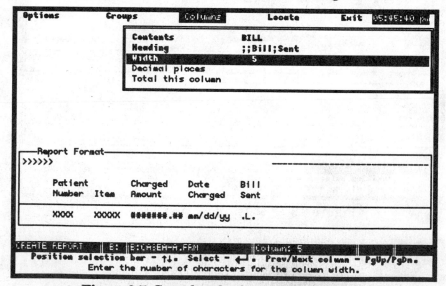

**Figure 9.7 Completed column specifications**

## Displaying a Report

This report form (template) can now be used to display any subset of the data in the specified form. To display a report using the report template, select **Retrieve Report**, the proper drive, and CASEA-A.FRM. To display a report of all the records, select **Execute**. Press [Ctrl] S to stop the scrolling of a report. Press any key to continue scrolling. To generate a report of only the records for January 1, again select **Retrieve Report**, the proper drive, and

CASEA-A.FRM, then select **Build a search condition** CHARG_DATE = 01/01/90. The dot prompt equivalent is REPORT FORM B:CASEA-A FOR CHARG_DATE = CTOD('01/01/90') TO PRINT. The output should look like Figure 9.8.

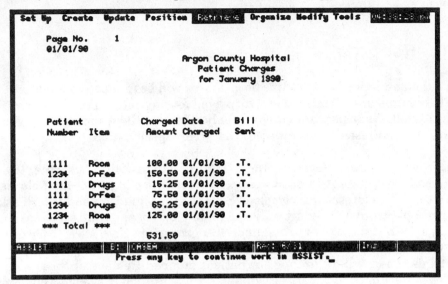

**Figure 9.8 Completed report**

## Modifying a Report Form

You can change any of the report specifications with **Modify Report**. Use **Modify Report B: CASEA-A.FRM** to modify the report form file. The next screen is just like the Create Report screen, except that MODIFY REPORT appears on the status line. Select **Page title**, change the second line of the title to Patient Charges in Transaction Order. **Locate** lets you move directly to any column on the report by selecting it from the list of column contents, which is convenient when a report has many columns. Use **Locate** to move to CHARG_DATE and edit the column heading to change it to ;;Charge; Date. The space between the ; and Date will move the word Date one character to the right in the column heading, which will make the column heading appear to be centered. Change the column width to 11. Use [PgUp] to move to the column containing ITEM and change the column width to 7. You can change any of the existing settings or entries by replacing them with new settings or entries.

You can also insert or delete columns. Move to the AMT_CHARG column and use [Ctrl] U to delete the column. CHARG_DATE, which was in column 4, is now in column 3, and the other columns have been similarly shifted left. Move to column 5 and reenter **Contents** of AMT_CHARG, with a column **Heading** of ;;Amount;Charged, the **Width** of 10, **Decimal places** of 2 and Yes for **Total this column**. If you forget how to insert or delete columns, the [F1] key toggles between displaying the report format and displaying the control screen that provides the commands for inserting and deleting. It is easy to accidentally insert an empty column, which causes dBASE to give a syntax error message when you try to display the report. If you get such an error message, you probably have an empty column. Use **Exit Save** to save the revised report form file when the changes are complete, and reissue the command used above to print the records for 01/01/90.

It is common to use an existing report form as the basis of another report with slightly different settings. This is done by copying the original .FRM file to a new .FRM file, which is then modified. You must close dBASE files before you can copy them, so [Esc] to the dot prompt and enter CLEAR ALL to close all the open files. Enter COPY FILE

CASEA-A.FRM TO CASEA-B.FRM at the dot prompt to copy the original report form to a new file. The equivalent Assistant command sequence is to select **Tools Copy file B: CASEA-A.FRM B:** CASEA-B.FRM. Open CASEA.DBF and use MODIFY REPORT CASEA-B.FRM to modify the new report file.

## Grouping Records

The Groups submenu lets you determine how records will be grouped. Subtotals of the groups and subgroups are calculated and displayed for any column in the report for which totals are calculated. **Groups** works properly only when the file is indexed or sorted with the same primary key expression contained in the group specification.

To see how this works, move to **Groups,** select **Group on expression,** and enter the expression PAT_NUM, either by typing it in or by using [F10] and selecting from the field list. Press ↵ to tell dBASE that the expression is complete. Select **Group heading** and enter Patient Number. Leave both **Summary report only** and **Page eject after group** set to **No** and do not enter anything in **Sub-group on expression** or **Sub-group heading.** Move to **Options** and select **Page title,** where you will change the second line of the title to Charges by Patient to indicate that this report will be grouped by patient number. Remember that using clear, accurate titles is part of good report design and documentation. Save your changes and leave the MODIFY REPORT mode using **Exit Save.**

Because the new report specification includes the grouping by patient number, the file must be organized in order of patient number to get the desired results. Since we already created an index in order of patient number, PAT.NDX, reopen CASEA with PAT.NDX as the Master index (USE CASEA INDEX PAT) and LIST the records to make sure they are in patient-number order. Use REPORT FORM CASEA-B FOR CHARG_DATE=CTOD ('01/01/90') to display a report of the data for 01/01/90 grouped by patient number. The equivalent command sequence from the Assist menu is **Retrieve Report B: CASEA-B.FRM Build Search CHARG_DATE =01/01/90 Execute.** The results are shown in Figure 9.9.

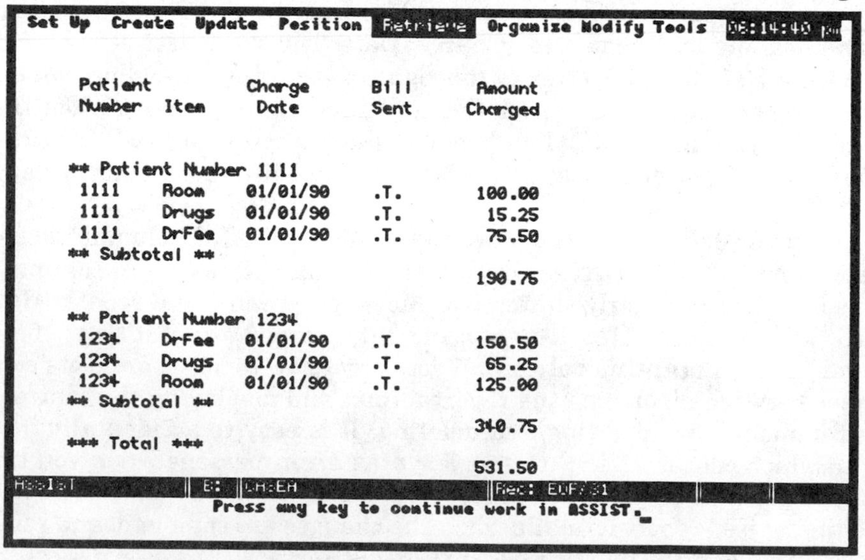

Figure 9.9 Report grouped by patient and date

Notice that the report also includes subheadings for each patient by number and subtotals of the charges for each patient. If you run the grouped report without the data organized in the proper order, dBASE begins a new group each time it encounters a new PAT_NUM. Try this to see the results. By now, you should be comfortable enough to begin exploring various dBASE features on your own.

A report of charges grouped by day would also be useful, so create one named CASEA-C.FRM. Remember to close the open files before you try to copy them, then follow the steps used above to make a copy of CASEA-A.FRM named CASEA-C.FRM. After making the copy, reopen CASEA.DBF without an index, then create a new index by charge date (DATE.NDX) to be used with CASEA-C.FRM. Change the second line of the report title for CASEA-C.FRM to Patient Charges by Day, group on the CHARG_DATE field, and enter Charge Date as the group heading. Display or print the report to make sure it works correctly.

A report with subgroups requires the file to be indexed using a key expression that includes both the group and the subgroup expression. In the index key expression, the group expression must be first, followed by the subgroup expression. A report grouped by patient, with subgroups by date within patient, would be useful. Close all the files, copy CASEA-B.FRM to CASEA-D.FRM, and modify CASEA-D.FRM. Change the second line of the title to Charges by Patient and Date. Keep PAT_NUM as the expression to be grouped on. Under **Groups**, select **Sub-group on expression** and enter CHARG_DATE as the expression to be used for subgroups, then select **Sub-group heading** and enter Charge Date. Exit and save the modified report form. Make a new index, PAT-DATE.NDX, using the index key expression PAT_NUM + DTOC(CHARG_DATE) or SET INDEX TO PAT-DATE to use the PAT-DATE.NDX created earlier. Print the report using CASEA-D.FRM. The dot prompt command is REPORT FORM CASEA-D TO PRINT.

Although the dBASE report generator provides for only two levels of groupings and subtotals, the records can be further organized within subgroups by using a more complex index key expression. To organize records by item within date within patient, SET INDEX TO PA-DA-IT. If you need to, make another index, PA-DA-IT.NDX, using the index key expression PAT_NUM + DTOC(CHARG_DATE) + ITEM. Generate the report again after the PA-DA-IT index is active and note the difference in how records are organized within the subgroup. The first section of the report, for only patient number 1111, is shown in Figure 9.10.

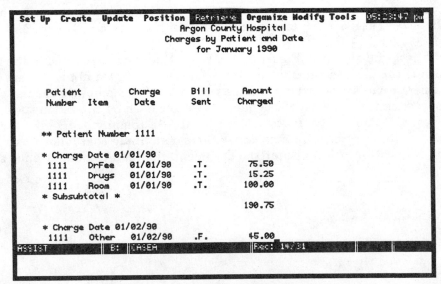

**Figure 9.10 Reports with subgroups**

# Brief Introduction to dBASE Programming

Although indexing and report generation have addressed several of the controller's needs, a few tasks remain to be completed. Report generation needs to be simplified so that it can be delegated to clerical personnel, and the automated invoicing system must be developed. These require using the dBASE programming capabilities.

## Creating and Running a Program

Since a report that contains groupings also requires the file to be organized in a manner consistent with the groups, you must remember to select the appropriate Master index before running a report. You can make dBASE take care of that kind of detail by writing a simple program.

dBASE stores programs in files with the extension .PRG, which are also referred to as Command files. These are ASCII (text) files, which can be created with most word processors or text editors. There is a rather limited text editor for creating programs within dBASE, which this book assumes you are using. However, you can use a different word processor to create the program files if you prefer. Within dBASE, programs must be created and modified from the dot prompt.

You have decided to write a program to generate the report "Charges by Patient," using the report form CASEA-B.FRM. Create a program file named REPORTB.PRG by entering MODIFY COMMAND REPORTB at the dot prompt. (Since you can abbreviate dBASE commands to the first four letters of the command, this can also be entered as MODI COMM REPORTB.) Telling dBASE to modify a file that does not exist causes it to create a new, empty file with that name. If no file extension is specified, dBASE assumes that the extension is .PRG. The top portion of the program entry and edit screen shown in Figure 9.11 should appear. The body of the screen will be blank. In the future, if an empty screen appears instead of the program you want to modify, use [Esc] to exit and reenter the filename. It is most likely that you misspelled the filename or failed to specify the correct disk drive. In either case, dBASE creates a new file with the name you entered.

Now enter the program shown in Figure 9.11. The first thing to be entered in the file is documentation of the file and what the program does. As discussed in the context of Lotus reports, documentation is a record of what the program is for and how to use the program. Since documentation is for the benefit of human users, it must be entered in such a way that dBASE will ignore it and not try to execute it as a dBASE command. dBASE ignores any line in a program that begins with an asterisk (*) and anything that follows two ampersands (&&) within a line. Enter the documentation and command lines shown in Figure 9.11.

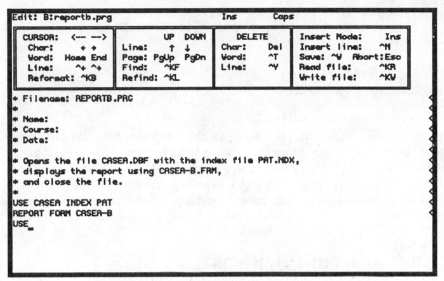

**Figure 9.11 REPORTB program screen**

The commands are all ones you have used before, either by typing them at the dot prompt or by using Assist. The first command line opens the data file CASEA.DBF with the PAT.NDX index. The next line uses the report form CASEA-B to generate the report of Charges by Patient. The last command line closes all the files. When the program is complete and appears to be correct, use [Ctrl] [End] to save it and return to the dot prompt.

To run or execute the program, enter DO REPORTB at the dot prompt, and dBASE executes the commands contained in the file REPORTB.PRG. If the program is correct, the report of Charges by Patient should be displayed on the screen. If you made any data-entry errors in the command lines, the program may not run. If this happens, you will get a message that tells you that the file does not exist, that dBASE encountered an unrecognized command verb, or some other error message. The line of the program that is listed and the location of the question mark above it provide clues as to where the error is located. The Navigation line will contain **Cancel, Ignore, or Suspend? (C, I, S)**. Typically, you will enter C to cancel execution of the program, use ↑ twice (or as many times as needed) and ↵ to reenter the command MODI COMM REPORTB, and fix the program by editing the command lines on the screen. Repeat this sequence until the program executes successfully by displaying the report.

Similar programs can be developed for each of the other reports by copying REPORTB.PRG to other files, similar to the process used for copying report form files. Copy REPORTB.PRG to three other files named REPORTA.PRG, REPORTC.PRG, and REPORTD.PRG. Modify the resulting files as necessary to get them to generate reports A, C, and D. The items to be changed are the filename, the index filename, and the report form filename in both the documentation and the actual dBASE commands. For example, COPY FILE B:REPORTB.PRG TO B:REPORTA.PRG, then MODI COMM REPORTA, and change the file contents to

```
* REPORTA.PRG
*
* Name:
* Course:
* Date:
*
```

```
* Opens the file CASEA.DBF,
* displays the report using CASEA-A.FRM,
* and closes the file.
*
USE CASEA
REPORT FORM CASEA-A
USE
```

Save the file with [Ctrl] [End] when the changes are complete. Run the program using DO REPORTA and check the output to make sure it works properly. Keep changing the program until it works. Use the same process to modify the program files REPORTC.PRG and REPORTD.PRG to display the other two reports, CASEA-C.FRM and CASEA-D.FRM. Test each program thoroughly to make sure it works properly, before trying to do the MENU program below.

## Printing Output from Programs

There are several ways to send the results of programs to the printer. Which way will be most effective in a given circumstance depends on the nature of the task you are trying to accomplish. Several easy ways to print the report incorporate the print commands within the program. Unfortunately, this requires you to be connected to a printer to use the program. While this might be reasonable to assume in a hospital, it is not reasonable to assume for all student users, so the commands were not incorporated in the programs here.

One alternative is to add the phrase TO PRINT to the Report command, as was done with List commands. For example, in REPORTB.PRG, the second command would become REPORT FORM CASEA-B TO PRINT. Another alternative is to add the commands SET PRINT ON just before the Report command and SET PRINT OFF just after the Report command. The first of these commands directs that whatever is displayed on the screen is also sent to the printer; the second command returns to screen only output.

If you want to let the user determine where output is sent, there are (at least) two alternatives. The easier of these is for the user to enter the command SET PRINT ON before entering the DO REPORTB command and to enter SET PRINT OFF when printing is finished. Use this method to print your reports now if a printer is available. This prints the command DO REPORTB as well as the report. The other alternative is to add a section to the menu program that asks the user whether to send the reports to the printer or not. This is beyond the level of sophistication of a brief introduction and will not be covered here.

## Memory Variables

dBASE stores data temporarily in memory variables, which are kept in main memory. A memory variable (which is abbreviated "memvar") usually contains a piece of data to be used in a program or to be displayed later. There are two ways to enter data in a memvar. The first is STORE *value* TO *memvar* and the other is *memvar* = *value*. The *value* can be a constant number, a literal string of characters enclosed in quotes, or a field name or combination of fields in an expression. The *memvar* name should not be the same as a field name. Memvars can have the same data types. The following are all legitimate commands to enter data values in memvars.

```
STORE value TO memvar              memvar = value
STORE 1 TO COUNTER                 COUNTER = 1
STORE 'Hello' TO GREETING          GREETING = 'Hello'
STORE AMT_CHARG TO THISCHARG       THISCHARG = AMT_CHARG
STORE ITEM TO THISITEM             THISITEM = ITEM
```

Enter one column of the commands to see how they work. The commands in both columns are equivalent. The first command stores the constant number 1 in the numeric memvar named COUNTER. The second command stores the literal string Hello in the character memvar named GREETING. If a file is open, you can also store the value of any field of the current record in a memvar. The third and fourth commands store the values of AMT_CHARG and ITEM of the current record of CASEA in the memvars THISCHARG and THISITEM. To check this, display the current record. You must be positioned at a record, not at the EOF, for a value to be stored. Each value entered in the memvar is displayed on the line immediately following the command.

Entering a ? followed by the name of a memvar displays the current value of the memvar on the following line. Enter ? GREETING to see this work. DISPLAY MEMORY displays all the memvars and their current values. The value in a memvar remains there until it is replaced with a new value or is cleared by a command such as RELEASE ALL or CLEAR ALL.

The results of AVERAGE, COUNT, and SUM may also be stored as memvars for display or use later. Suppose you want to compute the average bill of each patient at the hospital. The solution could be calculated by giving Average Charge the memvar name AVG_CHARG. Clear all existing memvars at the dot prompt with RELEASE ALL and enter AVERAGE AMT_CHARG TO AVG_CHARG. The screen display should indicate that 31 records were averaged and that the average AMT_CHARG is 76.75. To total all the charges, use SUM AMT_CHARG TO TOT_CHARG. Again, 31 records should be summed, and the total should be 2379.36. To display the average and the sum, enter ? AVG_CHARG, TOT_CHARG at the dot prompt. To display the results more clearly, enter ? 'Average amount charged was ', AVG_CHARG. dBASE will display "Average amount charged was 76.75."

## Creating Menus

Much of the work of entering data and printing out reports can be handled by clerical personnel if the interface is user friendly. While it is easier to generate reports by running the programs you developed than by having to enter the commands from the dot prompt or the Assistant each time, a menu system would make it even easier to generate reports. It is fairly easy to program menus in dBASE. By now, you should have four programs (REPORTA.PRG, REPORTB.PRG, REPORTC.PRG, and REPORTD.PRG) that generate the reports developed for the hospital in the preceding section. The next thing you will do is enter a program to display a menu from which a clerical user can select reports to be run. A program to generate a menu for displaying the reports is shown in Figure 9.12.

```
* Filename: MENU.PRG
*
* Name:
* Course:
* Date:
*
* Displays a menu to select which report should be generated.
*
CLEAR ALL
CHOICE = 'Z'
*
DO WHILE CHOICE <> 'X' .AND. CHOICE <> 'x'
CLEAR
?
?
?'  A    Display Patient Charges by Transaction Report'
?
?'  B    Display Charges by Patient Report'
?
?'  C    Display Charges by Date Report'
?
?'  D    Display Charges by Patient and Date Report'
?
?'  X    Leave the menu without generating a report.'
?
?
*
ACCEPT 'Enter the indicated letter to select a menu item:   ' TO CHOICE
*
DO CASE
    CASE CHOICE='A' .OR. CHOICE='a'
        CLEAR
        DO REPORTA
        WAIT 'Press any key to continue...'
    CASE CHOICE='B' .OR. CHOICE='b'
        CLEAR
        DO REPORTB
        WAIT 'Press any key to continue...'
    CASE CHOICE='C' .OR. CHOICE='c'
        CLEAR
        DO REPORTC
        WAIT 'Press any key to continue...'
    CASE CHOICE='D' .OR. CHOICE='d'
        CLEAR
        DO REPORTD
        WAIT 'Press any key to continue...'
    CASE CHOICE='X' .OR. CHOICE='x'
        RETURN
    OTHERWISE
        ? 'Not a valid menu selection.'
        WAIT 'Press any key to continue, then try again.'
ENDCASE
*
ENDDO
```

**Figure 9.12 Menu program**

The following discussion explains the purpose of each section of the program and what each command will cause the computer to do. Enter the documentation and commands shown in

Figure 9.12 in a program file named MENU.PRG as you read through the following sections. After you enter the program, you can print a copy of the program or any other text file by using the command TYPE *<filename>* TO PRINT. The *<filename>* means that the name of the specific file you want to print should be inserted in that position in the command. The command to print the menu program is TYPE MENU.PRG TO PRINT.

As already discussed, a program should contain both documentation to explain the program to the human user and commands to be executed by the computer. All lines that begin with * are documentation lines for human use only. The first several lines in a program file typically contain the name of the program file, the name of the person who wrote the program, and the date the program was written or last modified. Those lines that contain only a single * are used for spacing, to divide different sections of the program.

The first executable section of the program is typically used for general tasks, sometimes referred to as housekeeping. The first dBASE command in the program, CLEAR ALL, closes all open files and erases all memvar values. This keeps you from being surprised by the effects of leftover values from previously run commands. CHOICE is a memvar that soon will be used to hold the value that the user chooses from the menu. Although it is not necessary, it is a good idea to initialize each memvar by explicitly assigning it a value at the beginning of the program. This way, you know what value it contains and what the results of that value should be. The command CHOICE = 'Z' initializes the memvar CHOICE by entering the character Z.

You would like users to be able to select commands from the menu until they have generated all the reports they want to see. To do this, you must provide a way to make dBASE keep presenting the menu and letting users select items until they indicate to dBASE that they are finished. You also need a way for users to tell dBASE that they are finished.

The menu presentation will be repeated by using a DO WHILE loop. A loop is a set of commands that is repeated until the computer is told to stop repeating them. A DO WHILE loop keeps repeating the commands between the DO WHILE and the first ENDDO as long as (while) the specified conditions are met. The command line DO WHILE CHOICE <>'X' .AND. CHOICE <>'x' begins a loop that is executed as long as the value of CHOICE is anything except 'X' or 'x' (i.e., until the value of CHOICE is either 'X' or 'x'). The commands to be repeated within the DO WHILE loop are terminated by an ENDDO command, which is found on the last line of this program. DO WHILE loops can be contained within other DO WHILE loops, which is called **nesting** or **nested loops**. You will encounter an example of nesting below.

CLEAR clears the screen. (Notice the significant difference between CLEAR ALL and CLEAR!). It is common to clear the screen before displaying a menu. The next 13 lines that each begin with ? contain the text of the menu to be displayed on the screen. Recall that ? followed by a character string in quotes displays whatever is contained between the quotes. A ? followed by nothing or by blank spaces displays a blank line, which provides proper spacing for visual clarity and easy use of the menu.

Once these lines are entered, save your work with [Ctrl] [End] to return to the dot prompt. Enter DO MENU, which will run the part of the program that you have entered so far. The menu should appear on the screen, followed by the dot prompt, as shown in Figure 9.13.

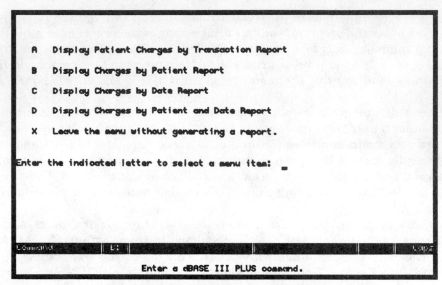

**Figure 9.13 Menu screen display**

Because there is no end to the DO WHILE loop yet, the program returns you to the dot prompt when it encounters the end of the program file. If a program ever appears to keep running endlessly, it is likely that you have created an infinite loop, which you can stop by pressing [Esc]. It is common to test programs one piece at a time, because it is easier to locate and fix an error in a few commands than in a long program.

Enter MODI COMM MENU again to continue working on the program. Fix any spelling or other errors before continuing with the next command, ACCEPT 'Enter the indicated letter to select a menu item: ' TO CHOICE. The ACCEPT command lets the user enter data from the keyboard. The command displays the character string contained within the quotes, which acts as a prompt to the user, and stores whatever is next entered from the keyboard in the named memvar.

The DO CASE command is often used in dBASE to implement menus. The DO CASE command begins a set of conditional statements. Each CASE statement contains one or more conditions, which dBASE evaluates. As soon as dBASE encounters a true CASE statement, the statements following it (up to but not including the next CASE statement) are executed, and control then is passed to the ENDCASE statement.

The first case statement says that if the memvar CHOICE contains either an uppercase or a lowercase letter A, the following commands up to, but not including, the next CASE command, should be executed. If CHOICE contains an A, the screen is cleared by the command CLEAR, and the REPORTA.PRG program is run by the command DO REPORTA. Note that a program (such as REPORTA.PRG) can be run by a command within another program (MENU.PRG). After REPORTA.PRG has made dBASE display report A, control is returned to the next command line in MENU.PRG after the last one that was executed.

The WAIT command displays the prompt contained within quotes and then waits for the user to press any key before continuing to execute commands. The prompt "Press any key to continue..." is displayed on the screen, and dBASE waits until a key is pressed to continue the program execution. Unlike ACCEPT, WAIT does not enter in a memvar the value of the key that the user presses.

The next three CASE statements are identical to the first one, except that they each call a different program to produce a different report. The fifth CASE, which is executed if CHOICE = X or x, leaves the program and returns to the dot prompt. Another command that could have been used to get back to the dot prompt is CANCEL. The difference between the two commands is that RETURN sends control back to another program if the current program was called or run by one, whereas CANCEL returns directly to the dot prompt.

If no CASE command is encountered that contains a true condition, the statements following the OTHERWISE command are executed, if an OTHERWISE command is included. Although it is not required, the OTHERWISE command is good for detecting data-entry errors and allowing the user to be notified of them. Including an OTHERWISE statement for this purpose makes it easier to use the program properly and thus contributes to efficiency and good internal control. If the user enters a character other than one of the valid menu options, then none of the CASE commands is true. The statements following the OTHERWISE tell the user that the entry is invalid and to try again. Every DO CASE must be accompanied by one or more CASE commands and an ENDCASE; an OTHERWISE is optional.

Finish entering the MENU program. Test and correct it until it works properly. Make sure you understand what it is doing at every step and how each command works.

## Creating Output Documents

The next task is to use dBASE to generate accurate, understandable invoices, to save time and reduce the chance of human error in copying the charges to the invoices. Although some of the data needed for an invoice are not contained in the data file CASEA, you will work with what is there to develop part of the invoice. Obtaining the remaining data from other files is addressed in the next chapter.

To manually prepare an invoice, you would organize the data in order of patient number and by date within patient. Beginning at the top of the list, you would then write down the patient number, copy each charge for that patient onto the invoice, and mark each charge on the list as billed once it is copied onto the invoice. When there are no more charges for the first patient, you would sum and write down the total charges for the patient. The invoice would look like the one shown in Figure 9.14.

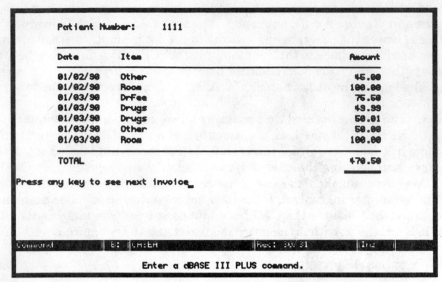

**Figure 9.14 Invoice output**

You would then continue through the list, repeating these steps for all patients, until you reached the end of the list of patient charges.

Instead of preparing the invoice manually, write a program to make dBASE organize the data in the desired order and total and display the charges. One program that will accomplish this is contained in Figure 9.15.

```
* Filename: INVOICE.PRG
*
* Name:
* Course:
* Date:
*
* This program generates invoices for all charges not yet billed,
* and marks them as billed after adding them to the invoice.
*
CLEAR ALL                              && Close any open files
COPY FILE CASEA.DBK TO CASEA.DBF       && Copy from backup data file
USE CASEA INDEX PA-DA-IT               && Open file by Patient Date Item
SET TALK OFF                           && Display output not commands
SET FILTER TO .NOT. BILL               && Process only charges not billed
GO TOP                                 && Go to first logical record
** Insert relations here
*
DO WHILE .NOT. EOF()                   && Repeat until EOF reached
   CLEAR                               && Clear the screen
   M_INVTOT=0                          && Store zero (0) in M_INVTOT
   M_NUM = PAT_NUM                     && Store value of PAT_NUM in
   @ 1,8 SAY 'Patient Number: '        &&    current record to M_NUM
   @ 1,28 SAY PAT_NUM                  && Print Patient number
   ** Insert name and address display here
   @ ROW()+2,8 TO ROW()+2,69           && Draw a horizontal line
   @ ROW()+1,8 SAY 'Date'              && Enter column headings for
   @ ROW(),20 SAY 'Item'               &&  Date, Item and Amount
   @ ROW(),60 SAY 'Amount'
   @ ROW()+1,8 TO ROW()+1,69           && Draw a horizontal line
   DO WHILE PAT_NUM=M_NUM              && For this Patient
      @ ROW()+1,8 SAY CHARG_DATE       && Print Date
      @ ROW(),20 SAY ITEM              && Print Item
      @ ROW(),60 SAY AMT_CHARG         && Print charge amount
      M_INVTOT=M_INVTOT+AMT_CHARG      && Add amount to total
      REPLACE BILL WITH .T.            && Change Bill to true
      SKIP                             && Move to next record
   ENDDO                               && Return to last DO
   @ ROW()+1,8 TO ROW()+1,69           && Draw a single line
   @ ROW()+1,8 SAY 'TOTAL'             && Print "TOTAL"
   @ ROW(),57 SAY M_INVTOT             && Print total amount
   @ ROW()+1,63 TO ROW()+1,69 DOUBLE   && Double underline total
   WAIT 'Press any key to see next invoice'    && Prompt & wait
ENDDO                                  && Return to related DO
*
CLEAR ALL                              && Close any open files
SET TALK ON                            && Display commands
CLEAR                                  && Clear the screen
@ 10,25 SAY 'All invoices were displayed'    && Invoices done
RETURN                                 && Return to dot prompt
```

**Figure 9.15 Invoice program**

The first section contains the familiar introductory documentation on the lines beginning with an *. Another way of documenting is illustrated on the following lines. When dBASE

executes a command line, it ignores anything that follows &&. The purpose of each
command is explained in the documentation following the && on each line.

Although many of the commands in this program are familiar to you by now, others are
new and require explanation. The CLEAR ALL command closes any files that might be
open and erases all memvars. The next command copies a backup file CASEA.DBK to
CASEA.DBF, the file you will use. This lets you begin with a correct and complete data file
that contains the charges that have not been billed each time you run the program. When
this program is debugged and ready for the hospital environment, this command would be
replaced with one that creates a backup copy of the main.DBF file because we will bill and
change the BILL value only once. The next familiar command opens the data file CASEA
indexed in patient number, date, and item order.

The next command, SET TALK OFF, is new. It stops the results of several types of
commands, such as SUM and INDEX, from being displayed on the screen as they are
executed. To see the effect of including this command, run the program with the command,
then modify the program to place an * at the beginning of the command of interest. Run the
program again and notice the difference in how it runs. Remember to take the * out before
continuing, if you want to keep the command active.

The command SET FILTER TO .NOT. BILL is also new. It makes dBASE limit its
activities to only those records in which the BILL field does not contain .T. This is done
because only the charges that have not yet been billed should be put on the invoice. Setting a
filter imposes the same type of condition that is invoked with a FOR in a dot prompt
command or **Build search** in the Assistant. The difference is that the filter applies to all
data display and processing that are done after it is set, whereas the search conditions
apply only to the single command in which they are included. The condition imposed by
the filter remains in effect until it is cancelled by closing the data file or entering the SET
FILTER TO command, which resets the filter to the default of processing all records. The
following GO TOP moves the record pointer to the first logical record of the filtered data.
The following documentation line that begins with ** is used as a reminder to the
programmer that this is where to place the commands to establish links with the file that
contains the name and address. A similar documentation line beginning with ** is
included later in the program to show where to insert the lines to print the name and
address. These commands will be added to the program in Chapter 10, after the use of
multiple files has been introduced.

The next line begins a DO loop that tells dBASE to keep repeating the commands contained
within the loop until the EOF is reached. Since the index has put the records in the desired
order for processing, and the pointer was moved to the logical top of the file (the first record
in index order), you are ready for dBASE to begin processing. CLEAR erases anything on
the screen. The next command stores 0 (the value zero) in the memvar M_INVTOT. This
variable is used to accumulate the total charges for the invoice, which will be printed at the
bottom of the invoice. Each time we begin a new invoice for a new patient, the M_INVTOT
must be set to 0 to get rid of the total from the previous patient. The next command stores the
value from the PAT_NUM field of the current record in the memvar M_NUM. Starting the
names of memvars with M_ is a useful way to distinguish them from field names.

The next line displays the words Patient Number, and the following line displays the
patient number of the current record on row 1, beginning in column 8 of the screen. This is
where the name and address of the patient are displayed when they become available in
Chapter 10. The @...SAY statement is used to display items on the screen or the printer.
The form of the full command is @ Row,Column SAY *expression* PICTURE *format*.

On most screens, the rows are numbered from 0 to 24 and the columns from 0 to 79 (other computers may have smaller or larger screen dimensions.). The @...SAY command writes the expression at row R and column C on the screen or printer. Rows and columns can be indicated by numbers or by reference to the current row or column number. The functions ROW(), COL(), PROW(), and PCOL() yield the values of the current screen row, screen column, printer row, and printer column, respectively. Using relative row and column references makes it much easier to modify the positioning of output if necessary. At the end of the last command, ROW() was 4, so the ROW() + 2 in the next command will cause the output to be displayed on row 6.

The next command, which is somewhat different from an @...SAY command, is used to draw lines and boxes. When the row is the same both before and after the TO, it results in a horizontal line. The next command displays column headings for the various columns to be listed on the invoice and is followed by another line.

An expression in an @...SAY command can be a character string, constant, memvar, or field(s). dBASE allows only one data type in any @...SAY command. You can convert among data types using STR() to convert numbers to characters and DTOC() to convert dates to characters. This is useful if you wanted to display, for example, @ ROW(), COL() SAY 'The date was' + DTOC(CHARG_DATE). The same thing can be accomplished by using two separate @...SAY commands, @ ROW(), COL() SAY 'The date was' followed by @ ROW(), COL() + 14 SAY CHARG_DATE.

The next line begins another DO WHILE loop, which is *nested*, or totally contained, within the first DO loop. This second DO loop will be executed only for the current patient, i.e.,WHILE the PAT_NUM remains the same as the value of M_NUM. Since you set the value of M_NUM to be equal to PAT_NUM just a few commands earlier and have done nothing since to change either of the values involved, the condition is certainly met for the first record. The next three commands output the CHARG_DATE, ITEM, and AMT_CHARG on the next row. The next command adds the value of AMT_CHARG in the current record to the current value of M_INVTOT, to accumulate the total charges for the invoice. The command REPLACE BILL WITH .T. changes the value in the BILL field of the current record to .T., because it has now been billed. The command SKIP tells dBASE to move to the next record in the file, since processing of the current record has been completed.

The ENDDO tells dBASE that the end of the most recent DO WHILE loop has been reached and to go back to the DO WHILE statement to see if the condition is still true. As long as the condition is true, dBASE will continue repeating the commands between the DO WHILE and the ENDDO. Since PAT_NUM is still 1111 for the second logical record of the file, this record is also displayed on the invoice. dBASE will continue to display these fields of each record as long as PAT_NUM is still 1111.

When a record is reached that has a new patient number, you want dBASE to output the total for the current patient's invoice before beginning an invoice for the new patient. The next four commands draw a line to separate the detail from the total line, display TOTAL and the total amount, and put a double underline (for good accounting formatting) under the total amount. The next command makes dBASE notify the user that the invoice is complete and waits for the user to press any key before it goes on to do the next invoice. The following ENDDO returns control to the DO WHILE NOT EOF() command to do the next invoice.

The final commands close the open files and erase the memvars, return the talk to its default status of ON, notify the user that all invoices have been displayed, and return the user to the dot prompt. These commands are executed only when all records have been processed and invoices have been completed for all patients. Again, correct the program until it works properly and make sure you understand exactly what each command does. You will need to use comparable commands and program structures to complete the practice exercises and to follow the work in the next chapter.

# Chapter Review

This chapter covered organizing data, generating reports using the dBASE report generator, and writing simple programs for a variety of purposes. Although this gives you quite a lot of power and flexibility, you still have not tapped the power of dBASE as a DBMS to use data from several files in a single application. The next chapter continues the invoice-programming process to make dBASE display patient name and address data from a separate file on the invoice.

# Practice Exercises

Exercise 9-1

**Filename: EX1.DBF**
(Continuation of Exercise 8-1)

1. Create a single field index to organize records in order of customer number. Name the index file CUST and print a list of records in this order.
2. Create a multifield index file named CUSTDATE to organize the records grouped by customer number and in date order within customer. Print a list of the records in this order.
3. Create a report named EX1.FRM with the page title and headings shown below. Set all column widths to 10 and total check amounts.

```
                     Darwin Department Store
                       Cash Receipts File
                       for February 1990

                 Date
Customer         Check          Check          Check
Number           Recorded       Number         Amount
```

Print the report in order of check amount.
4. Make a second report template called EX1A.FRM by copying the form EX1.FRM. Modify it to group records by customers with totals on amount, change the title to Cash Receipts by Customer, and move the Check Amount column to between Date Check Recorded and Check Number. Print the report only for customers with numbers below 100.
5. Create and print a memvar named M_ENDDAT that contains the date 2/28/90. Make sure it is a date, not a character memvar.
6. Write a program to display a Statement of Customer Payments for each customer with a customer number less than 150. Use the invoice program in the chapter

(Figure 9.15) as a model. A sample statement for customer number 0076 is shown below. Print a copy of the program and the output from the program for customer 51.

```
Customer Number:   0076


-------------------------------------------------------------
Date Received        Check Number            Payment Amount
-------------------------------------------------------------
02/05/90                  433                      137.83
02/28/90                  452                       84.37
-------------------------------------------------------------
Total Payments                                     222.20
```

## Reminders

1. INDEX ON CUST TO CUST then LIST TO PRINT.
2. INDEX ON CUST + DTOC(DATE_RECD) TO CUSTDATE then print.
3. CREATE REPORT EX1.FRM. The page title is entered using **Options Page title** and entering the page title shown above. The following settings will generate the column headings.

   | Column: | Contents | Heading | Width | Dec | Total |
   |---|---|---|---|---|---|
   | 1 | CUST | ;;Customer;Number | 10 | | |
   | 2 | DATE_RECD | ;Date;Check;Recorded | 10 | | |
   | 3 | CHECK | ;; Check;Number | 10 | | |
   | 4 | AMOUNT | ;; Check;Amount | 10 | 2 | Yes |

   INDEX ON AMOUNT TO AMOUNT and use **Retrieve Report** from the Assistant or REPORT FORM EX1 from the dot prompt.
4. Copy the report form EX1.FRM to EX1A.FRM. Modify EX1A.FRM using the Groups submenu to group records by CUST and change the title using **Options Page title**. Delete the Check Amount column with [Ctrl] U and insert a new column number 3 with [CTRL] N. Reenter the specifications for the Check Amount column in this new location. Add the condition FOR CUST<'100' and the phrase TO PRINT to the REPORT FORM EX1A command.
5. M_ENDDATE = CTOD('02/28/90').
6. The first section will contain documentation. The next section will erase all previous memvars and close all files. Open the file EX1 with CUSTDATE.NDX as the Master index and set a filter to limit processing to customer numbers below 150. Initialize a memvar to track the current customer number. Use a DO WHILE .NOT. EOF() to stop the program when the end of the file is reached. Use a nested DO WHILE for the same customer to put all the payments for a single customer on one statement. Display each payment and calculate and display the TOTAL payments for each customer. Make sure each DO loop has an ENDDO. To get a printout of the program, use the dot prompt command TYPE PROG.PRG TO PRINT. Use [Shift] [PrtSc] to print a copy of the Customer Statement for customer 0051.

## Exercise 9-2

**Filename: EX2.DBF**
(Continuation of Exercise 8-2)

1. Create a single field index to organize records in order of member number. Name the index file MEMB and print a list of records in this order.
2. Create a multifield index to organize the records grouped by member number and in date order within member. Name the index file MEMBDATE. Print a listing of the records in this order.
3. Create a report named EX2.FRM with the following page title and headings:

```
              Moose Wings Flight Club
                Member Flight Log
               Week 1 - April 1990


                                               Time
                   Date       Type      Time     in
        Member      of         of        of     the
        Number     Flight     Plane    Takeoff   Air
```

Print the report in order of member number.
4. Make a second report template called EX2A.FRM that groups records by plane type, in order of member number within plane group, with totals for air time but not for time of takeoff. Print the report. Change the title to Plane Flight Log.
5. Create and display a memvar named M_CAIR to store the sum of the air times for the Cessna and the average takeoff time for the Lear named M_LOFF.
6. Write a program to display a statement of member flights for each member. Use the invoice program in the chapter (Figure 9.15) as a model. A sample statement for member number 1234 is shown below. Print a copy of the program and the output from the program.

```
Member Number:   1234

-----------------------------------------------------------------
Flight                  Time of         Time
Date          Plane     Takeoff         in Air
-----------------------------------------------------------------
04/01/90      C             625         2.75
04/04/90      P            1012         1.75
-----------------------------------------------------------------
Total                                   4.50
```

## Reminders

1. INDEX ON MEMB TO MEMB then LIST TO PRINT.
2. INDEX ON MEMB + DTOC(DATE) TO MEMBDATE then print.
3. CREATE REPORT EX2. Enter the page title using **Options Page title**. The following settings will generate the column headings.

```
Column:     Contents  Heading                    Width Dec Total
   1.       MEMB      ;;Member;Number               6
   2.       DATE      ; Date;  of;Flight            6
   3.       PL        ;Type;  of;Plane              5
   4.       T_OFF     ; Time;   of;Takeoff          7
   5.       T_AIR     Time; in;the;Air              4    2   Yes
```

With MEMB.NDX as the Master index, use **Retrieve Report** from the Assistant or REPORT FORM EX2 from the dot prompt.

4. Copy the report form EX2.FRM to EX2A.FRM. Modify EX2A using the **Groups** submenu to group records by plane (PL) and change the title using **Options Page title**. INDEX ON PL + MEMB TO PLMEMB. REPORT FORM EXA2 TO PRINT.

5. SUM T_AIR TO M_CAIR FOR PL='C'. AVERAGE T_OFF TO M_LOFF FOR PL='L'.

6. The first section will contain documentation. The next section will erase all previous memvars and close all files. Open the file EX2 with MEMBDATE.NDX as the Master index. Initialize a memvar to track the current member number. Use a DO WHILE .NOT. EOF() to stop the program when the end of the file is reached. Use a nested DO WHILE for the same member to put all the payments for a single member on one statement. Display each flight and calculate and display the Total hours for each member. Make sure each DO loop has and ENDDO. To get a printout of the program, use the dot prompt command TYPE PROG.PRG TO PRINT. Use [Shift] [PrtSc] to print a copy of the Member Statement for member number 126.


Exercise 9-3

**Filename: EX3.DBF**
(Continuation of Exercise 8-3)

1. Create a single field index to organize records in alphabetical order of item description. Name the index file DESC and print a list of records in this order.

2. Create a multifield index to organize the records grouped by unit of measure and in update order within code. Name the index file UNITDATE. Print a list of the records in this order.

3. Create a report named EX3.FRM with the following page title and headings:

```
                Appalachian Manufacturing Company
                   Raw Materials Inventory
                   Last up date: 9/21/90


                                          Unit
        Unit      Inventory     Unit       of        Last
        Code     Description    Cost     Measure     Update
```

Print the report in alphabetical order of item description.

4. Make a second report template called EX3A.FRM by copying EX3.FRM. Add two new columns with the headings shown below. Group records by unit of measure with totals for value of inventory (unit cost x quantity). Print the report.

```
                Appalachian Manufacturing Company
                     Raw Materials Inventory
                    Last up date: 9/21/90


                                          Unit
        Unit    Inventory    Unit          of        Last
        Code   Description   Cost    Quantity  Measure  Update    Value
```

5. Create and display a memvar named M_PINEAVG to store the average quantity
   for pine.
6. Write a program to produce an inventory card for each item in inventory. Use the
   invoice program in the chapter (Figure 9.15) as a model. A sample Inventory Card
   for Grade A Oak is shown below. Print a copy of the program and the output from the
   program.

```
Code Number:   WOA
Description:   Oak Grade A
Unit:          BdFt
-----------------------------------------------------
Last Update           Unit Cost              Quantity
-----------------------------------------------------
09/21/90                3.80                    151
-----------------------------------------------------
```

Exercise 9-4

**Filename: EX4.DBF**
(Continuation of Exercise 8-4)

1. Create a single field index to organize records in order of employee number. Name
   the index file EMPL and print a list of records in this order.
2. Create a multifield index to organize the records grouped by employee number and
   in order of pay week within employee. Name the index file EMPLWEEK. Print a
   list of the records in this order.
3. Create a report named EX4.FRM with the following page title and headings:

```
                      R & D Consulting
                       Payroll File
                       for June 1990


    Employee     Pay      Project      Pay      Hours      Project
    Number       Rate     Number       Week     Worked     Completed
```

Print the report in employee number order.
4. Make a second report template called EX4A.FRM that will group records by project
   with subgroups on week within project and totals and subtotals for hours
   worked.Change the Title to Job Report. Print the report.
5. Create and display a memvar named M_HOURS to store the total hours worked for
   project 133. Also store the employee number from record number 14 in a memvar
   named M_EMPLNUM.
6. Write a program to print out an employee work summary for each employee. Use
   the invoice program in the chapter (Figure 9.15) as a model. A sample summary for

employee number 234 is shown below. Print a copy of the program and the output from the program.

```
Employee Number:  234

-----------------------------------------------------------------
Pay Week          Pay Rate       Project Number       Hours Worked
-----------------------------------------------------------------
06/08/90          100.00                   133                  14
06/22/90          100.00                   133                  16
06/29/90          100.00                   150                   6
-----------------------------------------------------------------
Total Hours                                                     36
```

# Chapter 10: Integrating dBASE III PLUS with Other Software

The audit and systems-design functions that accountants perform require a good understanding of computerized transaction processing systems (TPS). This chapter introduces the use of multifile operations, which are important in implementing a TPS. Integration among different types of software is also becoming extremely important. The latter part of this chapter addresses why and how to transfer data among dBASE files, and to and from other types of applications such as Lotus 1-2-3 and word processors.

## Case Setting

Several activities remain to be completed for Argon County Hospital that involve using data in different dBASE files or transferring data among dBASE files and other applications. Patient names and addresses must be put on the invoices along with the data from the billings file. Also, at least two clerks must be able to enter billing data at the same time during the busy season. Several reports dBASE generates need to be transferred into a word-processing package for incorporation into larger reports that are primarily text. Finally, other data need to be transferred to Lotus for additional analysis. You have been assigned to explore how to complete these tasks using dBASE.

## Database Design and Relation Types

Database management system (DBMS) software, such as dBASE, allows a departure from the traditional approach to the design and implementation of accounting information systems. Different types of data can be kept in separate files to maximize storage efficiency and data control, yet still be easily accessed and related to the appropriate data in other files. This enables an organization to implement the concept of **information resource management**, which views information as an important asset of an organization and facilitates using information as a strategic weapon. Several factors must be considered in logically designing a database and in physically implementing the design using a specific DBMS.

### Design Considerations

A primary concern in designing a database is reducing **redundancy**, the unnecessary duplication of data. System design should begin with an assessment of the outputs that the system must provide, which determines the inputs that are needed. The database should be designed to store the data in a way that allows efficient production of the needed outputs. Designing a database requires determining all the necessary fields (attributes) for the records (entities) that will be contained in the database. If all the data needed for any purpose were contained in a single file, it would be unmanageably large (requiring excessive storage space and file-search times), and there would be much redundant data, leading to multiple updates and data inconsistency.

Some poorly designed systems do keep all the fields in a single massive file. Consider the practical consequences if such a design had been used in the hospital. If every record also included the patient's name, address, phone number, and insurance company data, the billing file would be huge. Incorrect data is more likely because the probability of data-entry errors increases with the number of items entered. Inconsistent data also become more likely, because one or more items are commonly missed when data must be modified in multiple places because a change occurred. Not only would redundant patient data appear within a file, other types of applications that need patient data (such as medical records) would also have to separately maintain their own patient data.

The problems of data redundancy, inaccuracy, and inconsistency are significantly reduced by **normalizing** the database. Normalization leads to storing different types of data in several smaller files that minimize the redundant data and take up less space than a single large file would require. It is common to record events in a **transaction** file (such as the charges contained in the hospital's billings file) and to keep the relatively permanent and space-consuming data about each patient or other item in a separate **master file**. Both files must contain a common unique field. This unique field is called a **primary key** and is represented in this case as the patient number, PAT_NUM. The primary key is used to link the records in the two files. dBASE can look up the permanent data in the patient (master) file for each entry in the billing (transaction) file. The two resulting files together are much smaller than a single file would be, even though the key field used to link the files must be contained in both files to allow them to be linked. A rule of thumb is that only primary-key fields should appear in more than one file.

In addition to the files discussed here, the hospital would also have other master files (such as insurance companies, doctors, treatments) and transaction files (such as sales, purchases, payroll) that can eventually be related in an integrated database. Substantial planning is required to design a database that provides flexibility, consistency, and minimum redundancy. The following sections show how to open more than one file at a time and how to relate those files and transfer data among them.

## Types of Relations

There are several possible types of **relations** between files. When two files are linked, a movement of the record pointer in one file causes the record pointer in the other file to move to the record with the same key (linking) value. In dBASE, only two files can be linked (related) directly, and the linkage works in only one direction. The type of relation depends on the number of records with the same key value in each file and which file the relation is set *from* and *into*. The type of relation affects how the files are linked using dBASE.

The simplest type of relation is a **one-to-one** relation, in which each record has at most one corresponding record in the other file. There may be no corresponding records, but there cannot be more than one. Often, one of the two related files has several records that contain the key value, whereas the other file has only a single record for each key value. This can lead to either a many-to-one or a one-to-many relation, depending on the direction of the link between the files. The **many-to-one** relation is a relatively simple type of relation to deal with. The billing-to-patient relation is many to one; there can be many transactions (charges) in the billing file with the same key value (patient number), but there can be only one record with that value in the patient file. With a many-to-one relation, a movement in the many file moves the record pointer directly to the one corresponding record in the one file.

The relation is **one to many** if one record in the *from* file is associated with many records in the *into* file. For example, each patient has many charges. The patient-to-billing relation is a one-to-many relation because each one of the patients in the patient master file may have many charges in the billing file. With a one-to-many relation, a movement in the one file moves the record pointer in the many file to the first of the many corresponding records. It is common to index the many file on the primary-key field used to link the two files and to use SKIP and WHILE to move through all the related records in the many file.

A **many-to-many** relation means that many records in one file can be related to many different records in the other file. Either file may have any number (including zero) of corresponding records in the other file. An example of this would be a file with patients and a second file with nurses. Each patient would have several nurses each day, and each nurse would serve several patients. dBASE does not deal directly with many-to-many relations; it would require these two files to be linked by a third file that specifies which patients are related to which nurses. Often, the two files with the many-to-many relation do not even contain a common key field. The intermediary linking file would contain keys to both files being linked, as well as any information that pertains to the intersection. This results in two one-to-many relations between the intermediary file and each of the other files.

The relation between raw materials and finished goods is a common accounting application that is a many-to-many relationship. Many raw materials are typically used in each finished good, and each raw material is used in many different finished goods. The linking file in this case is the bill of materials, which lists the raw material number and the quantity of each raw material used in each finished product.

# Using Multiple Files

Although you have accomplished many things using only one data file at a time, the real power of a DBMS is its ability to establish relationships among several files to process data. When related data are contained in more than one file, several files must be open at once, and the related data in the various files must be linked. This is much more efficient than the traditional approach, which requires yet a third file to be set up containing copies of the data from both of the original files. This section discusses how to open multiple files simultaneously and how to link them so that the appropriate data from the related files are available.

## Opening Multiple dBASE Files Simultaneously

When a new file is opened (with USE or **Set Up**), dBASE automatically closes the previously open file. To open several files at once, dBASE uses a separate work area to hold each file. dBASE has 10 work areas available, which means that up to 10 files can be open at once. When you first enter dBASE or immediately after a Clear All command, dBASE is in the first work area, with no files open. Up to this point, everything you did was in that first default work area referred to as area 1 or A.

Commonly, the user opens a file in the first work area, then moves to the second work area and opens the next file, continuing this pattern until all the needed files are open. To move to a different area, use the Select command, followed by the number or letter of the work area to be selected. Work areas can always be selected (moved to) by using the numbers 1 through 10 or the letters A through J. After a file has been opened in a work area, the area can also be selected by using the filename. This book uses a number to select a work area before a file is open, then uses the filename to select the work area once a file is open. Confusion is greatly reduced by using the filename rather than trying to remember which work area number or letter is used in a particular program. It is possible to assign another name, or **alias**, to a work area. Consult your dBASE manual if you are interested in this option. After you select a work area, you remain in that area until you select another area. There is no Assist command equivalent to SELECT. The Select command may not work properly with a database (.DBF) filename that begins with a number or contains a number following a hyphen.

Enter dBASE and open CASEA.DBF with the index PAT.NDX (with either the dot prompt command USE CASEA INDEX PAT or the Assistant menu sequence **Set Up Database B:CASEA.DBF Y PAT.NDX**). Return to the first logical record in the file with GO TOP. Since the records are now indexed, the logical top will be record 3/31.

A new file can be opened in any work area by moving to that area with SELECT and the area number or letter and opening the desired file with USE at the dot prompt or **Set Up** from the Assistant. Entering USE, followed by no filename, closes the file in the currently selected area only. Any files open in other areas remain open and unaffected. The commands discussed in preceding chapters affect only the data file in the currently selected (active) work area. The command CLEAR ALL closes all open files in all work areas, erases all memvars, and returns dBASE to the default area 1 (or A). This is the same state dBASE is in when you first open it.

Next, move to the second work area with the dot prompt command SELECT 2. Now open the file CASEB.DBF in the second work area, also indexed by patient number (USE CASEB INDEX B-PAT or the Assist sequence **Set Up Database B:CASEB.DBF Y B-PAT.NDX**). Use LIST or BROWSE to see that this file contains the patient number, name, address, and insurance for each patient number included in the billing file, plus several additional information patients. Return to the first logical record in this file with GO TOP and use DISPLAY to see that it is record number 4/8 and that PAT_NUM has a value of 0070. Each area has its own record pointer, which moves independently of the record pointers in other areas, unless two files are linked, as discussed below.

If you are uncertain which files are open or what area dBASE is currently using, the Display Status command or [F6] will inform you of the file and the area. Enter DISPLAY STATUS at the dot prompt to see the material displayed in Figure 10.1.

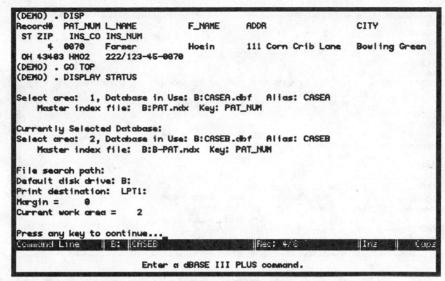

```
(DEMO) . DISP
Record#  PAT_NUM L_NAME              F_NAME      ADDR                    CITY
 ST ZIP    INS_CO INS_NUM
      4  0070      Farmer            Hoein       111 Corn Crib Lane      Bowling Green
 OH 43403 HM02    222/123-45-0070
(DEMO) . GO TOP
(DEMO) . DISPLAY STATUS

Select area:  1, Database in Use: B:CASEA.dbf   Alias: CASEA
    Master index file:  B:PAT.ndx  Key: PAT_NUM

Currently Selected Database:
Select area:  2, Database in Use: B:CASEB.dbf   Alias: CASEB
    Master index file:  B:B-PAT.ndx  Key: PAT_NUM

File search path:
Default disk drive: B:
Print destination:  LPT1:
Margin =     0
Current work area =    2

Press any key to continue...
Command Line      B:  CASEB                      Rec: 4/8         Ins      Caps
               Enter a dBASE III PLUS command.
```

**Figure 10.1 Display status with two open files**

The screen shows you which files are open in each area and what index, filter, format, and other files are active. Press any key to continue.

## Using Data from Other Areas

You can display and otherwise use data from any open file in any area. To use data from a file in an area other than the currently selected area, you must precede the field name with a prefix that explicitly specifies what area the desired data are in (using the filename or the area number or letter). The area indicator prefix is followed by -> (a hyphen and a greater-than sign), which is followed by the field name. There are no spaces between the prefix and the -> or between the -> and the expression. A prefix must precede data that come from another area; the current area prefix may also be specified, but is not necessary. When relations are set within a program, it is common to explicitly specify all prefixes, including the one for the current area. This prevents problems from occurring if the program is changed so that a different area is active.

Make sure you are at the top of the CASEB file in area 2, then move back to work area 1 with SELECT CASEA. Next, enter the command DISPLAY PAT_NUM, CASEB->PAT_NUM, CASEB->ADDR. This displays the record number and the value in the PAT_NUM field of the current record in the billing file (CASEA.DBF) and the values in the PAT_NUM and ADDR fields of the current record in the patient file (CASEB.DBF). Note that the patient numbers from the two files do not match, because no relation has been set. The command and results should appear as shown at the top of Figure 10.2.

```
(DEMO) .
(DEMO) .
(DEMO) .
(DEMO) .
(DEMO) . GO TOP
(DEMO) . SELE CASEA
(DEMO) . DISPLAY PAT_NUM, CASEB->PAT_NUM, CASEB->ADDR
Record#  PAT_NUM CASEB->PAT_NUM CASEB->ADDR
       3 1111    0070           111 Corn Crib Lane
(DEMO) .
(DEMO) . GOTO 7
(DEMO) . DISPLAY PAT_NUM, CASEB->PAT_NUM, CASEB->ADDR
Record#  PAT_NUM CASEB->PAT_NUM CASEB->ADDR
       7 2222    0070           111 Corn Crib Lane
(DEMO) .
(DEMO) . GO TOP
(DEMO) . SET RELATION TO PAT_NUM INTO CASEB
(DEMO) . DISPLAY PAT_NUM, CASEB->PAT_NUM, CASEB->ADDR
Record#  PAT_NUM CASEB->PAT_NUM CASEB->ADDR
       3 1111    1111           1234 Rasin Bagel Way
(DEMO) .
(DEMO) .
Command Line      B:  CASEA            Rec: 3/31      Ins      Caps
                 Enter a dBASE III PLUS command.
```

**Figure 10.2  Display of data from two files**

Although data from any area can be displayed or used, you cannot change the data in an area other than the one currently selected. To modify data with EDIT or REPLACE, the file in which the data are to be replaced must be in the currently selected active area.

As long as two open files are not linked, moving to a different record affects only the record pointer in the current area. To see this, move to record number 7 in the billing file (CASEA) with the command GOTO 7. Now reissue the command DISPLAY PAT_NUM, CASEB->PAT_NUM, CASEB->ADDR. (Remember that you can use ↑ to repeat a dot prompt command instead of retyping it.) This displays the current record number (7) and the value in the PAT_NUM field of this record (2222) in the currently selected file (CASEA.DBF) and the same values it previously displayed in the PAT_NUM (0070) and ADDR (111 Corn Crib Lane) fields of the current record in the patient file (CASEB.DBF). The results should appear as shown in the middle portion of Figure 10.2.

## Linking Files with SET RELATION TO

There are two ways to move the record pointer in a file that is not currently selected. One way is to select the area where that file is open and use a **position** command (such as GOTO or LOCATE) to move the record pointer. Another way is to establish a **link** between the currently selected file (billing) and the related file (patient) using the command SET RELATION TO. Although it is necessary to position for some purposes, it is most convenient to link the files whenever possible. When a relation has been set, a movement in the file the relation was set *from* causes the record pointer to move in the file the relation is set *into*.

In area 1, return to the first logical record in the billing file (CASEA.DBF) with GO TOP. Enter the command SET RELATION TO PAT_NUM INTO CASEB. This SET RELATION TO command causes the record pointer in CASEB (the file the relation is set into) to move to the first record that has the same key expression value (the value of the field PAT_NUM) as the current record in CASEA (the file the relation is set from). The key expression being used to link the two files must follow TO in the command. This is most often a single field name. The currently selected file (CASEA.DBF) is the file that the relation is set *from*, and the .DBF filename (CASEB) that follows the word INTO is the file the relation is set *into*. Each time dBASE moves to a new record in the CASEA file, the record pointer in the CASEB file automatically is moved to the first corresponding record. At the top of the CASEB file, DISPLAY PAT_NUM, CASEB->PAT_NUM, CASEB->ADDR, then move to record 7 and display the same fields. See how the results (also shown in Figure 10.2) now differ from the earlier results.

Although movement in the from file causes the record pointer to move in the into file, the reverse is not true. To see this, SELECT CASEB and GOTO 3. Now enter the command DISPLAY CASEA->PAT_NUM, PAT_NUM, ADDR. Note that this command is different from the ones entered above, although it does exactly the same thing, because the previous commands were issued from area 1 (CASEA). Since you are now in area 2, file designators are needed for the fields from area 1 (CASEA), but not for the fields from area 2, although file designators can always be used for the current area as well as other areas. Modify the preceding command to be DISPLAY CASEA->PAT_NUM, CASEB->PAT_NUM, CASEB->ADDR and enter it to see that it yields the same results. Explicitly including prefixes for all areas ensures that the same command will work from any area.

## Programming with Multiple Files

You can now modify the invoice program (created in Chapter 9) to include the patient name and address data contained in the patient master file (CASEB.DBF) on the invoice. This requires commands to open the patient data file, sets a relation from the billing to the patient file, and displays the name and address data. Since you have made dBASE display selected patient data on the screen already, it is just a matter of formatting the data to appear at the proper place on the invoice.

Issue the command CLEAR ALL to close all open files and return you to area 1. Next, enter MODI COMM INVOICE to modify the file developed in Chapter 9. To open and link the additional files, replace the documentation line "** Insert relations here" with the following command lines.

```
SELECT 2                                && Move to area 2
USE CASEB INDEX B-PAT                    && Open file by Patient Number
SELECT CASEA                            && Move to area 1
SET RELATION TO PAT_NUM INTO CASEB      && Link Patient to billing
```

To display the patient's name and address data from the patient master file, replace the documentation line "** Insert name and address display here" with the following command lines.

```
@1,40 SAY CASEA->PAT_NUM                     && Find PAT_NUM and print name
@ ROW()+2,8 SAY TRIM(CASEB->F_NAME)+' '+CASEB->L_NAME
@ ROW()+1,8 SAY CASEB->ADDR                  && Find ADDR and print address
@ ROW()+1,8 SAY TRIM(CASEB->CITY)+', '+CASEB->ST+' '+CASEB->ZIP
```

Note that the prefix is treated as part of the field name and therefore is contained within the parentheses of a dBASE function, such as TRIM(). The TRIM() function removes trailing blanks from a character variable. The +' '+ adds (concatenates) a blank space between the values of F_NAME and L_NAME. Similar spacing and punctuation are added between CITY, ST, and ZIP.

Make sure you understand the program, then continue to modify it until it works properly. When you have finished working with the program, use CLEAR ALL to return to area 1 and close all files and erase all memvars. The first invoice should appear as shown in Figure 10.3.

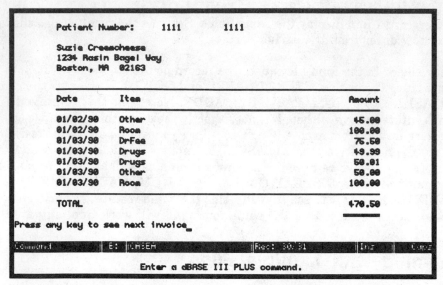

**Figure 10.3 Patient invoice with address**

This concludes the introduction to logically integrating several dBASE data files using relations. The ability to use multiple files and to link them provides the basis for using dBASE to develop integrated accounting information systems. The remainder of this chapter discusses physically transferring, instead of sharing, data among dBASE files and between dBASE and other applications software.

# Transferring Data among dBASE Files

Although the ability to link data in different files is a powerful feature, it is sometimes necessary to transfer data physically among dBASE files. Sometimes, data must be entered in several files by different employees and then combined in a single file. Other times, a portion of a data file needs to be copied to a separate file for other users. These capabilities are provided by the commands COPY TO and APPEND FROM.

## COPY TO Other dBASE Files

The hospital pharmacy wants to use some of the billing data for a service and utilization review it is conducting. Rather than have it use the billing files directly, make a copy of the part of the data that the pharmacy needs. Of course, your controls and procedures will allow access to the data (whether original or a copy) only if the pharmacy has a legitimate reason for requesting the data and if patient privacy and confidentiality will be preserved. If the hospital is electronically networked and has an integrated database, an alternative would be to allow the pharmacy to access the data via the electronic network using security and access codes.

The best way to copy all or part of a dBASE file to another dBASE file is with the command COPY TO. This command copies both the file structure and the specified data of the open file to another dBASE data file with the extension .DBF, unless another extension is specified. The command structure is COPY [FIELDS *<fields>*] [FOR *<conditions>*] TO

*<filename>*. The fields to be copied can be limited using FOR with a condition statement, FIELDS with a list of field names, or both. COPY TO is not available from the Assist menu. Note that COPY TO is different from COPY FILE, which was used in Chapter 7. COPY FILE cannot copy an open file. COPY FILE does the same thing as DOS COPY.

Open the billing file with USE CASEA in area 1 without an index. (For the remainder of the chapter, you will be working only in area 1.) The pharmacy needs only the data pertaining to drugs, and they do not need to know whether the charges have been billed. To copy just the needed data, enter COPY FIELDS PAT_NUM, ITEM, AMT_CHARG, CHARG_DATE FOR ITEM='Drugs' TO PHARMACY. When the copy is complete, USE PHARMACY and compare its contents to the specified criteria and the original file to see that the proper fields and records were copied.

## COPY STRUCTURE

It is common to have several employees enter data simultaneously, working on independent, stand-alone machines. The data they enter are then transferred to the main data file. This process also acts as an internal control mechanism, since the main data file is not used for editing and is less susceptible to damage in the case of human error, a power failure, or another disaster. Many individuals can enter data in separate files, which are then reviewed by a supervisor before the data are added to the main file.

The first step in this process typically is to copy the structure of the main data file to another file. COPY STRUCTURE TO *<filename>* copies the structure of the open data file to the new filename specified following TO. All fields of the file are copied unless a field list is specified. If a field list is specified, only the listed fields are copied. The command is COPY STRUCTURE TO *<filename>* [FIELDS *<field list>*].

Open CASEB and enter the command COPY STRUCTURE TO NEWDATA. Next, USE NEWDATA and LIST STRUCTURE to see that the structure is the same as that of CASEB. LIST the data to see that the file is empty. Enter the following records in NEWDATA.

```
3939 Kirk    James    PO Box 2001      Enterprise  OH   02001  BCBS  123/123-45-3939
4242 Darwin  Charles  678 Reptile Rd.  Seal Beach  CA   69696  HMO2  222/123-45-4242
```

## Adding Records with APPEND FROM

The command APPEND FROM is used to add data to the currently open file from an existing dBASE file. The structure of both files must match exactly, or no transfer of records can take place. To make dBASE add the two records from NEWDATA to CASEB, enter the command USE CASEB, then the command APPEND FROM NEWDATA. When the records have been appended, use BROWSE or LIST to see that the records have been added to the file.

It is common to USE the data-entry file (NEWDATA) and empty it using ZAP once the main data file (CASEB) has been checked and backed up. If you ZAP NEWDATA now, you will have to reenter the data to practice using APPEND FROM again. Also, remember that you will have several copies of the appended records in CASEB if you repeat the APPEND FROM command. Get rid of any extra records by marking them for deletion, then using PACK.

# Integrating dBASE with Other Software

Although dBASE is a powerful and flexible DBMS, it has virtually no other capabilities. If you need modeling capabilities, data must be exported to an electronic spreadsheet. To incorporate data from dBASE in written reports, data must be transferred to a word processor. If statistics or sophisticated graphics are desired, data must be sent to a statistical-analysis or graphics package. The primary mechanism in dBASE to facilitate such data transfer is a modification of the COPY TO command.

It is often necessary to bring data in from other types of software, such as mail-merge files from word processors and data files from statistical or spreadsheets packages. The command APPEND FROM can also be modified to accept inputs from types of files other than dBASE files. Although dBASE readily accepts data from other file types, the data must be structured to fit dBASE's rather rigid file structure. Another option for getting data into and out of dBASE is to use a file-translator program, such as the one in Lotus 1-2-3.

# Sending Data from dBASE with COPY TO

The best way to create a copy of all or part of a dBASE file for transfer to Lotus 1-2-3, a word processor, or another program is the command COPY TO. COPY TO, as used above, outputs data in other file formats if the appropriate modifier is added to the command.

Both the SDF (structured data format) and Delimited modifiers create ASCII files with the extension .TXT, which can be used in a word processor, imported into Lotus, or used by BASIC, COBOL, or FORTRAN programs. The output using the SDF option looks like the output of a LIST command, with the data in columns. It is useful for most word-processing tasks and for any programming language that can use data in that format. The Delimited option surrounds character field output with quotation marks (" "), and separates all fields with commas (,). This format can be imported easily into Lotus and can be used by the mail-merge programs of some word processors. Lotus 1-2-3 can also import SDF files, although it is easier to use the Delimited option. See Chapter 6 for more information on how to get ASCII data into Lotus.

It is also possible to create files directly in formats that 1-2-3, Multiplan and VisiCalc® can read. This is done by following the basic COPY command with TYPE, followed by WKS (for a Lotus file), SYLK (for a Multiplan file), or DIF (for a VisiCalc file). While this is a reasonably good alternative, dates are copied as labels (character data), which require conversion before date manipulations can be performed. Numeric and Label data may appear a bit strange at first, because of the column-width settings. To see the results of the various options, enter the following commands at the dot prompt, using CASEA.

```
COPY TO OUTSDF SDF
COPY TO OUTDEL DELIMITED
COPY TO OUT123 TYPE WKS
```

The results of the first two commands can be viewed on screen from within dBASE with TYPE OUTSDF.TXT and TYPE OUTDEL.TXT. The OUT123 file (which will be given the extension .WKS) must be retrieved into Lotus to be viewed with /File Retrieve.

## Bringing Data into dBASE

The command APPEND FROM adds data from another file to an existing dBASE file, using the same extensions as COPY TO. A data file must exist and be open to append from either a dBASE file or a foreign file. The structure of the open dBASE file must match the structure of the data being brought in. The file from which data are appended must contain only data; there can be no column headings or other items.

Files are on the student disk in ASCII delimited (INDEL.TXT), structured data (INSDF.TXT), and Lotus worksheet (IN123.WKS) formats. Enter TYPE B:INSDF.TXT to see what it contains; do the same for INDEL.TXT. Open NEWDATA and enter the command APPEND FROM INSDF SDF, then LIST or BROWSE the file to see the records that were added from INSDF.TXT. Use APPEND FROM INDEL DELIMITED and APPEND FROM IN123 TYPE WKS to add the records from each of these files to NEWDATA, and LIST or BROWSE again to see the added records. These records could also have been added to CASEB in the same way.

## LOTUS Translate

Lotus 1-2-3 (version 2.0 or higher) contains a Translate utility, available from the Lotus Access menu. (This feature is not included in the Student Edition of Lotus 1-2-3.) It not only translates Lotus files to other formats, it also translates to and from dBASE. Translate is essentially a stand-alone program, designed to translate among the two commonly used ASCII formats (SDF, DELIMITED) and special data file formats. The Translate utility is discussed in detail in Chapter 6.

## Other dBASE Capabilities

You should be aware of several dBASE capabilities not covered in this book. Some you will be able to learn on your own, others are likely to require additional courses. It is important that you feel comfortable referring to your dBASE manual or other dBASE reference book for further information. The manual and a user assistant in either a school computer lab or a corporate information center can often provide sufficient support to meet your needs.

Lists, reports, and other dBASE output can be sent to a file on disk by using SET ALTERNATE. The results can then be imported into a word processor or spreadsheet. REPORT has the ability to produce summary reports that contain only subtotals and totals, but not individual records. A common type of dBASE output is produced with LABEL. You can probably learn to use these features with the dBASE menus, manual, and Help facility.

The @...SAY commands used in the programs can be modified to provide much more control over the format in which the output is displayed. The Picture format allows you to add dollar signs, commas, and other formatting characters to the output. Using SET DEVICE TO PRINT before an @...SAY command sends the output of the @...SAY commands to the printer. There is also a command, @...GET, for full-screen data input.

A Catalog file can be used to identify which database and related index, form, and other files work together. Memo fields are a type of field that can contain long strings of text. They are generally difficult to work with, but they output neatly and can be useful if only a few records need long messages attached to them. There are several String Operators, which can be used to manipulate the contents of character fields and memvars. They can generate such results as the length of a data item or a specified substring from the beginning or end of a data item.

You will not need some of the more sophisticated dBASE capabilities unless you are developing a TPS using dBASE. Such development would require a greater knowledge of both dBASE and programming techniques than you have gained at this point. If you are interested in developing such skills, it would be appropriate to take a dBASE programming course. You can develop customized data-entry screens by creating and using a Format file. An Application Generator program is also included with dBASE, to facilitate development of TPS programs.

# Chapter Review

This chapter concludes the introduction to dBASE by using and integrating multiple dBASE files and transferring data to and from dBASE. The material covered in this and the preceding chapters provides you with a solid base of microcomputer skills to use in your accounting career. If you have learned the technical skills and how to apply them to management and accounting situations, you are well prepared to take advantage of the new information technology in the coming decades.

# Practice Exercises

Exercise 10-1

**Filename: EX1.DBF**
(Continuation of Exercise 9-1)

In addition to the dBASE Cash Receipts file used in previous exercises, Darwin Department Store has its customer mailing list in a word processor that can generate ASCII files. They want to transfer this data into dBASE, transfer dBASE data to other types of files, and use multiple files to add customer names and addresses to the statements of cash receipts.

1. The secretary who maintains the customer mailing list has generated two files that each contain part of the customer data, because you are not sure which type of file would work best. The file named EX1ASDF.TXT has data structured in columns (SDF), and the file named EX1ADEL.TXT has character data enclosed in quotes and items are separated by commas (DELIMITED). Display the contents of each file on the screen. Open the dBASE data file named EX1A.DBF and list its structure. Append the data from EX1ASDF.TXT to EX1A.DBF (which is an empty file that has an appropriate file structure), then append the data from EX1ADEL.TXT to EX1A.DBF. Print the resulting EX1A.DBF data in order of customer number.
2. The marketing department wants a data file to use for market research and special mailings to customers with credit limits of $500 or more. Copy the records (from EX1A.DBF) of only customers that meet this credit limit criterion to a file named EX1MKT.DBF and print the results.
3. The clerical personnel will now enter new customer data directly into a dBASE file when credit is approved. Copy the structure of the customer master file (EX1A.DBF) to EX1NEW.DBF and print the structure of the new file.

4. The secretary needs a copy of the cash receipts from customer numbers 322 and 354 to incorporate in a letter she is composing on the word processor. Make an ASCII SDF file named EX1WP.TXT that contains just this data from EX1.DBF. (To see the results, enter TYPE EX1WP.TXT or retrieve it with a word processor.)
5. Generate a Lotus file (EX1FIN.WKS) that contains just the customer numbers and credit limits for all customers, to be used by the financial analysis department. Retrieve the resulting file in Lotus 1-2-3.
6. Open EX1 in area 1 and EX1A in area 2. Link the two files so that movement in EX1 causes the pointer in EX1A to move to records with the same customer number. Print the customer number, name, credit limit, check amount, and check data for all receipts in customer number order.
7. Modify the program written in part 6 of Exercise 9-1 to link the Cash receipts file EX1.DBF to the customer master file EX1A.DBF and display the customer name, address, and credit limit, in addition to the customer number and other data already shown. Print a copy of the revised program and the output. The statement of customer payments for customer 0076 is shown below.

```
Customer Number:  0076
Credit Limit:      100

Peggy Spaulding
519 Maple Drive
Eugene, OR    97405


-----------------------------------------------------------
Date Received      Check Number          Payment Amount
-----------------------------------------------------------
02/05/90                  433                    137.83
02/28/90                  452                     84.37
-----------------------------------------------------------
Total Payments:                                  222.20
```

## Reminders

1. TYPE EX1ASDF.TXT and TYPE EX1ADEL.TXT. USE EX1A.LISTSTRUCTURE. APPEND FROM EX1ASDF SDF, then APPEND FROM EX1ADEL DELIMITED. INDEX ON CUST TO EX1A and LIST TO PRINT.
2. USE EX1A then COPY TO EX1MKT FOR CREDLIM>=500.
3. USE EX1A then COPY STRUCTURE TO EX1NEW. USE EX1NEW and LIST STRUCTURE TO PRINT
4. USE EX1 and COPY TO EX1WP SDF FOR CUST='0322' .OR. CUST='0354'. TYPE EX1WP.TXT.
5. USE EX1A and COPY CUST.CREDLIMTO EXFIN WKS. In Lotus, /File Retrieve EXFIN.
6. USE EX1; SELE 2; USE EX1A; INDEX ON CUST TO EX1ACUST (or another index filename); SELE 1; INDEX ON CUST TO EXICUST SET RELATION TO CUST INTO EX1A; LIST CUST, EX1A->F_NAME, EX1A->L_NAME, EX1A->CREDLIM, AMOUNT, DATE_RECD.
7. Make sure you have a backup of the program and MODI COMM EX1. Add the commands to open the customer master data file (EX1A.DBF) in area 2 and set a relation based on customer number from the cash receipts into the customer master file. Add the commands to display the needed data from the customer master file on the statement of customer payments.

Exercise 10-2

**Filename: EX2.DBF**
(Continuation of Exercise 9-2)

In addition to the dBASE Flight Log file, Moose Wings Flight Club has the plane rental fees in a word processor. They want to transfer this data into dBASE, transfer existing dBASE data to other types of files, and use multiple files to add the rental fees to the statements of member flights.

1. The club secretary, who maintains the plane rental fees schedule, has generated an SDF file (EX2ASDF.TXT) that contains the plane data. Display the contents of this file. Open EX2A.DBF, which is an empty file that has an appropriate file structure. Append the data from EX2ASDF.TXT to EX2A.DBF. Print the resulting EX2A.DBF data in alphabetical order by name.
2. The Cessna users' group wants recent flight data for the Cessna. Copy the records of only the Cessna flights from the flight log (EX2.DBF) to a file named EX2CESS.DBF and print the results.
3. From now on, the hangar attendant will enter flight log data directly into a dBASE file as flights are taken. Copy the structure of the Flight Log file (EX2.DBF) to a file named EX2NEWFL.DBF. Print the new file structure.
4. The club secretary wants a copy of the flight log for use in a word processor, to incorporate it in the monthly report to the board of directors. Make an ASCII SDF file named EX2.TXT that contains the data from EX2.DBF in date order. (Type EX2.TXT on the screen or retrieve it with a word processor to see the results.)
5. Generate a Lotus file (EX2.WKS) that contains just the PL, T_OFF, and T_AIR, to be used for analyzing plane usage. Retrieve the resulting file in Lotus 1-2-3.
6. Open EX2 in area 1 and EX2A in area 2. Link the two files so that movement in EX2 causes the pointer in EX2A to move to the record for the same plane. Print the member number, flight date, plane name, takeoff time, time in air, and rental rate for all flights in member number order.
7. Modify the program written in part 6 of Exercise 9-2 to link the Flight Log file EX2.DBF to the Rental Fees file (EX2A.DBF). Display the hourly rental fee and flight rental charge (rental fee, RENT, multiplied by the time in air, T_AIR), in addition to the data already shown. Print a copy of the revised program and the output. The revised statement of member flights for the first member is shown below. (For additional practice, you could also create member data and display the member names and addresses on the statements.)

```
Member Number:   1234

-----------------------------------------------------------------
Flight                 Time of      Time      Rental      Rental
Date         Plane     Takeoff      in Air     Rate       Charge
-----------------------------------------------------------------
04/01/90     Cessna       625        2.75        59       162.25
04/04/90     Piper       1012        1.75        32        56.00
-----------------------------------------------------------------
Total                                4.50                 218.25
```

**Reminders**

1. TYPE EX2SDF.TXT. USE EX2A and APPEND FROM EX2ASDF SDF. INDEX ON NAME TO EX2PNAME and LIST TO PRINT.
2. USE EX2, then COPY TO EX2CESS FOR PL='C'. USE EX2CESS and LIST TO PRINT.
3. USE EX2, then COPY STRUCTURE TO EX2NEWFL. USE EX2NEWFL and LIST STRU TO PRINT.
4. USE EX2. INDEX ON DATE TO EX2DATE and COPY TO EX2.SDF. TYPE EX2.TXT.
5. USE EX2 and COPY FIELDS PL, T_OFF, T_AIR TO EX2.WKS. In Lotus, /File Retrieve EX2.
6. USE EX2; SELE 2; USE EX2A; INDEX ON PL TO EX2APL.NDX (or another index filename); SELE 1; SET RELATION TO PL INTO EX2A; INDEX ON MEMB TO EX2-MEMB.NDX; LIST DATE, EX2A->NAME, T_OFF, T_AIR, EX2A->RENT.
7. Make sure you have a backup and MODI COMM EX2. Add commands to open the Plane file (EX2A.DBF) in area 2 and set the relation based on plane (PL) from the flight log into the Plane file. Add the commands to display the hourly rental rates from the Plane file, to calculate and display the amount of charges for each flight, and to calculate and display the total charge for the member on the statement of member flights.

Exercise 10-3

**Filename: EX3.DBF**
(Continuation of Exercise 9-3)

In addition to its dBASE Inventory file, Appalachian Manufacturing Company has a Raw Materials Activity file (which contains the purchases and withdrawals from raw material inventory) in a word processor that can generate ASCII files. They want to transfer this data into dBASE, transfer existing dBASE data to other types of files, and use the Activity file data to update the Inventory file.

1. The clerk, who maintains the Raw Materials Activity file in a word processor, has generated a delimited file (EX3ADEL.TXT) that contains purchases of and withdrawals from inventory. Display the file contents. Note that withdrawals are entered as a negative QUAN number, since they must be deducted from inventory. Append the data from EX3ADEL.TXT to EX3A.DBF (which is an empty file with an appropriate file structure). Print the resulting EX3A.DBF data grouped in alphabetical order by COD.
2. The production supervisor wants to review the data on purchases and withdrawals of pine. Copy the records for all activities involving pine from the Activities file (EX3A.DBF) to a file named EX3APINE.DBF and print the results.
3. The receiving clerk will now enter data on purchases and withdrawals directly into a dBASE file when the activity takes place. Copy the structure of the Activities file (EX3A.DBF) to a file named EX3ANEW.DBF and enter the three records shown below in the new file. Append the records from EX3NEW.DBF to EX3A.DBF. Print EX3NEW.DBF and the updated EX3A.DBF.

| Record# | COD | DATE | QUAN |
|---------|-----|----------|------|
| 1 | SLA | 09/28/90 | 20 |
| 2 | WOA | 09/28/90 | -58 |

```
3        WPC      09/28/90      -94
```

4. The secretary wants a copy of the inventory for use in a word processor. Make an ASCII SDF file named EX3.TXT that contains the data from EX3.DBF and print the results with TYPE EX3.TXT TO PRINT.

5. Generate a Lotus file (EX3.WKS) that contains just COD, U_COST, and QUAN to be used for inventory analysis by the inventory manager. Retrieve the resulting file in Lotus 1-2-3.

6. Open EX3 in area 1 and EX3A in area 2. Link the two files so that movement in EX3A causes the pointer in EX3 to move to the first record for the same Code (COD) in the Activity file. Display the code, unit cost, and amount of activity for all birch (WBA and WBB).

7. Write a program to display the beginning inventory (from EX3.DBF) followed by the purchases and withdrawal data (from EX3A.DBF) for each inventory item. The output for inventory item WOA is shown below. Print a copy of the program and the output.

```
Code Number:   WOA
Description:   Oak Grade A
Unit:          BdFt
Unit cost:     3.80
-----------------------------------
Date           Quantity      Balance
-----------------------------------
09/21/90                       151
09/24/90         200           351
09/25/90        -109           243
09/28/90         -58           185
-----------------------------------
```

## Exercise 10-4

**Filename: EX4.DBF**
(Continuation of Exercise 9-4)

In addition to the dBASE Time Summary file, the payroll clerk for R&D Consulting has the Employee master file in Lotus. R&D management wants to transfer this data into dBASE, transfer existing dBASE data to other types of files, and use multiple files to add the customer names and addresses to the employee work summary.

1. The clerk who maintains the Employee master file has generated a Lotus file, EX4AWKS.WKS, that contains the employee data. Use the empty dBASE data file named EX4A.DBF and append the data from EX4AWKS.WKS. Print the resulting EX4A.DBF data in order of employee number.

2. The personnel department wants a dBASE file of employees who earn more than $75 per hour. Copy from EX4A.DBF only the records that meet this hourly rate criterion to a file named EX4APERS.DBF and print the results.

3. The payroll clerk will now enter the employee data directly into a dBASE file when a new employee is hired. Copy the structure of the Employee master file (EX4A.DBF) to a file named EX4ANEW.DBF and print a listing of the structure of the new file.

4. Generate a Lotus file (EX4.WKS) that contains the employee numbers, pay week, hours worked, and pay rates for all employees, to be used in personnel planning and budgeting. Retrieve the resulting file in Lotus 1-2-3.

5. Modify the program written in part 7 of Exercise 9-4 to link the Time Summary file EX4.DBF to the Employee master file (EX4A.DBF) and display the employee name, address, and pay rate, and to calculate and display gross pay, in addition to the employee number and other data already shown. Print a copy of the revised program and the output. Use the pay rate from the the Employee master file instead of the one in the Time Summary file. Now that the Employee master file is in dBASE, the database design can be improved by removing the pay rate from the Time Summary file and using the rate found in the master file. The employee work summary for employee 234 is shown below.

```
Jumpin' J. Flash
2 Koolakid Rd.
Patterson, NJ  07003

Employee Number: 234
Pay Rate:    $ 100.00
------------------------------------------------------------------
                  Project                 Hours               Gross
Pay Week          Number                  Worked                Pay
------------------------------------------------------------------
06/08/90            133                     14               1400.00
06/22/90            133                     16               1600.00
06/29/90            150                      6                600.00
------------------------------------------------------------------
Total                                       36               3600.00
```

# Appendix A: Lotus 1-2-3 @Functions

The @functions are built-in Lotus 1-2-3 formulas that perform specialized calculations. The @functions can be used independently or in combination with other functions and formulas. The first section of this appendix deals with general information on @functions, the second section groups @functions by type, and the third section lists the @functions and their arguments with a short description. All sections are organized alphabetically by @function.

## General Information

The general format of a Lotus 1-2-3 @function is @FUNCTION (*argument1,argument2,...*). The @function begins with the "at" sign (@) followed by the function name. The function name tells Lotus which calculation to perform followed by the *arguments*. The *arguments* are used by Lotus for the calculations. Each @function returns a single value from the @function name and arguments. Here, the function names are in uppercase letters (Lotus converts them to uppercase automatically), and the *arguments* are in italic lowercase letters.

Different types of @functions require different types of arguments. There are three types of **arguments**. The types of argument are numeric values (numeric value of *x*), range values (one or more ranges of numeric values for *list*), and string values (text string value for *string*).

General rules are as follows:
- Enclose arguments in parentheses.
- Insert no spaces within arguments.
- Separate arguments with a comma (,) or a semicolon (;), never a space.
- Enclose string arguments in double quotes (" ").

Errors in @function entry will cause the computer to beep, put you in EDIT mode, and move the cursor to error location.

## Group Types

### Mathematical @Functions

| | | | | | |
|---|---|---|---|---|---|
| @ABS | @ACOS | @ASIN | @ATAN | @ATAN2 | @COS |
| @EXP | @INT | @LN | @LOG | @MOD | @PI |
| @RAND | @ROUND | @SIN | @SQRT | @TAN | |

### Logical @Functions

| | | | | |
|---|---|---|---|---|
| @FALSE | @IF | @ISERR | @ISNA | @ISNUMBER |
| @ISSTRING | @TRUE | | | |

**Special @Functions**

| @@ | @CELL | @CELLPOINTER | @CHOOSE | @COLS |
| @ERR | @HLOOKUP | @INDEX | @NA | @ROWS |
| @VLOOKUP | | | | |

**String @Functions**

| @EXTRACT | @FIND | @LEFT | @LENGTH | @LOWER | @MID |
| @N | @PROPER | @REPEAT | @REPLACE | @RIGHT | @S |
| @STRING | @TRIM | @UPPER | @VALUE | | |

**Date and Time @Functions**

| @DATE | @DATEVALUE | @DAY | @MONTH | @YEAR |
| @NOW | @TIME | @TIMEVALUE | @HOUR | |
| @MINUTE | @SECOND | | | |

**Financial @Functions**

| @CTERM | @DDB | @FV | @IRR | @NPV | @PMT |
| @PV | @RATE | @SLN | @SYD | @TERM | |

**Statistical @Functions**

| @AVG | @COUNT | @MAX | @MIN | @STD | @SUM |
| @VAR | | | | | |

**Database Statistical @Functions**

| @DAVG | @DCOUNT | @DMAX | @DMIN | @DSTD | @DSUM |
| @DVAR | | | | | |

# Alphabetical List of @Functions

| Function | Description |
|---|---|
| @@(*cell address*) | returns value of cell referenced by *cell address* |
| @ABS($x$) | returns absolute, or positive, value of $x$ |
| @ACOS($x$) | computes arc cosine of angle |
| @ASIN($x$) | computes arc sine of angle |
| @ATAN($x$) | computes second-quadrant arc tangent of angle |
| @ATAN2($x,y$) | computes fourth-quadrant arc tangent of angle |
| @AVG(*list*) | returns average value of cells in *list* |
| @CELL(*attribute,range*) | too complex to discuss here; check Lotus manual |
| @CELLPOINTER(*attribute*) | information about the current cell; see @CELL |
| @CHAR($x$) | returns ASCII code corresponding to first character in *string* |
| @CHOOSE($x,v0,v1,...,vn$) | returns value $x$ from a list $v0,v1,...,vn$ |
| @CODE(*string*) | returns ASCII character corresponding to $x$ |
| @COLS(*range*) | returns number of columns in *range* |
| @COS($x$) | returns cosine of angle $x$ |

| @COUNT(*list*) | returns number of nonblank cells in *list* |
|---|---|
| @CTERM(*int,fv,*) | computes compounding periods of *present value* to grow to a *future value* based on a fixed *interest* rate |
| @DATE(*year,month,day*) | returns serial date for the year, month, day |
| @DATAVALUE(*date-string*) | returns serial date for the string value of year, month, day |
| @DAVG(*input,offset,criterion*) | averages *offset* column of *input* range that meets the *criterion* |
| @DAY(*date number*) | returns day number of month from 1 to 31 |
| @DCOUNT(*input,offset,criterion*) | counts nonblank cells in *offset* column of *input* range that meet *criterion* |
| @DDB(*cost,salvage,life,period*) | computes depreciation on an asset for specific period based on double-declining balance |
| @DMAX(*input,offset,criterion*) | finds highest value in *offset* column of *input* range that meets *criterion* |
| @DMIN(*input,offset,criterion*) | finds the lowest value in the *offset* column of the *input* range that meets *criterion* |
| @DSTD(*input,offset,criterion*) | computes the standard deviation for values in *offset* column of *input* range that meets the *criterion* |
| @DSUM(*input,offset,criterion*) | adds values in *offset* column of *input* range that meet *criterion* |
| @DVAR(*input,offset,criterion*) | computes variance for values in *offset* column of *input* range that meet *criterion* |
| @ERR | returns the value ERR (error). |
| @EXACT(*string1,string2*) | compares two strings for exact match |
| @EXP(*x*) | returns number *e*, raised to the *x*th power |
| @FALSE | returns value 0 |
| @FIND(*search-string,string,start-number*) | position of first occurrence of search string |
| @FV(*pmt,int,term*) | returns future value based on equal *payments* at the given *interest* rate for a specific *term* |
| @HLOOKUP(*x,range,row-number*) | compares *x* to each cell in index row of *range*, moves down the column by specified offset or *row-number*, returning contents of cell |
| @HOUR(*time number*) | returns hour value from *time number* from 0 through 23 |
| @IF(*condition,x,y*) | returns value *x* if true condition, value *y* if false condition |
| @INDEX(*range,column,row*) | returns value of cell in *range* at intersection of *column* and *row* |
| @INT(*x*) | returns integer portion of *x* |
| @IRR(*guess,range*) | returns internal rate of return for range of cash flows, given a guess to start computation |
| @ISERR(*x*) | returns 1 if value of *x* is ERR, 0 if not |
| @ISNA(*x*) | returns 1 if value of *x* is NA, 0 if not |

| | |
|---|---|
| @ISNUMBER(*x*) | returns 1 if *x* is a number of formula, 0 if not |
| @ISSTRING(*x*) | returns 1 if *x* is a string value, 0 if not |
| @LEFT(*string,n*) | returns first *n* characters in *string* |
| @LENGTH(*string*) | returns number of characters found in *string* |
| @LN(*x*) | computes natural logarithm (base *e*) of *x* |
| @LOG(*x*) | computes common logarithm (base 10) of *x* |
| @LOWER(*string*) | converts all characters in *string* to lowercase |
| @MAX(*list*) | returns highest single value in *list* |
| @MID(*string,start number,n*) | extracts *n* characters from *string* at *start number* |
| @MIN(list) | returns lowest single value in *list* |
| @MINUTE(*time number*) | returns minute value from *time number* from 0 through 59 |
| @MOD(*x,y*) | returns remainder, or modulus, of *x/y* |
| @MONTH(*date number*) | returns month of the year from 1 through 12 |
| @N(*range*) | returns value of upper left cell in *range* |
| @NA | returns value NA (not available). |
| @NPV(*int,range*) | returns net present value of a range of future cash flows given fixed periodic interest rate |
| @NOW | returns serial number of current date and time |
| @NPV(*int,range*) | returns net present value |
| @PI | returns value of $\pi$ (about 3.141592653589794) |
| @PMT(*prin,int,term*) | returns periodic payment necessary for financing of a *principal* amount at given *interest* rate for a *term* |
| @PROPER(*string*) | capitalizes first letter of every word in *string* |
| @PV(*pmt,int,term*) | returns present value based on equal *payments* at given *interest* rate for a *term* |
| @RAND | generates a random number between 0 and 1 |
| @RATE(*fv,pmt,term*) | returns periodic interest necessary for a *future value* to grow to a *future value* for a *term* |
| @REPEAT(*string,n*) | duplicate *string, n* number of times |
| @REPLACE (*original string,start-number,n,new string*) | removes *n* characters at *start-number* and replaces with *new string* |
| @RIGHT(*string,n*) | returns last *n* characters in *string* |
| @ROUND(*x,n*) | rounds number *x* to *n* places |
| @ROWS(*range*) | returns number of rows in a *range* |
| @S(*range*) | returns upper left cell in *range* as a string |
| @SECOND(*time number*) | returns second value from *time number* from 0 through 59 |
| @SIN(*x*) | returns sine of angle *x* |

@SLN(*cost,salvage,life*)                    computes straight-line deprecation of an
                                             asset

@SQRT(*x*)                                   returns square root of *x*

@STD(*list*)                                 returns standard deviation of the values
                                             in *list*

@STRING(*x,n*)                               converts *x* to a string with *n* places right
                                             of decimal

@SUM(*list*)                                 adds values found in *list*

@SYD(*cost,salvage,life,period*)             returns sum-of-the-years'-digits
                                             deprecation for specified period

@TAN(*x*)                                    returns tangent of angle *x*

@TERM(*pmt, int,fv*)                         returns number of payment periods based
                                             on equal *payments*, *interest* rate, and
                                             *future value*

@TIME(*hr,min,sec*)                          returns serial time of *hour, minute,
                                             second*

@TIMEVALUE(*hr,min,sec*)                     returns serial time of string value for
                                             *hour, minute, second*

@TRIM(*string*)                              removes excess spaces from *string*

@TRUE                                        returns value 1

@UPPER(*string,*)                            converts all letters in *string* to uppercase

@VALUE(*string,*)                            converts number *string* back to numeric
                                             value

@VAR(*list*)                                 returns variance of values in *list*

@VLOOKUP(*x,range,column-number*)            compares *x* to each cell in index column
                                             of *range*, moves across the row by
                                             specified offset or *column-number*,
                                             returning contents of cell

@YEAR(*date number*)                         returns year number from 0 through 199

# Appendix B: Lotus 1-2-3 Versions

Lotus 1-2-3 versions are as follows: 1A, 2.0, 2.01, 2.2, 3, Student 1, Student 2. A worksheet created with one version can always run on a higher version; the opposite is not true, i.e., you cannot run a worksheet created under version 3 on version 2 software. This is true of most software, including operating systems. Most later versions of software have an option for saving files in a format that can be used on a lower version of the software. If you have access to a machine at home or work, but also sometimes use machines and software in a school or commercial lab, this may be important to you.

Different versions of Lotus 1-2-3 have different size worksheets. The grids have different numbers of rows and columns. The maximum size of a completed worksheet is limited by two factors: (1) the size of memory and (2) the version of the software.

There are many operations and functions contained in version 2 and the Student version 2 that are not available in the lower numbered versions. The following operations covered in this book are not supported by Lotus 1-2-3 version 1:

> Hiding columns (Chapter 4)
> @IF with labels (Chapter 4)
> Parse (Chapter 6)
> Translate (Chapter 6)
> System (Chapter 6)

If you are using version 1 to do most of your work, it is suggested that you complete all the other activities in the cases and exercises using version 1. Take the resulting file to a computer lab that has a version of Lotus 1-2-3 that will allow you to complete the remaining activities, and complete your work. Save the work in a file named with the file extension (.WK1 or .WKE) used by the newer version of Lotus 1-2-3. You will not be able to retrieve the resulting final worksheet using version 1, but the .WKS file containing all the rest of your work will still be on the disk and can be retrieved using version 1.

# Appendix C: dBASE III PLUS File Types

dBASE III PLUS uses several different file types, and each has its own file extension to indicate what type of file it is. dBASE file extensions are as follows:

| Extension | FILE | Purpose |
| --- | --- | --- |
| .CAT | Catalog | names of all related files for a database |
| .DBF | Database | transactions or happenings |
| .DBT | Memo | large blocks of text |
| .FMT | Format | custom screens or report forms |
| .FRM | Form | creating stored report forms |
| .LBL | Label | printing with LABEL command |
| .MEM | Memory | holding results of computations in memory |
| .NDX | Index | sorted entries |
| .PRG | Program | programmed commands (batch processing) |
| .QRY | Query | conditions to display records |
| .SCR | Screen | screen layout of custom data-entry form |
| .TXT | Text | copied data from another package |
| .VUE | View | relating database files with their indexes |

# Appendix D: dBASE III PLUS Versions

The database management system developed by Ashton-Tate has evolved over the years. This evolution is reflected in revisions and new versions. Each version is more powerful than its predecessor.

dBASE II was the first version to be marketed by Ashton-Tate and served as a command-language DBMS that allowed programmers to create application programs . A command language is typically represented by the procedural languages such as COBAL, FORTRAN, and PASCAL. These third-generation languages required an extensive knowledge of programming techniques and structure.

dBASE III was introduced with more power and a more user-friendly interface, and was quickly followed by dBASE III PLUS, which is in most common use today. You have seen the power of the PLUS version, which includes the Assistant as the user interface. The combination of both a menu-driven interface for those who are infrequent users of dBASE and the dot prompt alternative for individuals who are frequent users of the program gives the best of both worlds to the novice and the power user.

The latest version to be marketed is dBASE IV. There were problems bringing this version to market, which Ashton-Tate is still trying to resolve at this writing. You can look forward to many more versions and revisions of dBASE, each more powerful and versatile than the preceding one.